SOVIET MILITARY INTERVENTIONS
SINCE 1945

СОВЕТСКИЕ ВОЕННЫЕ ОПЕРАЦИИ ЗА РУЬЕЖОМ С 1945г
ОБЗОР ХАРАКТЕРНЫХ СЛУЧАЕВ

АЛЕКС П. СМИД и ЭЛЛЕН БЕРЕНДС

SOVIET MILITARY INTERVENTIONS SINCE 1945

With a Summary in Russian

Alex P. Schmid

With Case Studies by Ellen Berends

Transaction Books
New Brunswick (U.S.A.) and Oxford (U.K.)

Library of Congress Catalog Number: 85-8424
ISBN 0-88738-063-8 (cloth)
Printed in the United States of America

Library of Congress Cataloging in Publication Data

Schmid, Alex Peter.
  Soviet military interventions since 1945.

  Bibliography: p.
  Includes index.
  1. Soviet Union—Military relations—Foreign countries. 2. Soviet
Union—Foreign relations—1945-   . 3. World politics—1945-   .
4. Military history, Modern—20th century. 5. Soviet Union—History,
Military—1917-   . I. Berends, Ellen. II. Title.
UA770.S328   1985   947.085   85-8424
ISBN 0-88738-063-8

The publication of this book was supported by the Center for the Study of Social Conflicts (C.O.M.T.), State University of Leiden, Hooigracht 15, 2312
KM Leiden, The Netherlands.

Everyone is entitled to his own views.
No one is entitled to his own facts.

— James Schlesinger

TABLE OF CONTENTS

Foreword by Milton Leitenberg   xi
Introduction   xvii
Acknowledgements   xix

I   INTRABLOC CONFLICTS : THE SOVIET UNION'S OCCUPATION
    OF EASTERN EUROPE AND THE SPECIAL CASE OF CHINA
                 Introduction   1
                 Stalin's Policy for Eastern Europe   1
                 The Prague Coup of 1948   6
                 The Popular Uprisings in the Post-Stalin Era   10
                 China - A Special Case   14
                 Conclusion   15
Case Study I   The Incorporation of the Baltic Republics into
                 the Soviet Union (1940-1949)   18
Case Study II   The East German Uprising (1953)   23
Case Study III   The Hungarian Uprising (1956)   26
Case Study IV   Warsaw Pact Intervention in Czechoslovakia
                 (1968)   30
Case Study V   The Sino-Soviet Border Dispute (1960s)   35

II INTERBLOC CONFLICTS: MILITARY ASPECTS OF THE
    EAST-WEST CONFLICT
                 Introduction   39
                 The Spectre of a Soviet Invasion of Western
                 Europe   40
                 Early Cold War Conflicts (1946-1949)   42
                 From the Korean War to the Cuban Missile Crisis 45
                 The USSR and Vietnam   49
                 Conclusion   50
Case Study VI   The Iranian Crisis (1945-1946)   54
Case Study VII   The Greek Civil War (1944-1949) - A Case of
                 Soviet Non-Intervention   59
Case Study VIII The Korean War (1950-1953)   63
Case Study IX   The Soviet Role in the Allied Occupation of
                 Austria (1945-1955)   69

III EXTRABLOC CONFLICTS: SOVIET MILITARY INVOLVEMENT
    IN THIRD WORLD CONFLICTS
                 Introduction   73
                 Soviet Military Involvement in the Third World 75
                 The Period 1945-1955   75
                 The Period 1955-1965   77
                 The Period 1965-1980s   84
                 Latin America   85
                 Asia   86
                 The Middle East   91

	Soviet Naval Interest, Arms Transfers and Bases	91
	Soviet Military Interventions	93
	The Soviet Union in Africa	100
	The Cuban-Soviet Intervention in Angola	102
	The Soviet Union and the Ogaden War in the Horn of Africa	110
	Conclusion	117
Case Study X	The Soviet Intervention into Afghanistan (1979-)	127

IV EPILOGUE: PAST AND FUTURE OF SOVIET MILITARY INTER-
    VENTIONS

	Introduction	133
	Intrabloc Interventions	137
	Interbloc Interventions	144
	Extrabloc Interventions	149
	Conclusion: The Soviet Union - Expansionist or not?	158

	Notes	163
	Bibliography	191
	Index	211
	Summary in Russian	217
	Summary in English	221

LIST OF TABLES

I	Foreign Military Forces in Europe, early 1980s	38
II	How the Cold War Was Played, according to Brzezinski	51
III	Structure of World Trade, 1979	72
IV	Export of Major Weapons to Third World, according to SIPRI (1980)	92
V	Types of Military Assistance and Military Intervention	123
VI	Foreign Interventions in the Soviet Union Since 1917	133
VII	Size of British, French and Russian Empires (in skm)	134
VIII	Soviet Military Interventions and Annexations, 1918-1945	135
IX	A Survey of Soviet Intrabloc Military Interventions Since 1945 (including China)	138
X	A Survey of Soviet "Interbloc" (NATO + 'Western') Military Interventions Since 1945	145
XI	Soviet Domination Versus War	148
XII	A Survey of Soviet Extrabloc Military Interventions Since 1945	150
XIII	Soviet Weapon Deliveries to Non-Socialist Countries, 1976-1980	153
XIV	Foreign Military (Technicians, Advisers, Troops) Stationed Outside Europe, 1982-83	154
XV	War Proneness of Countries, according to Cold War Orientation	155
XVI	Gains and Losses for the Soviet Union, 1945-1979	156
XVII	Soviet Military Interventions in the Postwar Period, according to Periods and Locations	158

FOREWORD BY MILTON LEITENBERG

This book is a very necessary one from many points of view. Both the majority of political scientists who concern themselves with world peace and the public peace movements are overwhelmingly concerned with arms control. They think most often about military balance estimates: strategic balances of nuclear warheads and missile launchers, numbers of troops and of conventional weapons possessed by the opposing alliances in Europe, perhaps even military doctrines for the use of these forces, and so on. They rarely concern themselves with the large number and wide variety of foreign military interventions in the post-World War II years. Nevertheless, if a military confrontation between the nuclear powers should ever develop, it will most likely result from the intervention by one or the other in a third country.

This book is also needed because we still do not understand the USSR and its foreign policy at all well. The interpretation of that policy is made on the basis of an extremely confusing mix of components: national and territorial goals of pre-revolutionary Czarist regimes, the heritage of ideological and doctrinal statements from the time of the Soviet revolution and the writings of Lenin, the policies of the Comintern and Cominform, the post-war military occupation of Eastern Europe, assumptions of realpolitik, and the visible evidence of Soviet external engagements. Particular additional problems compounding the interpretation of Soviet policies are the frequent major shifts in those policies - as occurred between 1939 and 1941 - and the very major role that "disinformation" plays in the functioning of the Soviet government, in some aspects virtually a necessity for its operation.

Of course, when it is a matter of invading other states, every nation employs euphemisms. On December 29, 1979, on the fourth day of the occupation of Afghanistan, the Soviet government announced that it had been invited by the Afghan government to protect it against the counter-revolution supported by China, Pakistan, and the United States. The joint aim of these three governments was described as seeking to crush the Afghan revolution, and the Afghan groups allegedly armed by them were said to constitute "... a serious threat to the very existence of Afghanistan as an independent state." *) The

----

*) A Soviet political spokesman explained in late 1983 (in private conversations) that the USSR had to invade - that is "go in [to] ... Afghanistan, things were getting out of hand, the Afghan government was loosing control and the USSR faced an uncertain future with a neighbouring country. It would all take time. The USSR had not pacified Central Asia until 1934. It was not only the bandits in Afghanistan, it was also the people, ... but they will learn. It will take time."

similarity to German statements upon occupying Norway and Denmark in the Second World War is striking. On April 9, 1940, the German Foreign Ministry announced that due to the prior violations of Danish and Norwegian neutrality, Germany has assumed the responsibility for defending the neutrality of the two countries. Nevertheless, everyone - including very likely the invader - understood that Norway and Denmark had been invaded by Germany.

In another event pertaining to the USSR, one finds that the official Soviet chronology of international events notes for August 21, 1968: "Entry into Czechoslovakia... of Soviets military units... to help the working people of that country safeguard their revolutionary achievements against encroachments by internal and external enemies of socialism."

However, the "Convention for the Definition of Aggression", signed between the USSR and Czechoslovakia on July 3, 1933, stated in its Annex:

> "No act of aggression within the meaning of this Convention can be justified on any of the following grounds, among others:
> A. The internal condition of a state, for example: its political, economic or social structure, alleged defects in its administration, disturbances due to strikes, revolution, counterrevolutions or civil war..."

If this looks back to documents prior to 1968, point 6, "Non-Intervention in Internal Affairs", of the first section of the Final Act of the Conference on Security and Cooperation in Europe, signed in 1975, states

> "The participating States will refrain from any intervention, direct or indirect, individual or collective, in the internal or external affairs falling within the domestic jurisdiction of another participating State, regardless of their mutual relations. They will accordingly refrain from any form of armed intervention or threat of such intervention against another participating State."

The sentences are repeated again in the section of the Final Act on "Matters Related to Giving Effect to Certain of the Above Principles". It is perhaps for this reason that in the parlance of Soviet diplomatic language, military intervention, such as the invasion of Czechoslovakia in 1968, is termed "fraternal solidarity and support".

At the end of the Second World War, the USSR had been a bit more blunt in its explanations. Foreign Minister Molotov told the Finnish negotiators in 1944, "The basic purpose of our war is to re-extablish our old boundaries", and it was to restore the pre-revolutionary Czarist boundaries that the USSR carried out the occupations and invasions of 1939. In explaining to the Finns the Soviet desire for a naval base at Hanko, on Finnish territory, Molotov stated:

> "Great Britain has had Gibraltar in her possession for a couple of centuries, but no one, not even Spain, has considered this fact as being odd, although Britain's own security does not depend on Gibraltar as ours does on Hanko." (1)

The USSR has now been in existence for 68 years. When WW II ended in 1945, only 28 years had passed since 1917. In the 40 years since 1945, the Soviet Union has to all intents and purposes held its nominal East European allies (with the exception of Bulgaria and Romania) under a form of military occupation. The USSR shows no indication of relieving that occupation in its own long term interests, as some political analysts began to suspect by the mid-1970 that it might. Its repeated military interventions in Eastern Europe to maintain the status quo makes that clear. One of the most significant aspects of the Soviet decision to invade Afghanistan in 1979 - as well as the decision to support the prior Marxist coup in 1978 - is precisely the indication of willingness to exchange a neutral independent buffer state for a highly unstable and bitterly hostile vassal under military occupation. That is a clear choice in the direction opposite to the one that might be considered most judicious and desirable from the USSR's own long term political point of view. If one calculates that the large scale United States intervention in Indochina began in 1963 or 1964 and ended in 1975, the United States was occupied in a full scale war in that theatre for eleven or twelve years. The USSR has been involved on a somewhat smaller scale in Afghanistan for over five years now. The domestic internal pressures that helped force the United States out of Indochina do not exist in the USSR in regard to Afghanistan. Similarly, external international pressure on the USSR regarding its war is also far less significant. The USSR had carried out major external military interventions in the pre-World War II period, particularly in 1934-38 in China's Sinkiang province. And of course, the USSR invaded or occupied Finland, Poland, Latvia, Lithuania and Estonia in the months following the announcement of the Soviet-German Non-Aggression Pact on August 24, 1939. Beginning in July 1933, the USSR signed a "Convention for the Definition of Aggression" of its own initiation with each of these countries. According to this convention the subsequent Soviet actions were forbidden. Nevertheless, as we examine previous historic parallels, and as we learn considerably more about the USSR with the passing years, we simultaneously find Soviet capabilities and behavior changing as well. It seems unquestionable that the USSR is now able to effect military events around the world in a way it had not been able to do previously. Along with major improvements in its capabilities - the navy, long-distance aviation, forward bases in foreign territories - there has come an increased willingness to intervene in military operations in states distant from Soviet frontiers as well as those close by. Alex Schmid has been able to clearly demonstrate the progression of those changes over time in his study.

In carrying out their research, Dr. Schmid and Drs. Berends were also forced to think about what the term "foreign military intervention" meant. Was it to be used only to denote a major invasion - large scale expeditionary military forces sent abroad - or should it include a variety of other smaller scale external military activities of one country in another, either during combat or in peacetime? It is extremely important to understand the frequency with which social scientists use definitions to exclude very basic segments of the subject they are ostensibly studying. I can provide a very relevant example. In a recent discussion at a West European research institute, one researcher argued that "Poland could not, or should not, be considered in a study of the USSR and its neighbours since it was occupied by the USSR. It was [therefore] not a classical neighbour." "Classical" neighbours were presumably defined as unoccupied or uninvaded neighbours. But since the purpose of the study under discussion was to investigate the relations of one state to another, and among other things to examine which of its neighbours that country had invaded or not, and why, it would have been an extremely odd study if one had begun by removing all those neighbours already invaded or occupied. The behaviours considered by Alex Schmid in his survey are sufficiently broad that this problem is clearly overcome, and the reader is provided with the maximum of empirical information. If it subsequently seems more correct that some of the categories of external involvement subsumed under "military intervention" should be reinterpreted as legitimate "military assistance", they can afterwards be excluded.

With the diversification of both donors and recipients of military support, the phenomenon of intervention is increasing and spreading throughout the world. While it is certainly not the only military and political problem facing the world, understanding the nature and objectives of the Soviet state, or any other interventionary state, is crucial to hopes for future world peace. The purpose of this book is to examine these questions for the USSR. No reader should think for a second that the authors are not fully conscious of the post World War II history of foreign military intervention by the United States, Great Britain, France, and in more recent years even by a new generation of third-world interventionary states. (See, for instance, my forthcoming survey of these and other interventions in "Aspects of Military Intervention and the Projection of Military Power" (2).) That other nations besides the USSR are also guilty of gross external military intervention does not reduce any less the need to document and to study Soviet external military intervention. In addition to its own direct activities, the USSR provides major aid and support to Vietnam, Cuba, Libya, and Syria, all heavily engaged in foreign military intervention under varying circumstances.

If the description of Sir Curtis Keeble should be correct, that the USSR is

> "... a continental imperial power, newly risen to superpower status and faced with the need to consolidate the areas under its control, to sap the strength of its opponents and to develop the means for worldwide projection of power.
> ... a power which, over the centuries has sought security against the threat and the reality of invasion across open land frontiers by the constant extension of its power into areas beyond those frontiers. Having done so, it has found the need to secure tranquility within those areas newly brought under control, as well as stable, compliant administration in them adjacent to the imperial frontier." (3)

then the prognosis for international peace, at least as far as this factor is concerned, is not particularly promising. With the doctrinaire Soviet interpretation of most international events as a conflict between socialism and capitalism and the natural course of events being considered the triumph of socialism as a "logical consequence", interference with the natural course of events requires action on the part of "the peace-loving policy of the Soviet Union" to "promote... the triumph of the new and revolutionary over the old and obsolete" (4). Marxist-Leninist doctrine provides a convenient justification for the use of Soviet power outside the boundaries of the Soviet state, and the 1933-1936 non-aggression treaties signed by the USSR and its neighbours are then to be interpreted as a Leninist change of tactics and flexibility.

A historical review of the engagements of the USSR outside its borders in the post-World War II period leaves one with an interpretation of Soviet international behavior as a combination of historical tradition, post revolutionary doctrinal precept, and the more recent acquisition of military naval and air capabilities which enable the USSR to carry out military activities further from its own borders when it decides to do so.

This volume is an excellent introduction which provides the reader with a wealth of detailed information to assist him in understanding a neglected area of Soviet foreign policy.

Milton Leitenberg

The Swedish Institute of International Affairs

February 1985

Notes

1) Cit. Thede Palm, The Finnish-Soviet Armistice Negotiations of 1944 (Stockholm, Almquist & Wiksell, 1971) p. 92.
2) M. Leitenberg, "Aspects of Military Intervention and the Projection of Military Power", Paris, short version in press. Longer version: Frankfurt a.M., HSFK, 1985; see also: Richard Dean Burns and Milton Leitenberg, The Wars in Vietnam, Cambodia, and Laos, 1945-1982: A Bibliographic Guide (Santa Barbara, ABC-CLIO, 1983).
3) Curtis Keeble, "The Roots of Soviet Foreign Policy", International Affairs, 60:4 (Autumn 1984), 561-578.
4) A.A. Gromyko and B.N. Ponomarev, Soviet Foreign Policy (Moscow, Progress Publishers, 4th Edition, 1981) p. 22.

INTRODUCTION

The principal method to obtain and maintain national security today is through reliance on military strength, often in alliance with geographically adjacent states. Together they form military blocs, usually under the leadership of the strongest member. Before the Second World War there were eight nations with superior military strength. In terms of size of their military budgets they could be grouped in three tiers. On top stood the United States. In the second tier ranked France, the United Kingdom and the Soviet Union. In the third tier came Germany, Italy, Japan and Poland (1). World War II started on the third tier and gradually moved up. The war, in which ultimately 45 other nations became involved, ended with the third tier militarily eliminated, one second tier power enhanced to the first tier, and the remaining two second tier nations joining forces with the prewar top tier occupant. The result was a bipolar world with two major military powers dominating much of the world. Before the great war the Soviet Union and the United States had accounted for no more than one quarter of the world's military expenditures together; after the war their share rose to over half of the world military budget (in 1983 $ 637 billion). The two superpowers formed military blocs (the North Atlantic Treaty Organization - NATO and the Treaty of Friendship, Mutual Assistance and Cooperation - WTO) with now 16 and 7 allied nations respectively. These two blocs spend 72 percent of the world total military expenditures (NATO: $ 307 billion; WTO more than $ 151 billion; rest of the world ca. $ 178 billion) (2).

Military conflicts in the postwar period can be categorized in relation to bloc-membership. We shall term conflicts between these two blocs inter-bloc conflicts; conflicts within these blocs intra-bloc conflicts and conflicts outside them extra-bloc conflicts. In the present study we look at the military interventions of the Soviet Union in these three conflict constellations for the postwar period. In doing so we have used the term 'intervention' in a broad sense as indicated by Table V (see p. 123).

There are certain aspects which the present study does not cover. Soviet nuclear threats have been excluded from this study since these are dealt with separately in an article by Schmid to be published next year. Soviet instigations to and support of coups d'etats by local (military) forces are also not analyzed here although there are some references to these as in the case of Afghanistan. The whole field of foreign-led or supported (military) coups d'etat deserves special treatment - and not only in relation to the Soviet Union - although the subject is a difficult one due to problems of data reliability. Excluded from this study are also secret service activities in the field of subversion, destabilization, assassination and state-supported terrorism. Here the record is even more shady than in the field of coups. In a sense these are, however, all forms of foreign intervention which should not be shied away from by students of international relations. Aware of these varieties of intervention, we have in the present study focussed our attention on various types of direct military interventions.

Our choice of case studies is to some extent subjective. We have, for instance, no case study on Soviet military intervention in Poland in 1956 while we have one case study on the Greek Civil War. This despite the fact that the degree of Soviet military involvement in 1956 was much higher than in 1946-1949 in Greece. The reason why we included the latter was that it formed the pretext for the American policy of Containment and thereby became historically important in a way the 1956 military movements of Soviet troops in Poland were not. Another case study whose inclusion needs explanation is the one dealing with the Soviet post-war occupation of Austria. A legacy from World War II, it cannot be placed on the same level as the occupation of the Baltic states or Afghanistan. The main interest of the Austrian case is that the fait accompli situation of 1945 proved reversible after a decade. A case study on the Finnish experience would have been equally appropriate to illustrate the exception to the general pattern of Soviet rule in Europe. In this sense, our selection of case studies was subjective.

Some of the omitted cases are dealt with in the course of the general survey, though usually at lesser depth. The structure of this study is such that certain aspects are treated in the main text as well as in the case studies. The alternative would have been a multitude of cross-references which would have been even more cumbersome for the reader. This structure of the text is a result of a division of labour between the authors. All but one of the ten case studies (the exception being the one on the Greek Civil War), were written by E. Berends, while the general survey was authored by A.P. Schmid. The latter consists of three separate chapters dealing with Soviet intrabloc, interbloc and extrabloc military involvement respectively. In the first chapter the role of Soviet arms and armed forces in the postwar period are described in relation to conflicts in Eastern Europe and with China. The second chapter offers an analysis of military aspects of the East-West conflict. A study of the Soviet military role in the Third World is provided in the third chapter. The final chapter summarizes the findings on Soviet foreign military involvement and discusses the future of Soviet intervention.

The historical survey is based on secondary studies. A broad range of Western and a smaller selection of Soviet sources were utilized, the latter in translations, except for the case studies for which official Soviet sources were also consulted. The notes and the bibliography are attached at the end of this study.

ACKNOWLEDGEMENTS

The present study is an outgrowth of a broader study on the applicability of non-military resistance measures for contemporary conflicts. A source of support for this joint study has been the Dutch foundation 'Synthesis'. Through a timely grant this foundation made it possible that the case studies could be written.

In terms of intellectual stimulation our greatest debt goes to Milton Leitenberg, presently at the Swedish Institute for International Affairs.

At the State University of Leiden André Köbben, director of the Center for the Study of Social Conflicts (C.O.M.T.) gave us his full support. Without his good services, the material basis for this study would have been absent.

Special thanks are due to Jan Brand for assisting in many ways; to Peter G. Riddell and to Luyke Wittermans for correcting our English.

There are also many others who in one way or another contributed to this study through their work or advice. We will list only some of them: Berto Jongman, Hans Oversloot, Maart Wildeman, Angela van der Poel, Marie Verdel, Anke van Tuyll.

While they all helped to make this a richer study, the responsibility for any shortcomings and opinions expressed rests with us alone.

E. Berends
A.P. Schmid

Chapter I

INTRABLOC CONFLICTS: THE SOVIET UNION'S OCCUPATION OF EASTERN EUROPE AND THE SPECIAL CASE OF CHINA

Introduction

The liberation of Eastern and Southern Europe from German occupation brought about social transformations spearheaded by the Communist parties and guaranteed by the Soviet Red Army. The continuing Soviet postwar presence and involvement in national affairs evoked resistance. On a number of occasions such resistance, both popular or led by national elites, endangered the Soviet hegemony and was met with the threatened or actual deployment of military forces. In the Soviet Republics themselves, the military had to be deployed in the Baltic states and the Ukraine in the immediate postwar period. Guerrilla-type resistance also appears to have taken place in Poland. Twice, in 1949 and in 1950, Yugoslavia feared Soviet military intervention. In 1956, Soviet-led forces almost clashed with Polish forces organized by the 'national' communist Gomulka. Albania was subjected to Soviet threats in 1960-1961, and so was Poland in 1980-1981. In 1953 and 1956 popular uprisings in East Germany and Hungary were suppressed by Soviet troops. The most important deployment of military might, however, was the invasion of Czechoslovakia on August 20, 1968, when sixteen Soviet, three Polish, two Hungarian, two East German and one Bulgarian division intervened to put an end to "socialism with a human face". At that time Leonid Brezhnev gave a revealing explanation to the Czech leaders:

> "Your country is situated in the region where Soviet soldiers set foot in the Second World War; we have paid for that with great sacrifices, and we will never leave. Your borders are our borders as well. And if you do not obey us, we feel threatened. In the name of our dead from the Second World War, who have given their lives for your liberty, we are fully justified to send out soldiers to you so that we can feel factually secure within our borders. Whether there is a direct threat is secondary as this is a question of principle. And that is the way it will be from the Second World War onwards 'to eternity'." (1)

In the following pages, an attempt will be made to chronicle the Soviet Union's intrabloc conflicts in the postwar period. Five case studies treat these in greater depth.

Stalin's Policy for Eastern Europe

The territorial gains of the Soviet Union in Central and Southern Europe following World War II were considerable: half of Poland's territory amounting to 179,000 square kilometres went to the Soviet Union, the northern Bukovina and Bessarabia passed from Romania to the USSR. Czechoslovakia lost its northern province Ruthenia (Carpatho-Ukraine) to the Soviet Union. Half of East Prussia passed into the possession of the Soviet Union, the other half going to the resurrected Polish state now stretching as far west as the Oder-Neisse. Finland, which had regained some of the territories lost in the Winter War of 1940 with German help, was defeated again in 1944 and lost Western Karelia and the ice-free Port of Petsamo in the north, which gave the Soviet Union a common border with Norway. The Baltic states were reconquered. All told Soviet annexations involved a total of 472,000 square kilometres inhabited by nearly 24 million people.

Annexations such as these, however, were the exception. Most of the countries liberated from Nazi rule were granted formal independence and sovereignty, although controlled by Soviet military and Communist party presence. These indirect gains were even more substantial, involving 1,017,330 square kilometres of territory (without Yugoslavia) and nearly 93 million people (2). Whether this was a planned or an ad hoc result of Soviet policy is unclear. Yet there are no indications that Stalin's dreams were as ambitious as the ultimate result: the control of Eastern Europe - an area larger than France and West Germany combined.

There is almost no historical material available which would reveal what Stalin's intentions for the postwar period were with regard to the conquered territories. A few indications can be gained from writings of Yugoslavian authors. At one point Stalin apparently thought about creating a series of federations in the Balkan and in Eastern Europe, linked with the Soviet Union. When the dispute with Yugoslavia broke out in 1948 the substance of a discussion between a close associate of Tito and the Soviet ambassador in Belgrade, held in 1945, surfaced. Therein it was stated that "Soviet-Yugoslav relations should be based on the prospect of Yugoslavia's incorporation in the Soviet Union". In April 1945, Stalin told Milovan Djilas, the Yugoslavian liaison man of Tito in Moscow, that "This war is not as in the past; whoever occupies a territory also imposes on it his social system. Everyone imposes his own system as far as his army can reach." (3).

In October 1944, a secret understanding had been reached between Churchill and Stalin which laid down the spheres of interest of the Soviet Union on the one hand and Great Britain (with the United States) on the other for the Balkan and Eastern Europe. Greece was declared to be for 90 percent in the Western sphere and Yugoslavia for 50 percent. Soviet influence was to be 75 percent in Bulgaria, 50 percent in Hungary, and 90 percent in Romania. No agreement was reached on Poland, the country Great Britain entered the war for and the country Stalin had divided up with Hitler. The Americans, for whom Churchill also pretended to speak, did not commit themselves to this wartime agreement (4). With regard to Poland, Stalin was prepared to see it restored as a nation provided it ceded its eastern territories to the Soviet Union, accepted a regime to Moscow's liking and generally would serve as a buffer state. At Yalta, in February

4-11, 1945, the Western allies did not counter the Russian demand resolutely and contented themselves with empty promises of fair and early elections (5). It soon turned out that the London-based Polish exile government was no match for the Soviet-backed Lublin group. The popular front which they formed together in a provisional government was quickly transformed, after electoral frauds, into a "Democratic Bloc" which in turn became the "United Workers Party". Stanislav Mikolayczyk, the leader of the Polish Peasant Party (which counted 600,000 members - three times as many as the communist party in 1946), was back in exile by 1947. The new minister of Defence of Poland's army was a Soviet general of Polish descent, Marshal Konstantin Rokossowski, and he was appointed by Stalin.

It took only two to three years before Soviet control over Eastern Europe was established through secret police and Communist party coercion in the shadow of the Soviet occupation divisions. In Poland, the armed resistance against the Communist regime between 1945 and 1948 cost some 20,000 lives, including those of 4,000 Soviet soldiers. Another 50,000 resistance fighters were captured and deported to Siberia (6). In the case of Yugoslavia, which to a large extent had liberated itself from Nazi rule, Stalin did not succeed in establishing control. Tito rejected the incorporation of functionaries in his government apparatus who were primarily loyal to Moscow. Nor did he grant Soviet diplomats and advisors a privileged role in the reconstruction of Yugoslavia. The absence of a common border with the Soviet Union, the popularity of Tito, and the loyalty which military and party members showed to him, in combination with the economic and political support Tito was obtaining from the West, allowed Yugoslavia to survive its expulsion from the Cominform and heavy Soviet pressures. Between 1949 and 1952 there was a build-up of Soviet forces on the borders of Bulgaria and Hungary which reportedly led to more than 5,000 armed incidents. Specific Soviet preparations for invasion were registered by Yugoslavian intelligence both in the autumns of 1949 and 1950. One author, Vladimir Dedijer, also reported a Soviet invasion plan immediately following Stalin's death (7).

Hungary, which had fought on the side of the Axis until December 1944, was occupied by Soviet troops. There were only about 600 Communist party members in Hungary in 1945 and at the parliamentary elections in November 1945 the Communist and the Social Democrats together polled only 17 percent while the Smallholders Party won 57,5 percent. The occupation force, however, insisted on a coalition government. With the help of the Soviet army (numbering one million soldiers) Máthyás Rákosi and his exile group of 160 men, upon return from Moscow, bit by bit - the term salami tactics was Rákosi's - gained power in the coalition government (8). With the control of the Ministry of the Interior, and thereby the secret police (Allamvédelmi Osztály - AVO), in the hands of the Communists, a regime of torture and disappearances begun. Yet the Soviets were also directly involved. The secretary-general of the Smallholders, Bela Kovâcs, was abducted on February 27, 1947, by the Red Army's police and deported to Siberia (9). According to one account, no less than 600,000 Hungarians were deported to Siberia and Mongolia in these years (10). The Allied control Commission's Western representatives protested in vain. As in Romania, B··lgaria and Finland, a Soviet General receiving his instructions from Moscow was in command of the Control Commission. The 1947 elections were rigged and some members of the non-Communist parties were accused of plots and put on trial which induced others to go into exile.

In Romania, a country which had changed sides in the war after a coup d'etat led by King Michael I. on August 23, 1944, Soviet treatment was hardly different. Some 250,000 civilians and 180,000 soldiers were transported to the Soviet "Main Administration of Corrective Labour Camps", acronymed GULAG (11). With the political opposition dealt with in such a way it was difficult to imagine how the West could retain a 10 percent influence in Romania and a 50 percent influence in Hungary as Stalin had agreed with Churchill in October 1944. In Romania, the charge levelled against the peasant leader Ion Maniu was that he had been plotting against the state with British and American agents. The charge was not completely off the mark. Great Britain and the United States had sizeable oil investments in Romania. There had been an earlier attempt to organize a counter coup against the pro-Communist premier Petru Groza. However this conspiracy between the American members of the Allied Control Commission in Bukarest and King Michael in 1945 came to nothing. If there was a plot in 1947 it misfired as well. The 74 year-old Maniu was given a life sentence on November 11, 1947 and the King was forced to abdicate at gunpoint before the year ended (12).

The events in Bulgaria resembled those in Romania despite the fact that it had not increased its territory at Russia's expense the way Romania had done. Although it had not been at war with the Soviet Union (only with the Western powers), the Red Army entered the country on September 9, 1944, and within a week a pro-Communist coup took place in Sofia. A popular front government was formed, with the Communists demanding the ministries of Justice and the Interior. This in turn led to the formation of a people's militia under the new minister of the Interior. A reign of terror followed with tens of thousands of political opponents ending up in concentration camps. Among those executed was Nicola Petkov, the leader of the Agrarian Party which had gained almost one quarter of the votes in the 1946 elections. He was arrested in June 1947 with others and hanged on September 24, in the central prison of Sofia (13).

How systematic the deportations from Hungary and Romania were is difficult to assess but it might well be that the same sort of planning was applied which had been prescribed for the Baltic states in 1940. There the security forces of the NKVD - the acronym of the 'People's Commissariat for State Security' - drew up lists with 29 categories of persons to be "registered for later arrest or deportation to Russia". These categories included Social Democrats, Liberals, Zionists, Freemasons, public officials, aristocrats, members of the diplomatic service, representatives of foreign firms, officials of the Red Cross, and their families, as well as relatives of people who had gone into exile (14). This programme for the Baltic states, interrupted by the

German invasion in the summer of 1941, was to be resumed after the reconquest of the Baltic states, with hundreds of thousands of people to be deported in the years thereafter, with peasants being a major category of victims (see case study I).

The sovietization and repression did meet some resistance both inside and outside Russia's prewar borders, in the Ukraine (until 1947) and Byelorussia as well as in Poland and the Baltic States. In Lithuania about 20,000 Soviet troops were killed in the years 1944-1948 by local partisans, according to a Soviet source (15). In the Baltic States guerrilla formations were still active in the early 1950s and the latest recorded resistance fighter killed in action was reported in Lithuania in 1965 (16). Apart from armed resistance there was also passive resistance in the Baltic States. One author writes with regard to the postwar reimposition of Soviet rule:

> "...there was a considerable degree of passive resistance from peasants and religious groups, which resulted in massive deportations in 1949-50. At the same time, numbers of leading figures in the three States were purged. As a result of these purges, Russians and Soviet-born Balts came to occupy leading positions in Estonia and Latvia." (17)

Purges were generally occurring at the end of the takeovers in Eastern Europe. There was a certain pattern to the communist seizures of power. Malcolm Mackintosh, a British analyst and former officer with the Allied Control Commission in the Balkans, described it as a five step sequence:

(1) First came the establishment of a political coalition called a "National Front", a "Patriotic Front", or something similar, with major Communist Party participation. Communists were placed in control of the Interior Ministry as well. (...)

(2) Second, the Soviets forcibly merged the non-Communist, left-wing, or agrarian parties with the local Communist Party. (...)

(3) Third came the isolation of the center or right-wing parties. Here the normal procedure was to purge and bring to trial some leaders and to force others into exile. (...)

(4) Fourth, with the political system firmly in the hands of the Communist Party, elections were held on a single list of candidates. (...) The various elections and the formation of Communist government were followed by pleas for international diplomatic recognition and by the signature of peace treaties with the ex-enemy countries in 1947.

(5) The fifth stage, and the most brutal one, was when Stalin turned upon the "internal" Communist Party opposition in each of these countries, destroyed their resistance leaders, including the people who admired Tito, and indeed all Communist leaders who did not have a "Muscovite" background. (18)

In some respects these steps, carried out over a period of roughly five years, mirrored the developments in the Soviet Union in the two decades between the World Wars. The Soviet model, based on collectivization, industrialization and police terror was reproduced, with little or no consideration for local circumstances (except in

Poland with regard to collectivization) and with equally little concern whether the nations concerned had been on the Allies' or the Axis' side in the World War. As far as the Red Army was present this process worked, with minor exceptions. Finland was not swallowed up. The Allied Control Commission was headed by a Russian, but the country was not militarily occupied, except for the Porkkala base leased to the USSR. After the 1948 election in which the Communists did badly, they were dropped from the coalition without Stalin putting up a show of force. He had required a recognition of the special relationship between Finland and the Soviet Union which precluded the possibility that Finland would join a Western bloc and this assurance he had obtained before these elections. The Finnish communists had prepared a coup but received no Soviet backing. Stalin got all he wanted without them (19). Stalin himself was once quoted as saying that he chose this course because he knew that the Americans "had a thing" about Finland and that he did not want to risk trouble with them about this 'peanut'. Perhaps Stalin also "had a thing" about Finland. The granting of independence to Finland in 1917 was done by Stalin himself in his function as Commissar for the nationalities (20). A less sentimental reason for not absorbing Finland in toto was that an annexation would have jeopardized Sweden's neutrality and driven Sweden into a Western alliance, something hardly desireable to Stalin.

Albania and Yugoslavia were beyond the postwar reach of the Red Army (although the latter had helped to liberate Belgrado). Czechoslovakia, on the other hand, was a special case. With the treason of the West of 1938 at Munich fresh on their minds, many Czechs and Slovaks had warm feelings towards the Red Army when it arrived. The Communist takeover of Czechoslovakia occurred without sizeable Soviet Army presence in the country. Stalin once admitted that a freely elected government in any of the countries surrounding the USSR "would be anti-Soviet, and that we cannot allow" (21) but in Czechoslovakia, at least, there was genuine popular support for the Communist party in the beginning. Austria and Germany were also special cases since a zonal occupation by the four powers had been agreed upon during wartime already. In Austria the Communists could not get sufficient local support which would have allowed the Red Army to strengthen them. The situation was different in the Eastern Zone of Germany, where the Communists merged with the Social Democrats to form the Socialist Unity Party (SED) whereupon developments resembled those in the rest of Central Europe.

This, in brief, is the general picture of Communist takeovers in Eastern Europe and the Balkans. However, it is worthwhile to look at one case in more detail. The Communist-takeover of Czechoslovakia, with the invisible Soviet military pressure during the coup of 1948 and the strong Soviet support for the new regime after this event, is especially interesting.

The Prague Coup of 1948

In prewar Czechoslovakia the communists had polled some 10 percent of the votes (1935), eleven years later they became the biggest single party in a four-party political landscape, polling 38 percent of the votes in 1946. The main Czech exile leaders, Eduard Benes and Klemens Gottwald, met in 1943 in Moscow to discuss postwar arrangements. Eduard Benes, taking into account the geopolitical position of his country and the lesson from Munich in 1938, was convinced that the Soviet Union had to be accommodated. So he conceded five ministries to the Czech communists who under Gottwald had 'unconditionally' claimed the Interior (with the police), Defence, Information, Education and Agriculture. In a second meeting in March 1945 in Moscow the Slovak communists were also promised three government posts from a total of 25 to be distributed. When the exile government entered the country at Košice in the footsteps of the Red Army in April 1945 the new 'National Front' begun its work as a "democracy without opposition", excluding collaborators as well as representatives of domestic resistance. The communists were the most active in solidifying their position. As one writer described it:

> "And so they travelled from Košice in Soviet army vans loaded with propaganda material including stacks of application forms for Party membership. (...) The nation was to see that the Communists were the most active and the most capable. They used Soviet help and local enthusiasm to restore water supplies, clear the débris of war, obtain emergency food supplies, set up the administration, round up the Germans, arrest quislings and generally get things going. Local government and Communist leadership became irreversibly intertwined. By July 1945 the Party had almost half-a-million members (a remarkable progress from the less than 40,000 who had survived the war) and at the end of the year membership stood at over 800,000." (22)

In addition to local government successes, communists also became heavily represented in the top of youth organizations, trade unions, co-operative movements, farmer and veteran organizations and the like.
Czechoslovakia had emerged relatively undamaged from the war and its industrial base was a promising asset. Workers' militia were formed and armed to protect the factories, ostensibly against Sudeten-German sabotage, but they also formed a counterweight to the Army which was never fully under communist control (23). The new minister of Defence, General Ludvík Svoboda, was, for tactical reasons, not a card-carrying communist but his relationship with Klemens Gottwald, the premier, was a very close one. After the 1946 elections the Communists held, together with the Social Democrats, a slight majority of 153 parliamentary seats out of 300. The coalition government formed the year before in the 'Kosice agreement' remained in power, although the composition slightly changed. The communists held two of the key ministries, Interior and Information, in their hands. Although there were no deportations and arrests without charges and trials in the pre-1948 period, the police was put to good use by the Communists and so was the ministry of Information (24). The Red Army, however, played no visible role. Most of the 100,000 - 300,000 Soviet troops in Czechoslovakia had been withdrawn in November 1945 following a proposal of mutual

American and Soviet troops withdrawal made by President Truman (in September 1945 the USSR had still demanded winter quarters for 400,000 men in Czechoslovakia) (25). However, there were the unequal treaties which gave the Soviet Union economic advantages in its trade relations. Of special importance were the uranium mines of Czechoslovakia for the nuclear programme of the Soviet Union. The Czech price for uranium was such that the Soviet Union saved two billion dollars in its purchases in comparison with world market prices (26). The country's freedom of action was limited as became clear when the government, upon a direct order from Stalin, had to revoke its participation in the discussion on Marshall plan aid (27). Such Western aid was, of course, only available at a political price. When in 1947 the harvest was bad, the Americans made the delivery of grain conditional to a change in the country's political stance, and the deal did not materialize. In their place, the Russians offered 600,000 tons of grain, thereby boosting the image of the Communists. However, their popularity was not so big that they could hope on a parliamentary road to socialism. In fact, one poll conducted by the Prague Institute for Public Opinion forecasted in January 1948 a Communist vote slice of only 28 percent, ten percent less than two years earlier. In the face of deteriorating electoral prospects, the Communist Party's Central Committee had already in late November 1947 decided to prepare for taking state power.

On February 20, 1948, the politburo of the CSCP decided that "the Rubicon had been crossed" (Gottwald) (28). A tactical blunder of non-communist ministers who resigned from office on that date, out of protest over a refusal to dismiss eight newly-appointed Communist police officers in Prague, opened the door for the Communists. To the amazement of the departing ministers their resignations were accepted by President Benes after five days of wavering. Benes was old and very ill and afraid of war. He had been blackmailed by Gottwald on Stalin's orders with the threat of a Soviet military invasion. In addition, Rudolf Slanský, the Secretary General of the Communist Party, had threatened to shoot the bourgeois ministers (who were under house arrest), if Benes refused to sign the new cabinet list and accept the resignation of the ten ministers.

Following the resignation of these ministers the Communists effectively gained control over public reactions to the resignation. The non-Communist parties did not obtain access to radio to explain their position on orders from the Communist minister of Information. The newspapers of the coalition partners were kept from being distributed or were not even printed through the obstruction of Communist workers. All over the country Soviets in the form of "Action Committees of the National Front" were mushrooming whose demand was for a regenerated National Front without the bourgeois parties (29). Workers' militia, armed by comrades from the factories, marched through the streets, while the army stayed in the barracks. Having their agents in the other political parties, in preparation for the May elections, the Communists were informed about these parties reactions. The other parties were unable to mobilize popular support which would have tipped the balance. On February 25, Benes agreed to the formation of a communist-dominated government after

Gottwald had shown him a "liquidation list" of democratic politicians who would be executed if the President's hesitation would lead to bloodshed. Jan Masaryk, the foreign minister, agreed to stay on the post.

On the face of it, there was nothing unconstitutional about this Communist taking of state power. No violence had been used - although the police had intimidated political opponents. No general strike had been staged and the Soviet Army had not entered the picture, although there had been rumours of Soviet intervention. On February 19, 1948, the Deputy Foreign Secretary of the Soviet Union, Valerian Zorin, had arrived in Prague, ostensibly for discussing grain deliveries, and he conferred with communist ministers. To Klemens Gottwald, he let it be known that "the Soviet Union would not allow the West to interfere in Czechoslovakia's internal affairs". Zorin had come with orders from Stalin to use the minister crisis for beating the bourgeois parties decisively. He even recommended to Gottwald to ask for Soviet military assistance. The Soviet armies on the Austrian, Hungarian and East German borders, Zorin said, were prepared for intervention (30). Western intelligence was ignorant of this move. The American ambassador pointed out that "There was no evidence of any Soviet troop concentrations on the borders of Czechoslovakia" (31), and Bruce Lockhart, a British intelligence officer, concluded that the Soviet Union had not provoked the February crisis although it could have forced a decision if it had wished. Gottwald, while using the intervention threat as a means of blackmailing Benes, felt confident that he could succeed without direct outside military assistance. Stalin later forgave him for having acted on his own: "Excellent, comrade, excellent. You have liquidated the bourgeoisie with velvet gloves. But you have also had luck on your side." (32)

Once the takeover was a fact, the arrests and purges were carried out with Soviet encouragement and even with specific directions. Altogether some 350,000 Czechs and Slovaks were subsequently imprisoned or put into labour camps (33). On March 10 Jan Masaryk committed "suicide" by falling out of a window, reminiscent of the events of 1618, when a defenestration in Prague had marked the beginning of the Thirty Years' War. More than anything else this caused alarm in the West and, in the words of the American President, "sent a shock-wave through the civilized world" (34).

In fact the fate of Czechoslovakia had been sealed earlier. In April 1945, U.S. General George S. Patton, coming from Bavaria, had offered to liberate Prague with his tank corps which stood only 90 kilometres outside Prague when the Red Army was still 170 kilometres away. Neither General Eisenhower nor President Truman would allow him to proceed beyond Pilsen. The tanks of the Red Army arrived only on May 9 in the capital (which had liberated itself with the help of anti-communist Russians from the Vlassov Army two days before). In the subsequent years polarization between the blocs had led to the expulsion of the communist parties from the government in France and Italy the year before and everywhere a realignment of forces took place which left no room for the dream of Edward Benes that his country could serve as a bridge between East and West. Czechoslovakia was not allowed to participate in the Marshall Plan of economic aid which had been offered to "everything west of Asia" (G. C. Marshall), including the Soviet Union. On July 10, 1947, Stalin had vetoed Czechoslovak participation in the recovery programme. To counter the Plan, Stalin set up the Information Buros of the Communist and Workers' Parties (Cominform) in September 1947. Benes who was very ill and practically under house arrest outside the capital, resigned on June 7, 1948. On his death bed he confessed: "My biggest mistake was that I refused to believe until the end that Stalin lied to me cynically and in cold blood." (35) His funeral in September was the occasion for a large-scale anti-government demonstration but an increase of repression in the form of forced labor-camps broke the spirit of resistance for the time being. In one of these camps, which was attached to the uranium mines, the sons of the "capitalist and middle class families" were drafted to dig uranium for the socialist atomic bombs (36).

The events in Prague and the subsequent Berlin blockade in June 1948 rallied the forces of the Western democracies and speeded up the process of economic and military reconstruction.

The Popular Uprisings in the Post-Stalin Era

Immediately after the war Stalin had conceeded that there could be various roads to Socialism (but not various socialisms). However, after the defection of Yugoslavia, control over the other socialist countries was strengthened and the measures taken in Czechoslovakia after the February 1948 Putsch were one expression of this. Stalin mistrusted local communists and preferred communists which had spent their years in Moscow where they had acquired enough fear if not respect to stay in line with whatever Stalin held to be good. One of the "national" communists fortunate enough to survive, Imre Nagy, wrote in 1955 that Stalin and his Hungarian henchman Mátyás Rákosi had "exterminated" party members opposing the establishment of a Stalinist dictatorship and the subordination of Hungarian interests to Soviet hegemony (37). The "Muscovites", whose first loyalty was to the "socialist motherland" rather than to their own country, were not so numerous that they could have run the satellite countries, and from their co-operation with home-grown communists tensions arose. On a deeper level the tensions were those between loyalty towards the Soviet Union and loyalty towards one's own nation of origin, between the Soviet model of development and local solutions to local problems. As long as Stalin reigned, the national communists had no chance: Gomulka in Poland, Rajk in Hungary, Kostov in Bulgaria and others were removed from office. However, after the death of Stalin on March 5, 1953, the struggle for power in the Kremlin and the steps towards destalinization of the Soviet Union itself, brought about changes in the countries of Eastern Europe.

The power struggles within the communist party in the Soviet Union and the other socialist countries between Stalinists and anti-Stalinists, between Muscovites and nationalist reformers, were not synchronized, which produced unholy alliances and unstable situations. The struggle between Muscovites and national communists was one for positions as well as for reforms. As Christopher Jones put it:

> "They [the reformers] also had to emphasize those reforms that had the political effect of reducing the power of the Muscovites. The most effective weapon of the reformers was "truth" - public revelations of the incompetence, illegalities, and hypocrisies of the Muscovites, and public relevations of past instances of Soviet interference in the internal affairs of their country. These relevations gave the intraparty feud the quality of a moral struggle between truth and falsehood. In this battle over "truth", control of the information media became crucial." (38)

Khrushchev's rapprochement with Tito in 1955 signalled to other communist leaders that the Soviet Union seemed prepared to accept various socialisms. In 1961 Albania, with the support of China, managed to wrestle itself from Soviet influence and Romania also succeeded to detach itself after the Red Army was withdrawn in 1958. However, what was possible on the Soviet Union's Southern flank, was not allowed on the Western flank. In Germany, Hungary, Czechoslovakia and Poland reformist trends, backed by popular support, were undone by the Soviet Union in the 1950s and thereafter.

In the case of Poland in 1956, the crisis had been triggered off by a strike action of some 30,000 workers in Poznan. In order to placate popular unrest, the national communist Wladyslaw Gomulka was brought back to power, after having spent five years in jail. When Khrushchev, flanked by eleven generals, arrived in Warsaw on 19 October, 1956, to bring back Poland under Soviet control, this was accompanied by troop movements of the Red Army both at the borders of Poland and within. Soviet strength in Poland was increased from three to seven divisions. In addition to Soviet troop deployments in East Germany and Byelorussia, a Soviet naval task force was sent to Gdansk. The new secretary-general of the Polish communist party refused to negotiate as long as Soviet and Polish troops under Marshall K. Rokossovsky marched towards the capital and he threatened to address the nation by radio (39). Although the Polish army was under the leadership of a Soviet General, Gomulka had the support of some military units. The Polish air force under General Frey-Bielecki declared that it was prepared to attack these troops if they advanced beyond a certain line. At one point Polish units actually opened fire on a Soviet regiment entering from East Germany. The internal security forces (numbering 50,000 men themselves) had armed factory workers and students in Warsaw. It must have been clear that the price for conformity with the Soviet Union was a bloodbath and this the Soviet leaders were not prepared to pay. During the negotiations it also dawned on Khrushchev and his Soviet colleagues that they were in fact hostages of Gomulka and his ally General Komar, the newly appointed head of the Polish security forces. From that point on the Soviet leaders became conciliatory (40). In October 1956 the national communists in Poland won the day and the Soviet-imposed Polish Minister of Defence returned to

Moscow for good. Their triumph directly encouraged the Hungarian reformers to try the same.

The reasons why the Soviet Union intervened militarily in Hungary but not in Poland can be brought down to a couple of crucial differences. One is sequential: the Polish reformers were a week ahead and could get away being the first defectors. (The same mechanism helped Cuba to get away from American hegemony but contributed to the intervention in the Dominican Republic in 1965.) The second reason is more important: in Poland power passed from one wing of the Communist party to the other. In Hungary the same seemed to happen and the Soviet Union was prepared to led Imre Nagy steer a more nationalist course. But Nagy was prepared to concede a multiparty coalition government not dominated by communists. In fact the popular uprising threatened the very survival of the Communist party and the armed intervention by ten Soviet divisions in early November 1956 was no longer one to save the Muscovite faction from the nationalist one, but to rescue the remains of the Communist Party (41) (see case study III).

The subsequent developments in Hungary and Poland showed that the victory of Gomulka and the defeat of Nagy were later to some extent reversed. Gomulka gradually returned to the Soviet line and, according to one account, even pleaded in 1970 for a Soviet intervention to save his tottering regime after the outbreak of food riots (42). Janos Kádár who was imposed by the Red Army in Hungary in 1956, on the other hand, was able to introduce important reforms and achieve a measure of popular acceptance in the 1970s which few East European leaders ever could enjoy.

The East German rising of June 1953 came too soon after Stalin's death to allow for wavering or flexibility in Soviet reactions. Its outcome was also paradoxical to some extent. Walter Ulbricht, who was about to lose his position in the central committee, saw his rule consolidated for almost two decades as a consequence of the uprising (see case study II).

The most drawn-out conflict between reformers and Muscovites occurred in Czechoslovakia in 1968 with the Prague spring and the Soviet intervention in August as highlights. In contrast to Hungary twelve years before, there was no direct threat of a Communist party losing power. The Soviet leaders nevertheless labelled Dubček's policies dangerous "right-wing deviation". They were apparently afraid of a "second Yugoslavia" with potential contagious effects not only for other satellite countries but even for the annexed Baltic states and for the Ukraine. The Kremlin decided that it was too risky to leave Czechoslovakia unchecked and intervened with half a million Warsaw Pact troops on August 21, 1968. Although no military resistance was offered, it took no less than eight months - and the threat of a second invasion - to place power back in the hands of Muscovites. Despite the military presence of the occupation armies it proved, in the beginning, hard to find anybody willing to act as their puppets. That, however, was a prerequisite to success. As Christopher Jones writes: "The Soviet leaders require a fifth column in the East European party to legitimize the use of Soviet troops and to form a new government" (43). The restauration of orthodox communism after a short period of "communism with a human face" in Czechoslovakia after 1968 has not taken the form of "kádárization". Rather, the policy has been one of depoliticizing public life and of letting the attention of the masses go to their private affairs by means of a relatively modest cultivation of consumerism (see case study IV).

Although the methods have changed since Stalin, the nature of Soviet control has in many ways remained the same. Nomenclatura - the right to appoint officials to the higher party and state offices in Eastern Europe - has not been renounced by Stalin's successors and the East European armies are integrated into a Warsaw Pact command structure which makes their use for national defence against the "socialist motherland" an unlikely occurrence (44). Christopher Jones has made a case that Soviet military intervention took place in situations where the risk of war with the reformers was small. Where there was determined resistance and a credible threat of national resistance - such as in Yugoslavia after 1948 or in Poland in 1956, he argues, the Soviets backed down. In Albania in October 1961 Enver Hoxha also warned the USSR that "our glorious armed forces are fully in form and prepared to defend the Albanian People's Republic". In a similar fashion Nicola Ceausescu mobilized the Romanian army and distributed arms to militia at the time of the invasion into Czechoslovakia in order to signal determination to the Soviet leaders. In Hungary Imre Nagy's new government lacked the time to put up organized popular armed resistance. In Czechoslovakia, the government was lulled into a false sense of security after the Bratislava Declaration of August 3, 1968. After the invasion unexpectedly begun on August 20, 1968, the Dubcek government instructed its security forces to offer no armed resistance. Would arming the workers in the pre-invasion period have deterred Soviet intervention as was the case in Poland twelve years earlier? There is much plausibility to Jones' thesis that it made a difference:

> "Tito, Gomulka, Ceausescu, and Hoxha have shown that the Soviets will not use force to remove the leadership of a rebellious East European Communist party if the leaders of the party are willing to go to war in defense of their national sovereignty. What the leaders of the Czechoslovak party failed to do in 1968 was to mobilize their army and nation against the threat of Soviet military intervention."

However successful, deterrence of external intervention is not always enough. The Polish events since December 13, 1981 offer an example of self-occupation. The Polish army under general W. Jaruzelski took over state power after the Communist Party had disintegrated too much to offer hope for restauration of Soviet influence along civilian, party lines. While the military regime attempted to create the impression that it had saved the country from a Soviet military intervention, it is more likely that it acted as a kind of proxy, sharing common interests with the USSR.

If this interpretation is correct, it could signify that the armies of the Warsaw Pact partners of the Soviet Union have been successfully denationalized. The main function of the Pact for the USSR might be not to deter inter-bloc conflict but to prevent further intra-bloc secession. Or, as Alvin Rubinstein has put it cogently in his introduction to Christopher Jones path-breaking analysis of Soviet influence in Eastern Europe:

> "...first, in Bulgaria, Hungary, East Germany, Poland, and Czechoslovakia, Moscow uses the Warsaw Pact to reinforce Soviet influence by preventing national armed forces of the Pact countries "from adopting military policies that would give these national armies the capabilities of defending national territory by national means (italics added); and
> second, the national leaderships of Romania, Yugoslavia, and Albania, however, have been able to retain independent national control of their Communist Party organizations and effectively deter threatened Soviet military interventions "by demonstrating a capacity for prolonged resistance to a Soviet occupation" through the formation of military units able to mount a "territorial defense"." (45)

Today, forty years after the end of the Second World War, thirty-one Soviet divisions are still stationed in Eastern Europe with only Bulgaria and Romania forming exceptions among the Warsaw Pact countries.

China - a Special Case

The Brezhnev Doctrine, stressing the Soviet Union's right to intervene into another socialist state to avoid a return to capitalism, could not be applied to the People's Republic of China. The fact that China was so populous and so large and the fact that its social revolution had not been carried out behind the shield of the Soviet Red Army, precluded any military interference into the political structure of China. While there are parallels in the Sino-Soviet conflict with the one between Yugoslavia and the Soviet Union, Stalin was aware that he could not afford to treat Mao like Tito.

In 1945 Stalin had recognized the government of Chiang Kai-shek as the legitimate government of China in return for the latter's recognition of the "independence" of the Mongolian People's Republic and other concessions like a joint Sino-Soviet naval base at Port Arthur. However, the following year Soviet troops also came to the support of the newly founded East Turkestan Republic in the Kuldzha-Ili and Altai regions of Sinkiang. This military intervention (in which troops from Outer Mongolia also participated), was opposed by both Chinese nationalists and local Kazakh and Uighur groups. The Soviet troops retreated in 1947, two years before the Chinese Communists took control of Sinkiang. Stalin had aided the Chinese Communists by giving them the Japanese weapons captured in the Soviet occupation of Manchuria in 1945. At one point he urged them to enter into a coalition with the Chinese nationalists. While Mao's victory over his rival in 1949 was perceived as America's "loss of China", the Soviet Union's role in bringing this about had been negligible. In February 1950 a Sino-Soviet alliance against "Japan or any other State which should unite with Japan, directly or indirectly" was concluded between Stalin and Mao. Yet even Mao had to accept the independence of Mongolia. He was, as Khrushchev later observed, treated by Stalin "like a beggar".

While the nature of the Sino-Soviet collaboration during the Korean War is not well documented, it is generally accepted that after a period of relative cordiality until the mid-fifties, the relationship declined until Khrushchev withdrew all Soviet technicians in the summer of 1960. Ideological differences with regard to the prescribed course of relationships with the "imperialists" and the nations of the Third World played a role. The relative small amount of economic and military aid the Soviet Union was capable or willing to grant to China, coupled with Moscow's claim of leadership of the international Communist movement, contributed to the widening of the rift between the two Asian powers. During the Quemoy crisis of August-September 1958 the Chinese did not obtain the kind of Soviet support they thought they were entitled to due to their role in the Korean war. All they received was a nuclear guarantee for the case of an American nuclear attack. Coming, as it did, when the crisis was practically over, it was hardly more than an empty Soviet bluff in the eyes of China (46). Soviet policy towards India at the time of the Sino-Indian war of 1962 was also a sore point. In the ultimate analysis, however, it was a power rivalry between the first and the biggest socialist country, a rivalry poisoned by the heritage of the imperialist past when Czarist Russia in a series of "unequal treaties" concluded in 1858, 1869 and 1881 had obtained more than half a million square miles of Imperial Chinese territory in Central Asia and the maritime provinces of Siberia. Khrushchev's refusal to share the secret of the atomic bomb with China indicated to the Chinese leadership that the Soviet Union wanted China to remain a second-rate power, dependent in its contest with the United States over Taiwan on the nuclear shield of the Soviet Union. Unable to recover Taiwan, the leaders of the People's Republic of China raised the spectre of territorial claims on its Western border, when they demanded discussions on disputed border areas (47). The Soviet Union refused.

While border fighting initiated by the Chinese in the 1960s could be contained and apparently deterred by a nuclear threat, the Soviet Union has today almost as many troops on her border with China as in the Central European frontline states at the Iron Curtain (48). The Sino-Soviet alliance concluded in 1950 between Mao and Stalin, though long a dead letter, has not been renewed since it expired in April 1980. Relations between the two countries have been brought back to the level of "peaceful coexistence" at best, that is, on the same level as the relationship with imperialist powers and capitalist states (see case study V).

Conclusion

The speed with which the nations of postwar Eastern Europe were transformed into 'People's Democracies' must have amazed the Communists themselves. Within three years Communist party membership increased from 1,000 to 500,000 in Bulgaria; from 600 to 900,000 in Hungary; from about 2,000 to 940,000 in Romania; from 20,000 to 1,370,000 in Poland and from around 30,000 to 2,000,000 in

Czechoslovakia (49). With the external backing of the Red Army and the internal use of the secret police (in the cases of Bulgaria, Hungary and Romania hardly purged from fascist elements) effective Communist organizations were established and the opposition parties were split and destroyed. Once in power, many of the national Communist were purged, meeting a fate similar to the one of their political opponents. Ultimately it was not their being Communists that mattered to Stalin, but their being under his control. Control was the key: control by the Soviet Union to prevent future German influence in Eastern Europe; control to eradicate anti-Russians elements; control to extract economic recompensations for the Soviet losses suffered in the Great Patriotic War and control to prevent Capitalist influence (50). Kristian Gerner has assessed the Stalinist empire in these terms:

> "As for Central and South-East Europe, the treatment meted out by Stalin and the CPSU to the peoples of the conquered states shows that he regarded these peoples more as a nuisance and a potential threat than as an asset. Stalin's major interest was obviously in the territories of the countries in question. His political line was to deprive the subdued populations, as well as their communist rulers, of every possibility of influencing their own fate, not to allow them to interfere with his wish to station Soviet troops in the middle of Europe. Stalin showed that he knew how to control a territory by converting its inhabitants into prisoners. This method was fundamental to ensure the system's stability. When Khrushchev admitted that not only his own countrymen but also the peoples of the vassal states were human beings, a new foundation for the system had to be worked out." (51)

Stalin's successors have criticized him for many things but not for his foreign policy. They still seem committed to defend Stalin's empire - "the gains of socialism", as they euphemistically term it - against internal and external enemies. For this purpose the Warsaw Pact was created on May 14, 1955, linking Albania, Bulgaria, Czechoslovakia, the German Democratic Republic, Hungary, Poland and Romania militarily to the Soviet Union. It is this internal mission of the Warsaw Pact that constitutes the hidden aganda of the 'Greater Socialist Army' built around the Soviet Armed Forces under the control of the Soviet General Staff. T. Rakowska-Harmstone et al. have focussed on this neglected dimension of the alliance:

> "The organizational structure of the Warsaw Pact simultaneously meets Soviet requirements on both the internal and external fronts in Eastern Europe. There are three requirements on the INTERNAL front:
> 1. Maintaining a highly visible Soviet capability for internal military intervention against either anti-communist movements or national communist regimes seeking independence from the USSR;
> 2. Deterring a possible NATO military response to a Soviet intervention in Eastern Europe; in particular, a West German response to a Soviet intervention in the GDR;

3. Denying East European defence ministries the capability of defending either national communist regimes or anti-communist successor regimes. The denial of these capabilities results from a fragmentation of control over national armies. The East European political elites which ultimately depend on the assured capability for Soviet intervention support the Warsaw Pact policy of fragmentation of national control over national armed forces. They also support Soviet policies on the external front.

On the EXTERNAL front there is one basic requirement: keeping NATO on the defensive; in particular, keeping West Germany on the defensive. Soviet conventional and nuclear forces meet this requirement largely on their own, but the East European forces... contribute to the Soviet military threat against NATO." (52)

If it is true that without a strong army there can be no policy (General A. Beaufre), and if it is true that the armies of the Warsaw countries (except Romania) have been successfully decapitated and denationalized by the Soviet Union, Soviet military interference has been institutionalized to a degree which makes an armed conflict unlikely. It would mean that Soviet security stands on firm foundations, though not on the one of Article 8 of the Warsaw Treaty of Friendship, Cooperation and Mutual Assistance (1955) which refers to each member country's adherence "to the principle of respect for the independence and sovereignty, and of non-interference in their internal affairs." (53)

Case Study I

THE INCORPORATION OF THE BALTIC REPUBLICS INTO THE
SOVIET UNION (1940-1949)

At the end of the First World War Lithuania, Latvia and Estonia
became independent republics. The three countries had been
dominated by Russia for 100 to 250 years. In the recent past two of
them had been occupied by Germany (Estonia and Latvia in 1918). In
the wake of the Russian revolution they had experienced shortlived
Communist regimes, and had been invaded by the Soviets. The Baltic
nations had signed separate peace treaties with the Soviet Union in
1920 and their independence was generally recognized, though
Lithuania had some territorial disputes with Poland and Germany. The
three Baltic republics entered the League of Nations and adopted a
policy of neutrality. In the course of time they concluded
non-aggression pacts with the Soviet Union and in 1934 Lithuania
joined the Defence Alliance between Estonia and Latvia, after that
known as the Baltic Entente.
The Baltics largely faced the same internal problems. To expropriate
the big landlords, radical land reforms were carried out, especially in
Estonia and Latvia, and in the course of time the Baltic economy
became rather prosperous. Constitutionally, the Baltic republics
introduced reforms along western lines. Yet political experience and
democratic traditions were lacking and during the 1930s Estonia and
Latvia came to be governed by authoritarian regimes, as had been the
case in Lithuania from 1926 onwards.
The Baltic nations had gained independence at a time when both
Germany and Soviet Russia were defeated and they retained
independence only as long as these two neighbouring powers remained
weak (1). On August 23, 1939, the Molotov-Ribbentrop Pact of
Non-Aggression was concluded between the Soviet Union and
Germany. In a secret protocol that was part of the treaty and in the
supplements added during the following months, it was stated among
other things that all of Estonia and Latvia and virtually the whole of
Lithuania belonged to the Soviet sphere of interest. Declaring that
the Baltics were pursuing a pro-German, anti-Soviet policy and
pointing at their inability to prevent a German attack on the Soviet
Union through Baltic territory, Moscow demanded mutual assistance
pacts with the Baltic republics which were to make the former
non-aggression pacts invalid. The Baltic nations realized that
resistance was useless. The pacts which were signed in September and
October 1939 allowed the Soviet Union to maintain military bases on
Baltic territory. Soviet military maps printed in September 1939
already depicted the Baltic nations as Soviet republics and secret
basic instruction on the procedure regarding the deportation of Baltic
anti-Soviet elements was drafted in October 1939 (2). During that
same period of time, Germany and the Soviet Union - as agreed under
the Molotov-Ribbentrop pact - actually divided Poland between

themselves (September 1 and 17), and the Soviet Union attacked Finland (November 1939).

At the end of May 1940 the Soviet Union called upon the Lithuanian government in an official communiqué to put an end to its 'provocative acts' (3). On June 14 and 16 the Soviets demanded that the Baltic nations accept the stationing of more Soviet troops. In the night of June 14th, Soviet units marched into Lithuania, and on June 17 Latvia and Estonia were invaded. A.A. Zhdanov was put in special command of Estonia, A.Y. Vyshinsky of Latvia and V.G. Dekanozov of Lithuania; all three were outstanding members of the Communist Party of the Soviet Union. New, pro-Soviet 'popular' governments were installed, and in Soviet terms the socialist revolution had scored a victory. On July 14-15 general elections were held with single lists of Soviet-supported Communist candidates. Voting was recorded by a stamp in the voter's passport, and Communist majorities were obtained ranging from 93 to 99 per cent. The new Baltic parliaments immediately voted for incorporation into the Soviet Union. Their requests were accepted by the Supreme Soviet of the Soviet Union on August 3, 5 and 6, and Lithuania, Latvia and Estonia became the 14th, 15th and 16th Socialist Soviet Republic. During the same time Bessarabia and northern Bukovina were also incorporated. On August 7, 1940, the Supreme Soviet legalized the incorporations. The overwhelming majority of nations, including the United States and Great Britain, did not recognize the legality of the annexation of the Baltic nations into the Soviet Union. Baltic diplomatic and consular representatives abroad continued to function.

The former state structure of the Baltic republics and their legal systems were rapidly destroyed and a beginning was made with the sovietization of politics, economics, culture, education and other spheres of life. After the occupation the Soviet secret police immediately started to make arrests. The first mass arrests - affecting tens of thousands of Balts - took place between June 13-16, 1941. The deportations to the Soviet Union of most of the prisoners were described in the Soviet press as "voluntary migrations" (4). After the German invasion of the Baltics various mass graves were discovered. During the Soviet occupation in 1940-41 about 45,000 Lithuanians 60,000 Estonians and 35,000 Latvians were arrested, deported or killed (5). A similar policy was implemented in the Soviet-occupied part of Poland. From the point of view of Soviet ideology, the mass arrests were explained by the necessity to free the Baltic republics from capitalist remnants. Captives were accused of being anti-Soviet or counterrevolutionary elements, or renegade communists. In Western eyes, Soviet policy in the Baltics has to be seen against the background of the insanity of Stalinist terror.

Active resistance against the Soviet occupation of 1940-41 has apparently not been widespread in Estonia, Latvia and Lithuania. However, with the outbreak of the war between Germany and the Soviet Union on June 22, 1941, spontaneous demonstrations against Soviet domination occurred in the Baltics. At the same time Baltic units of the Red Army turned against the Russian soldiers. In Lithuania an estimated 100,000 insurgents seized control of several localities and on June 24 the restoration of the independent

Lithuanian state and the formation of a Provisional Government were proclaimed over the Kaunas radio. After a year of Soviet domination, many Balts were ready and willing to co-operate with the Germans. They greeted them as liberators, and the Baltic risings against the Soviets considerably facilitated the German invasion. Within a week after the beginning of the war the Baltic republics together with White Russia were incorporated into the German Reich as the new province of Ostland. The Germans soon forfeited the initial co-operation of the native population by ignoring the Baltic quest for independence and by their brutality. All in all about 577,000 Balts are estimated to have been killed or deported by the Germans, about half of them for being Jewish (6).

The Soviets started to reconquer the Baltics in early 1944. Like the Russians in 1941, the retreating Germans resorted to a scorched earth policy. A considerable number of Balts, many of them guerrillas, joined the so-called Volunteer Legions in German service to fight the Soviets. These units consisted of both volunteers and conscripts. The Nazi regime in the Baltics collapsed in the autumn of 1944. Estonians attempted in vain to declare their country free and independent, as did the Latvians in May 1945 just before the end of the Second World War. At least 250,000 Balts reportedly fled in fear before the advancing Soviet armies, mainly to Sweden and Germany. This invasion brought more Soviet troops into the Baltics than in 1940-41, and they often behaved like conquerors, engaging in looting and violence.

The Soviets reestablished communist governments. The purges were resumed immediately after the return of the Soviet security services, even before the Baltics had been entirely reconquered. In Lithuania the purge at first consisted of systematic arrests of individuals. These purges did not reach pre-war proportions until February 1946 when, as a result of intensified efforts to destroy armed resistance, the Soviets carried out mass arrests and mass reprisals (7). During their somewhat slower retreat from Estonia in 1941 the Soviets under the guise of mobilization had deported well over 42,000 young Estonian males. Now, all inhabitants of 12 years and older were screened. The purges seems to have been performed by way of arrests of individuals until March 1949 when, after a few years of preparative measures, the collectivization of agriculture was finally carried out.

In 1940 all land, banks, big and medium sized industries had been nationalized. Major reforms to sovietize Baltic society had not yet been introduced before the war, and the German occupation in some fields meant a step backward. After the war the Baltic economies were to be integrated into the Soviet system of planning. A small majority of the Baltic population was engaged in agriculture in medium and small holdings. Yet, according to Soviet statements, at least 80 per cent of the Latvian peasants in 1949, for instance, were considered 'kulaks' (8) and therefore subject to persecution. Collectivization could be implemented after a few hundred thousand Balts were taken away (9), most of them from the rural districts. In the houses of the uprooted farmers, who had provided the political base of the Baltic states, Russian peasants were settled. After 1949 deportations of Balts continued, though on a reduced scale. In addition, young Balts were forced to leave for labour service in the Soviet Union as "voluntary migrants". Most of the sentences for Baltic deportees lasted 10 to 25 years. The number of those released reportedly increased greatly after 1955/56 (10). The estimate of the return to the Baltics of 25-30 per cent of the deportees after Stalin's death (11) seems rather high, since death rates in Soviet punitive camps up to 1951 are said to have been 20-30 per cent a year (12). Moreover, quite a few of those released had to remain in exile, whether attached to or freed from their previous labour. A return of 15-20 per cent of the Baltic deportees therefore appears a more reliable estimate (13). The estimates of the total losses of the Baltic population under Soviet rule vary greatly from 500,000 deportees during 1941-1949, some 600,000 during 1940-1953, to almost 2 million killed or deported during 1940-1951 (14), i.e. from some 10 to more than 30 per cent of the population.

The agricultural collectivization dealt a great blow to the resistance movement in the Baltics, because it deprived the active partisans of the supply base and winter shelter previously provided by farmers. The active, fighting partisans generally lived in the dense forests and therefore were called 'forest brethren'. They received passive co-operation from supporters who lived ordinary lives. Organized partisan resistance lasted until 1953 in Lithuania, but there were still reports of incidental acts of armed resistance and non-violent opposition in the Baltics thereafter. In a case study on Lithuanian partisan resistance (15) it is stated that the movement developed spontaneously in Lithuania in the summer of 1944 and in less than a year numbered an estimated 30,000 active fighters. Lithuanian resistance to the Nazis had emphasized passive resistance, but against the Soviets struggle for independence resorted to violent means. At the same time the partisans illegally published papers and periodicals, maintained courts, established an underground government with a President and a Council of the Republic, etc. Most of the active fighters were young and the predominant social background was that of workers and farmers with medium-sized holdings. From early 1945 onwards the membership was restricted to native Lithuanians with only occasional exceptions being made for Latvians. Material support from the Western powers was negligible. A certain unification of the scattered partisan groups in Lithuania was achieved at the end of 1946. The Soviet security and army forces, however, had immediately started reprisals against the partisans, and the average life expectancy of the active partisans was said to be two years. During the partisan war some 20-30,000 partisans were reported killed along with a comparable number of Soviets and Lithuanian 'collaborators' (16). Many active partisans surrendered when they were promised amnesty during the first period of armed resistance. According to a refugee estimate there were still 20,000 partisan fighters in the Baltics in or just before 1951 (17). From the end of 1948 onwards, the Lithuanian partisans could no longer effectively paralyze the functioning of local soviets and prevent the establishment of kolkhozes, and four years later organized armed resistance in Lithuania was destroyed. It is not to be expected that the picture of guerrilla resistance in Estonia and Latvia differs greatly from that in Lithuania described above.

With the collapse of organized partisan resistance the situation in the Baltic republics stabilized. The 4th All Union Five Year Plan (1946-1950) was aimed at complete economic integration of the Baltics into the Soviet Union. Due to a large immigration of Russians the proportion of native Balts in Estonia and Latvia has declined sharply. The traditional anti-Russian feelings (especially in Estonia) continue to exist. Nowadays living standards in the Baltics are high compared with other regions in the country. There are indications that the Soviet government was, by the early 1980s, starting to deal more firmly with nationalism in the three Baltic republics by taking actions against dissidents and religious communities (18). The number of Balts living outside the Soviet Union in 1970 is estimated at 102,800 Estonians, 180,000 Latvians and almost 800,000 Lithuanians (19). The incorporation of the Baltic republics into the Soviet Union de jure has not been recognized by many Western countries, including the United States, Great Britain, France and the German Federal Republic.

Case Study II

THE EAST GERMAN UPRISING (1953)

In July 1952 the leaders of the Socialist Unity Party of Germany (the SED), with Stalin's permission and perhaps on his instigation, announced a new economic policy. The reforms aimed at the rapid construction of full socialism and included a program for the collectivization of agriculture and measures against self-employed artisans and small business men. The immediate result of the new policy was a sharp increase in the number of refugees.

As the party continued its policy of forced industrialization and agricultural collectivization, the economy continued to deteriorate and the number of refugees increased considerably. The food situation, which had been bad in the German Democratic Republic (GDR) ever since the end of the Second World War, grew worse. In late March 1953 the food crisis deepened and voices were raised in protest against the economic situation.

Early in April 1953, General Secretary of the Socialist Unity Party (SED) Walter Ulbricht asked the Soviet Union for economic aid. But no direct aid was granted and Soviet Prime Minister Georgi Malenkov advised the GDR on April 15 to adopt a New Course to mitigate its policy of socialization. After Stalin's death in March 1953, the new leaders of the Soviet Union had initiated a more moderate policy for the Socialist motherland herself. However, instead of launching a New Course, Ulbricht, in a speech to high SED officials on April 16, announced the continuation of the present economic policy and proposed a raise in industrial production standards.

The Central Committee of the SED, in line with Ulbricht's proposals, resolved on May 13-14 to raise production norms in construction and several other industries by ten per cent. When the decree was published on May 28, the workers received it with great indignation and during the first half of June some 60 local strikes occurred.

Moscow must have strongly disliked Ulbricht's deviation from its directions. It introduced some changes in the representation of Soviet officials in East Germany. When Vladimir Semyonov arrived in Berlin to fill the newly created post of Soviet High Commissioner to Germany on June 5, 1953, he carried with him instructions that were imperative.

On June 11 Neues Deutschland, the official party organ, published a declaration of the Council of Ministers promising to correct mistakes made in the past and to raise living standards. The compulsory agricultural deliveries were to be lowered, fugitive peasants were promised land if they returned, children of the middle class and the bourgeoisie were to be admitted to higher education again, discrimination in food distribution was to be reduced, etc. The new production standards, however, remained in force.

Discontent due to the economic crisis had grown within the SED as well. Two leading communist party members, Wilhelm Zaisser and Rudolf Herrnstadt, advocated a new policy stressing priority production of consumer goods along the lines of the programs carried out in Hungary by Nagy and in the Soviet Union by Stalin's successors. On June 16 the members of the East German Politbureau met to discuss the conflict between Ulbricht and the 'liberals'. The majority of the Politbureau must have supported Zaisser and Herrnstadt, who were evidently backed by Malenkov and the head of the Soviet political police (NKVD), Lavrentii Beria. Ulbricht appeared to be in a very precarious position, from which he was to be saved by the uprising in Berlin.

During the morning of June 16, 1953, the workers of Blok 40 of the Stalin Allee housing project laid down their tools in protest against the compulsory new production quotas which should not have taken effect until June 30 but which appeared to have been applied retrospectively from June 1st. A few hundred workers started to march through the streets and on their way their number grew to about 2,000 (1). After their arrival at the House of Ministers, representatives of the workers were kept waiting for quite a while before it was announced that production standards were to be lowered again. In the meantime, however, the spontaneous demonstration against the new work standards had already spread throughout the city and had assumed a political dimension. Placards appeared in town, calling not only for a reduction in the production quotas and a lowering of the prices but also for the resignation of the government and free and secret elections. Some of the placards even called for reunification with West Germany. Ulbricht announced a New Course on the same evening.

The following day, on June 17, the uprising in East Berlin became general. Early in the morning several thousand demonstrators tried to occupy public buildings and insulted and attacked communist officials. There were strikes and the red flag was taken down and burnt. Similar incidents occurred in other East German industrial centres like Dresden, Leipzig, Magdeburg, Jena, Halle, Rostock, Merseburg and Bitterfeld. In total at least 300,000 workers in 272 towns throughout East Germany were on strike during that day, that is 5.5 per cent of the 5.5 million employees (2).

Soviet units intervened that very day. Two or three mechanized divisions (3) sealed off East Berlin and occupied the city. The tanks moved very slowly into the crowds. Some of the demonstrators threw rocks and sticks, but most were soon forced to disperse and abandon their protests; "the demonstrators were not familiar with non-violent resistance methods" (4). Generally, the uprising had a disciplined and non-violent character. The Soviet Military Commander of Berlin declared martial law and in the evening East Berlin was quiet again with Soviet forces remaining in the streets. In other parts of the country demonstrations continued for several days before they could be entirely quelled.

There seem to have been few casualties due to the great restraint used in the dispersal of the crowds. According to one source, however, perhaps 1000 people had been killed or wounded (5). Reportedly, 25,000 persons were arrested and 42 of them were condemned to death by special courts of justice (6). The trade union elections after the June rising resulted in a change of 71.4 per cent of the personnel (7).

It is not quite clear why the East German authorities did not crush the risings all by themselves. The East German police consisted of the People's Police (VP) and the Security Police (SSD). The VP generally remained passive, though a few joined the rebels. Unless directly attacked, the hated SSD remained passive as well, perhaps deliberately held back by security chief Zaisser. The East German military establishment, the People's Police in Garrison (KVP), by 1953 consisted of a 100,000 men (8). In 1952 the Soviet Union had started to form a regular army out of the KVP but the transition was still very incomplete in June 1953. During the demonstrations the isolated KVP remained passive until it was put at the disposal of the Russian supreme command. It then became an effective instrument of repression, though the Soviet troops were the decisive factor in quelling the uprising.

Of the estimated 30 Soviet divisions in East European countries in the early fifties, 22 of them were stationed in the GDR, altogether about 400,000 men. The quality of these Soviet troops seemed to have been rather high (9). As far as Berlin was concerned, the Soviets and not the East German regime were legally in control (10).

The Soviets probably considered an intervention necessary because the SED seemed to be losing control of events. Added to this was the fact that the SED was a coalition of communists and socialists and strong resistance had developed within the SED to Ulbricht's hard line policy. Moscow may well have feared a change to a non-communist East German leadership. There was little reaction to the events in the East European countries. They faced the same kind of economic problems and in most of their press comments the incidents were blamed on western agents.

The uprising in June must have shown the Soviet leaders that they had not acted rapidly or forcefully enough in directing the East German leaders to a solution of the economic crisis. This might have been connected with the problems within the Soviet collective leadership after Stalin's death in March 1953. A few days after the intervention, Beria's fall was announced. He was to be charged with treason and conspiracy. Both the Soviet and the East German leaders were to denounce Beria's policy with regard to the GDR, accusing him of obstructing the consolidation of socialism in East Germany. The charge was extended to Malenkov as well, after his fall a few years later. Pointing to the previous secret contacts between Zaisser, Herrnstadt and Beria, it became easier for Ulbricht to eliminate the leaders of the opposition. However, Ulbricht had to carry out the New Course conscientiously. This task was greatly facilitated when the GDR was granted considerable financial aid from the Soviet Union some weeks after the uprising in June (11).

Case Study III

THE HUNGARIAN UPRISING (1956)

After Hungary became a one party state in 1948, reforms along the lines of the Soviet model were carried out under the leadership of the Stalinist First Secretary of the Party and Prime Minister, Máthyás Rákosi. Since these reforms were not tailored to Hungarian conditions, living standards dropped quickly. Public resentment against the regime increased rapidly, but remained silent because of great terror.

Stalin's death in March 1953 marked the beginning of modest changes in the political climate in Hungary as in the Soviet Union. Imre Nagy succeeded Rákosi as Prime Minister and announced a more liberal New Course. But despite great popular support it failed to become a success, mainly due to Nagy's lack of following in the still Stalinist party. After criticism from Moscow and the resignation of his supposed backer, Soviet Prime Minister Georgi Malenkov, Nagy had to resign as head of government in April 1955 and was also ousted from his party functions.

When the Soviet First Secretary of the Party N. Khrushchev denounced Stalinism in his secret speech to the 20th Party Congress in February 1956, the Hungarian administration was discredited. Rákosi was replaced by Ernö Gernö, who, however, was too closely linked to the old regime to make the half-hearted attempts of governmental reforms look credible. The opposition was gaining force. In the second half of October 1956 Poland managed to secure its own path to socialism under the guidance of Wladislaw Gomulka as First Secretary of the Party. Inspired by the Polish example, Hungarian writers and students in Budapest on October 22 distributed lampoons with 16 demands. Among these figured prominently the withdrawal of the Soviet troops from the country, free and secret elections, freedom to set up political parties, freedom of press and speech, the right to strike, economic reforms and reforms of the administration under the leadership of Nagy. On the next day political meetings and demonstrations were organized and some incidents occurred involving the deeply hated secret police AVH (usually called by the former acronym AVO). Tension increased. The rebels obtained weapons and the movement grew overtly anti-Russian.

At that time, two Soviet divisions were stationed in Hungary: the so-called Southern Group of Troops, about 20,000 men and 600 tanks encamped mainly around their headquarters in Szolnok (1).

On October 24 Nagy was appointed Prime Minister. He was compromised at once, since that very day summary justice was introduced and a few thousand Soviet troops, with less than a hundred tanks (2), marched into Budapest at the request of First Secretary of the Party Gernö. Bitter streetfighting and strikes followed and the revolt spread like a bushfire in and beyond the capital. The Soviet troops already stationed in Hungary were gradually reinforced by Soviet forces from Romania. The reinforcements probably started arriving before October 24 (3). Members of the Soviet Politbureau Michail Suslov and Anastas Mikoyan arrived at Budapest to mediate. János Kádár replaced Gernö as First Secretary of the Party. Nagy formed a coalition cabinet. Apparently, the relatively small scale armed intervention of the Soviet Union in Budapest on October 24, 1956, did not have a clear political objective. The Soviet troops did not yet seem to be prepared for effective military action. A ceasefire was declared on October 28 and the Soviets withdrew from Budapest.

To appease the armed insurgents the Nagy government gradually began to meet their demands. On October 30 the one party system was abolished. Two days later Nagy announced Hungary's secession from the Warsaw Treaty Organization, coupled with a strong protest against the growing military presence of the Soviet Union in Hungary. On November 2 Hungary officially requested the United Nations to recognize and protect its neutrality. The day after Nagy shuffled his cabinet so that the Communist members became a minority.

In the meantime the number of Soviet troops on Hungarian soil had been raised to 50-75,000 men by October 26 and to 8 divisions by November 2, totalling 200,000 troops and 2,000-2,500 tanks by the eve of November 4th. The Soviet leadership discussed the situation in Hungary in secret emergency-meetings with Poland, Czechoslovakia, Romania, Bulgaria, Yugoslavia and China (4). Very early in the morning of November 4th Soviet forces launched their second intervention. They had been invited by a pro-Soviet opposition government formed by Kádár c.s. three days earlier.

This time the military operations of the Soviet forces were carried out ruthlessly, unlike the rather hesitating conduct during the first intervention. It took the Soviets but a few days to crush the Hungarian revolt. The whole country was placed under control. In March 1957 the Russians started to withdraw some of their troops. The Hungarians must have mourned about 20,000 dead (5). According to official Hungarian sources, between October 23 and December 1 12,971 wounded received professional medical treatment (6). At least 200,000 Hungarians out of a population of 10 million crossed the Austrian and Yugoslavian borders and became refugees. Soviet fatalities were, according to one source, 7,000 (7).

As political terror in Hungary had decreased, the revolutionary movement had grown. Soon Nagy's liberal concessions could no longer appease the strong opposition which threatened to dislodge the communist regime. Within the span of a few days events in Hungary had developed much faster and further than in Poland. During the second intervention the Soviets faced violent resistance by thousands of rebels, while most of the population sympathized passively with the insurgents. The Hungarian army as such could not be deployed against Soviet troops, since the officers were split into pro-Soviet, uncommitted and patriotic groups. The rank and file, however, generally showed strong sympathy for the insurgents and many military men, headed by general Pál Maléter, as well as policemen joined the uprising. The Soviets met the strongest resistance in the working-class districts of Budapest and the industrial centres in the countryside. Moreover, the workers started a general strike all over Hungary that was to last for well over one month.

Strikes, demonstrations and acts of violence continued throughout November and December. 80 per cent of the army officers refused to sign pledges to the new regime after the Soviet interventions (8). The opposition movement as such was never an organized body, but on student instigation workers had organized themselves during the first Soviet intervention. The first workers' councils at factory level had been set up on October 24. The students were formed into a Students' Revolutionary Committee. In the course of the general strike during the second Soviet intervention, the workers set up councils at factory, district and city level, and planned to organize at national level as well. The major task of the factory workers' councils was the take-over of the management of their enterprises, while the district workers' councils were in essence political organs from the start. Most of the delegates at the Budapest city workers' council were young skilled workers. The Kádár government at first tried to win the co-operation of the workers' leaders. When this effort failed it started to use coercion and force against them. By January 1957 striking or inciting to strike was punishable by death. Although the organized power of the workers' councils had now been broken and resistance against the Kádár regime was under control, sabotage, passive resistance and even occasional strikes and demonstrations by workers continued throughout 1957. On November 17, 1957, the government dissolved all remaining workers' councils.

In the eyes of the Soviet government the Hungarian uprising was a counter-revolutionary revolt, organized by the international imperialistic reaction; the Hungarian people was in danger of losing all socialist achievements and was threatened by a fascist dictatorship. According to its obligations under the Warsaw Pact, the Soviet Union 'assisted the Hungarian people' to crush the fascist counter-revolution and to strengthen peace in the world. According to Khrushchev the show of force was also meant to make it clear to the Red Army that the present Soviet leaders were as strong as Stalin had been, and as unlikely to be mocked at (9).

In the West, the open show of force in Budapest destroyed illusions about a possible liberalization of the Soviet Union after Stalin. However, outside Europe the Soviet intervention did not have much impact at all, and in essence the reaction of the American, British and French governments remained quite moderate. Criticism of the Soviet Union was confined to a moral condemnation through the UN, and no political or military pressure was exercised. Obviously, Dulles' roll-back doctrine was not meant for Hungary, as Hungarian listeners to Radio Free Europe might have been hoping for. It has, however, been alleged that the American CIA and West German BND did supply a limited number of weapons to Hungarian insurgents (10). When the Soviets invaded Hungary for the second time the Western world was deeply preoccupied with the Suez crisis which deflected attention from the Hungarian tragedy. At the request of the USA, Great Britain and France, the Security Council had met on October 28 and November 2 to discuss the first Soviet intervention. When the Security Council met after the second invasion, the Russians vetoed the American resolution aiming at the withdrawal of Soviet troops from Hungary and proposing to render material assistance. The General Assembly, however, did pass the resolution and decided to send UN observers to Hungary. Red Cross convoys were given permission to cross the Hungarian border only after a week; the UN observers were not admitted at all. In January 1957 the UN established a Special Committee on the Problems of Hungary to investigate the uprising, without being admitted to the country. The General Assembly of the UN continued to pass resolutions on the Hungarian question throughout 1962 (11).

In Hungary the dominance of the renamed communist party was restored and in March 1957 Hungary's allegiance to the Warsaw Pact was reaffirmed. To realize the political aim of their intervention the Soviets had brought Kádár to power, though he had reportedly not been their first choice (12). Hated as a quisling, Kádár purged the country and crushed the political opposition. In January and February 1957, 2,000 people were executed and 20,000 were taken prisoner (13). On the other hand, Kádár removed leading Stalinists from their positions, deideologized daily life and concentrated with the support of the Soviet Union and other East European countries on economic development. Public opinion was neutralized, living standards were raised (especially after the economic reforms in 1968) and after ten years the Kádár government had become one of the more stable regimes in Eastern Europe.

Case Study IV

WARSAW PACT INTERVENTION IN CZECHOSLOVAKIA (1968)

When the Stalinist Antonín Novotny resigned as First Secretary of the Czechoslovakian Communist Party on January 5, 1968, he was replaced by the Slovak Party Secretary Alexander Dubček. Dubček's appointment initiated a period of reforms that came to be called the Prague Spring.

The desire for changes felt by the majority of the population had several roots. Discontent with the economic situation had existed ever since 1962, when economic growth had suddenly stagnated and the third Five Year Plan for 1961-65 had to be withdrawn. Due to strong opposition from supporters of Soviet-type centralized planning, major economic reforms reflecting ideas of Ota Šik could only be introduced in 1965/67. But the economic flexibility aimed at was no success and prices rose sharply. The belief began to gain ground that economic changes were inadequate without political liberalization. The desire for political liberalization found support in the memory of a strong democratic tradition that had existed in Czechoslovakia up till the communist seizure of power in 1948. Among the Slovaks, moreover, resentment of Novotny, a Czech, and his policy of centralization was growing, and demands were heard for federalist reforms of the state. In sum, during the 1960s a cleavage had developed in the party between conservatives and liberal reformers, resulting in the replacement of Novotny.

The Dubček regime enjoyed wide popular support, and backed by the Slovaks the 'liberals' also had a majority in the Central Committee of the Party. At the end of March the former Minister of Defence, general Ludvik Svoboda, replaced Novotny as President, and Oldšich Cerník became Prime Minister. In the first week of April a Party Action Program was approved to give, as it was stated, Czechoslovakian socialism a human face. The Action Program was moderate in some aspects, radical in others, and in Moscow and in the other East European countries the Czechoslovakian New Course no doubt caused deep concern. After the abolition of press censorship a wave of criticism had burst forth, unprecedented in any socialist country. It was feared that the new leaders would lose control of events, and that Czechoslovakia would eventually withdraw from the Comecon or the Warsaw Pact. Czechoslovakia's location was of strategic importance - a 'dagger in the heart of Europe', more specifically in the heart of Eastern Europe. Furthermore, the political situation in Czechoslovakia could endanger other socialist countries (notably Poland and the Ukrainian part of the Soviet Union), if the new spirit of freedom proved to be contagious. Strongest denunciation of events came from the GDR, fearing the worst from a Czechoslovakian change in attitude towards West Germany.

The new Czechoslovakian leaders were not aiming at an independent position like the Yugoslavians at that time, nor at the kind of liberties the Hungarians had longed for in 1956, nor even at the position of the Romanians. It appeared that Dubček himself was truly attempting to stay with the communist line, that he was only slowly advancing towards economical and political reforms and did not intend to weaken socialism. The Czechoslovakian press, however, turned more anti-communist and anti-Soviet by the day and it became obvious that the liberal forces strengthened by Dubček's ascendency to power were gradually heading for a more risky course. The cleavage between the reformers and the conservatives within the Czechoslovakian party widened as did the split between Czechoslovakia and the Soviet Union, especially when destalinization in Czechoslovakia began to reach those elements in the party, army and secret police that Moscow had been able to count on in the past. Ever since the last week of March, 1968, the Czechoslovak question was a topic at summits in Dresden and Moscow. The Soviet Union did not have troops in Czechoslovakia, but on May 14, 1968, joint Polish-East German-Hungarian-Soviet "staff exercises" of the Warsaw Treaty Organization (WTO) took place in the north of Czechoslovakia, which included large armoured and infantery contingents. The manoeuvres were due to end on June 30, but the Soviet troops were only slowly withdrawn. By the second week of July 16,000 Soviet men were reported to be still in Czechoslovakia (1). Except for the political and military pressure exerted on Czechoslovakia to turn the course of events, an extensive propaganda campaign was launched in the Soviet, East German and Polish press.

On June 27 Ludvík Vaculík's 'Two Thousand Words', signed by 70 intellectuals and a few workers, called for non-violent action to maintain and accelerate the evolution towards democracy and warned of foreign intervention. The manifesto caused immediate commotion in Czechoslovakia and embarrassed the regime. On July 15 the WTO countries, except Romania and Czechoslovakia, after a summit in Poland, presented the so-called Warsaw Letter, condemning the situation in Czechoslovakia as unacceptable to socialist countries. But after consulting the Central Committee Dubček soon rejected the WTO demands. In the last week of July extensive manoeuvres started along the western borders of the Soviet Union, including the Russian-Czechoslovakian border.

At the end of July and in the beginning of August meetings took place in Cierna Nad Tisou between Czechoslovakian and Soviet party leaders and in Bratislava between leaders of the WTO countries, except Romania. The Bratislava communiques contained only generalities but it was widely believed that a compromise had been reached. The crisis that had arisen after Dubček's rejection of the Warsaw Letter seemed to have been warded off. Shortly afterwards the last WTO troops, probably all or most of them Soviet, left Czechoslovakia (2).

Nevertheless the Czechoslovakian press continued to publish anti-Soviet articles. On August 10 the draft Party Statute was published. It introduced secret ballots for party elections. The Statute was to be adopted at the Party Congress on September 9, 1968, to confirm the liberal course of the Prague Spring. On August 11 new military manoeuvres around Czechoslovakia were announced and at 11 p.m. on August 20, 175,000-200,000 troops of the Soviet

Union, the GDR, Poland, Bulgaria and Hungary crossed four borders of Czechoslovakia at eighteen different points.

Primary targets were airports and important cities. The invaders did not try to assume full control or to carry out police functions as the Soviets had done in Hungary. Ultimately the invaders numbered between 400,000 and 500,000 men, the overwhelming majority of them being Soviet troops. Perhaps 150,000 to 200,000 men were deployed from the Soviet Union to augment the Soviet divisions stationed in Eastern Europe prior to the invasion. It is estimated that there were less than 50,000 Polish troops, less than 20,000 Hungarian and as many East German troops, and fewer than 10,000 Bulgarians (3).

There has been a great deal of speculation about the decision to intervene. In the early months of 1968 Moscow had seemed to be prepared to go along with Dubček, but the Action Program in April had made the Soviets realize that delaying tactics would not solve the problem. The Soviet Union has probably taken the decision to intervene somewhere between late July and mid-August, perhaps even before the summit in Cierna. The technical preparation for a possible invasion seems to have started as early as April 1968.

At the request of its government the Czechoslovakian army of 175,000 men offered no military resistance because of the imbalance of forces. Besides, the Czechoslovakian army was not reliable with its pro-Soviet generals and Soviet advisers, contrasted with its more liberal rank and file. Allegedly, the Soviets had succeeded in getting one of the top military leaders in Czechoslovakia dismissed prior to the intervention. They also had the Political Military Academy in Prague where the majority of the Dubček supporters were stationed closed (4). With no battles, there were relatively few casualties (some tens, at most a few hundred) and on the Soviet side there were no known casualties (5). Spontaneous, improvised nonviolent resistance to the invasion was widespread. Resistance was mobilized by clandestine radio transmitters and an illegal press, and was supported in public by party, government, police and military men. The Czechoslovak Politbureau adopted and published a resolution condemning the intervention, and the 'Extraordinary Fourteenth Party Congress' met to discuss events only a day after the invasion had started. All sections of society refused to cooperate with the invaders, and attempts were made to mislead them and to undermine the morale of the badly informed soldiers. However, though nonviolent resistance succeeded in seriously hampering the invaders, it could not stop them or persuade them to withdraw.

Among the socialist countries, strongest opposition to the WTO intervention came from Yugoslavia and Romania. Immediately after the news of the invasion broke, both countries placed their forces on alert. Public opinion in the West was outraged while governmental response was restrained. The United States condemned the intervention but recognized Czechoslovakia's location within the Soviet sphere of influence. The American government was determined not to endanger the prevailing détente. It was hoped that the visit of President Johnson to Moscow soon afterwards would lead to an effective beginning of the Strategic Arms Limitations Talks. The UN Security Council met on the evening of August 21st. The Soviets vetoed a resolution condemning the invasion of Czechoslovakia. Three members of the Council had abstained and the matter was not referred to the General Assembly.

Initially the Soviet Union had tried to present the invasion as a response to an invitation by loyal communists, but all responsible Czechoslovakian authorities denied that any request for assistance had been made. Since no one in Prague, not even among the most orthodox party conservatives, could be found to form a puppet government, the Soviets had to exert pressure on the legitimate Czechoslovakian government, whose members were at that time under arrest. On August 26 the Moscow Agreement was reached. Dubček was to remain First Secretary of the Party. Shortly afterwards the Soviet Union made another effort to justify the invasion by pointing at the danger posed by NATO, and more precisely by West Germany. It was said that counter-revolution, abetted from without by imperialism, had threatened Czechoslovakia and thus the indivisibility of the socialist system. The right, claimed by the Soviet Union, to intervene forcibly in the affairs of any member of the socialist Eastern block to protect class struggle and proletarian internationalism, was soon to be known as the Brezhnev doctrine. The idea behind the Brezhnev doctrine had already been formulated in the Warsaw Letter of July 1968, though no military means of enforcing it were then mentioned (6).

In the beginning the Moscow diktat seemed relatively mild. Dubček and his associates, on the other hand, gradually discredited themselves by dismantling their own reforms. With the Moscow Agreement, the Czechoslovakian leaders had accepted Soviet demands on key elements of internal and foreign policy, including the restoration of censorship, the banning of free assemblies and non-communist organizations, the reconfirmation of Czechoslovakian adherence to all existing treaties and a closer co-operation with the Soviet Union. In October 1968 the Czechoslovakian leaders had to assent to the stationing of troops in their country, allegedly because of a military threat from West Germany. The Soviet forces in Czechoslovakia stabilized in the following years at 5 divisions (about 75,000 men). The intervention in Czechoslovakia reinforced Soviet military power in Europe by connecting Soviet forces in Poland and the GDR with Soviet forces in Hungary, that is, the Northern Group of Troops with the Southern Group. The new Central Group in Czechoslovakia raised the total of Soviet forces stationed in Eastern Europe to 26 divisions (7).

The morale of Czechoslovak nationalism, however, was at first not easy to break. After the invasion 57.8 per cent of the officers under 30 left the army at their own request (8). There were repeated incidents like the self-immolation of Jan Palach, and on the anniversary of the invasion security and border troops rather than the regular army had to put down anti-Soviet disturbances. In the West, indignation over the Soviet intervention soon died down.

The Soviet intervention achieved the desired result, but only after a long delay. Gradually several liberal members of the Central Committee of the Party were replaced by pro-Soviet conservatives. On April 17, 1969, Dubček, not being able to satisfy either his supporters or his critics, was succeeded by Gustav Husak under whose leadership political, economic and cultural life in Czechoslovakia was to be 'normalized'. Governmental bodies were thoroughly purged, as was the party, loosing about one third (more than half a million) of its members, mostly as a consequence of purges. In 1970 and 1971 2313 persons were reportedly sentenced for political reasons, and in 1972 a new wave of political trials followed (9). Living standards and the political climate came to resemble the one in the Russian part of the Soviet Union, and public opinion in Czechoslovakia became very embittered. In 1971 Husak publicly thanked the Soviet Union for complying with the 'request of Czechoslovak communists' to intervene in 1968 (10).

Case Study V

THE SINO-SOVIET BORDER DISPUTE (1960s)

Border disputes between China and (Soviet-)Russia have been a recurrent phenomenon ever since the 17th century. After the communist take-over in China (1949) the problems seemed to have eased, though there are indications that China did not look upon the matter as having been settled: Chinese maps of the early 1950s listed various parts of Soviet Kazakhstan, Kirghizia and Tajikistan as belonging to the People's Republic of China. The border dispute revived when the friendly relationship between China and the Soviet Union started to deteriorate. The discord between the two countries centered around ideological issues and rivalry for power. The boundary question was initially merely a convenient way to express differences, but it gradually turned into a cause of Sino-Soviet dissension in its own right.

The border dispute itself had to do with the border treaty implementation, the border demarcation and the administration of the border area. The Chinese considered the treaties, by which Russia in the 19th century had acquired some 1,5 million square kilometres (580,000 sq. miles) from China, as being "unequal". China asserted that the Sino-Soviet boundary up to then had remained an unsettled question, but said that it was willing to accept the unequal treaties as the basis for determining the border line. However, China accused the Soviet Union of having crossed even this boundary line and of having occupied large areas of China. The Soviet Union rejected the Chinese demand of a troop withdrawal from the disputed areas, arguing that the border line which was claimed by the Chinese did not coincide with the one defined by the earlier Sino-Russian border treaties (1). Besides, any considerable retreat to the north would leave the Russians in "tundra and ice" (2). According to Chinese sources, the Soviet Union considered that, on historical grounds, the Sino-Soviet border should in many places be determined beyond the line stipulated by the 19th century treaties, the Soviets desiring to have the 'actual boundary' taken as the basis for solving the border dispute (3). Regarding Outer Mongolia, China effectively dropped its territorial claims by concluding a border treaty in 1962.

During negotiations in 1964 maps were exchanged between China and the Soviet Union on which each country had marked its version of the Sino-Soviet boundary. In the east, the border followed the path of the rivers Ussuri/Wusuli and Amur/Heilung. On the 19th century Peking Treaty Map, which had a scale of less than 1:1,000,000, the exact demarcation had remained unclear (4). The Chinese considered the centre of the main stream as the line of division. However, the Soviet Union identified the Chinese bank as border and thus by 1969 over 600 of the more than 700 islands in the rivers, or some 400 sq. miles claimed by China, were marked as Soviet territory (5).

In Central Asia various areas were in dispute. According to China, the Soviets had occupied 185 sq. miles during 1960-1969 and another

1,080 sq. miles during 1972-July 1977 (6). Moreover, China accused the Soviet Union of large scale subversion among the rebellious minority population in the Chinese province of Sinkiang, where the situation had become rather critical in connection with the Tibetan revolt (1959). Throughout the 1950s limited guerrilla activities and uprisings had occurred in Sinkiang amongst the Moslem Kazakhs, Uighurs and other nationalities, who resisted the suppression of their languages and religion and the large-scale settlement of ethnically Chinese people. Between mid-1962 and September 1963 about 50,000 inhabitants of Sinkiang fled to the Soviet Union.

The disputed areas along the Sino-Soviet border were themselves uninhabited or sparsely populated. However, the hinterland of China's north eastern border region belonged to a military district which also included the very populous Peking region, and Manchuria was China's major industrial base. Sinkiang housed nuclear test facilities and strategic resources. Much of the Soviet population in Siberia and the Far East was concentrated along the important Trans-Siberian railway at relatively short distance from the border.

In 1960, or perhaps already in 1959, border incidents started to occur with increasing frequency, quickly taking the form of minor tit-for-tat reprisals. According to Soviet statements, the Chinese violated the Soviet border over 5,000 times during 1960, and during 1963 this happened more than 4,000 times, involving over 100,000 Chinese (7). China accused the Soviet Union of provoking over 5,000 incidents between 1960 and late 1965 (8). Negotiations in 1964 were fruitless. Tensions increased with the Cultural Revolution in China from 1966 onwards. In October 1966 Moscow reported that an estimated 2 million Chinese had massed on the Soviet border, notably in the Far East, to demonstrate in support of China's territorial claims (9). On March 2, 1969, the Chinese provoked an incident at the small uninhabited Damansky or Chenpao Island in the Ussuri river. The Soviet army vigorously retaliated on March 15. Subsequently hundreds of clashes occurred along the entire Sino-Soviet border, reaching a peak in August of that year. Allegedly, nearly all incidents were initiated by the Soviet Union as part of a policy of coercive diplomacy towards China, consisting of a combination of political and military pressure. The Chinese launched a nuclear shelter-digging program, and on August 23, 1969, the Chinese communist party declared that war might break out any time (10).

The conflict was not to escalate to that height. In early August of 1969 an agreement had been reached on shipping on the Amur and Ussuri rivers, and afterwards the situation remained quiet in this section of the frontier. After a meeting at Peking airport between the Chinese and Soviet Prime Ministers Zhou Enlai and Aleksei Kosygin, September 11, border negotiations were resumed in October 1969. Although diplomatic relations were restored and economic links were tightened, the talks rapidly proved to be fruitless with regard to the border dispute. The status quo was apparently to be maintained until the exact demarcation could be agreed upon. The publicly reported incidents declined to a frequency of one to three a year and were much less severe than during the summer of 1969. In most cases no regular army units were involved. Later, there would be rumours that China's Minister of Defence Lin Biao in 1971 intended to make use of the border conflict with the Soviet Union in his factional struggle with the Chairman of the communist party, Mao Zedong. The alleged plans did not materialize (11). The events in Afghanistan from 1979 onwards threatened to reactivate the border dispute in the Chinese-Soviet-Afghan border area. Repeated new proposals and meetings after 1969 remained without tangible result.

During the decade of friendship between China and the Soviet Union a roughly balanced number of troops had been encamped along their joint borders, with the Chinese in greater number in the east and a Soviet preponderance in Central Asia. After 1960 China built up the size of its forces in the northern border districts, gaining an edge in numbers over the Soviets. The Soviet Union, however, remained superior in equipment, mobility and reserves.

This balance of power was upset from late 1965 onwards when the Soviet forces were brought to a higher level of readiness and received better equipment. In 1966, by renewing an older treaty with Mongolia, the Soviet Union acquired the right to station troops and to maintain bases on Mongolian soil. China only marginally countered the considerable build-up of Soviet power by redeploying four or five divisions to the north east and to Inner Mongolia. The Vietnam War demanded China's military attention in the south, and the Chinese army was purged shortly before as well as during the Cultural Revolution (1966-1969). During the latter period of time the tension in China along the Sino-Soviet frontier increased. Both countries tightened their border security.

After the breakdown of the 1969 negotiations both China and the Soviet Union started to build up the economy, to augment the population, and in the first place to enlarge the military strength in the border areas. The Soviet Union notably increased its divisions to an estimated 44 in 1979, including three in Mongolia. At full strength, this would mean over 500,000 troops (12). These were kept at a high level of readiness and had better equipment, including superior air forces and nuclear weapons. By 1983 108 SSs-20 were assumed to be stationed in the Asiatic part of the Soviet Union. In reaction to the Soviet measures after 1969 the Chinese at first regrouped their units closer to the border and upgraded their equipment. Because of internal difficulties China could not deploy a considerable number of additional ground forces until 1972. By 1974 or 1975 the force imbalance had to some extent been redressed. In 1979 China was estimated to have stationed 55 Main Force divisions (forces which were directly commanded by the Ministry of National Defence) and 25 Local Force divisions in the north east, and 15 Main Force and 8 Local Force divisions in the north west. At full strength this would amount to about one million troops (13). In both countries additional forces could be deployed quickly in a case of emergency. All in all, China outweighted the Soviet Union in numbers, but notwithstanding Chinese nuclear efforts the Soviet Union remains far superior in terms of equipment.

Up till now the Sino-Soviet boundary question remains unsettled. Yet while China did not dare to speak or move too decisively during the height of the conflict, it took the liberty of behaving more aggressively in the late 1970s and early 1980s. As Robinson pointed out, the Soviet Union evidently overreacted to the March 2, 1969 incident, a reaction which appeared to be unforeseen by China. According to Robinson, China had to curtail the Cultural Revolution as an immediate result (14), and China's policy became increasingly centred upon its conflict with the Soviet Union. By decisively solving their short-term security problem in the given context of a bad overall Sino-Soviet relationship, the Soviets created a much larger long-term threat. China turned even more anti-Soviet. At a Congress of the Communist Party in 1977, Chairman Hua Guofeng denounced the Soviet Union as the most dangerous source of world war (15). The 30-year Treaty of Friendship between China and the Soviet Union was allowed to lapse in 1981. China abandoned its policy of self-imposed isolation. In 1978 a Sino-Japanese treaty was concluded. The relationship between China and the United States improved and from 1979 onwards both countries were engaging in a joint intelligence project and were preparing joint military planning. After 1981 the Sino-Soviet relationship seemed to improve somewhat and it was decided to resume border negotiations, which resulted in the opening of some boundary posts (16). By the 1980s, however, the situation had undergone a considerable change. China had moved from possessing a minimal deterrence in the 1960s to a more favourable position with nuclear missiles aimed at the Soviet homeland. To quote Robinson again, "whereas the Soviet Union was unable to convert its commanding military presence in Northeast Asia into a decisive political and economic influence in the rest of Asia, the Soviet military instrument shaped the Asian balance of power, political and military, if not economic" (17).

Chapter II

INTER-BLOC CONFLICTS: MILITARY ASPECTS OF THE EAST-WEST CONFLICT

Introduction

The attempt to trace the military confrontations in the Cold War conflict is faced with the seeming paradox that on the central front, along the "Iron Curtain" from the Baltic to the Adriatic, no actual East-West clashes have taken place except for some minor aerial incidents. Yet the most quiet Cold War front is at the same time the most heavily armed: along the East-West demarcation line over 15,000 nuclear weapons are allocated for nuclear war in Europe, and troops and advisers of the superpowers are stationed in forward positions (see Table I).

Table I: Foreign Military Forces in Europe, early 1980s

	USSR	USA	Other
Warsaw Pact			
Czechoslovakia	78,000		
East Germany	406,000		
Hungary	50,000		
Poland	50,000		
TOTAL	584,000		
Nato Countries			
Belgium		2,390	
West Germany		257,980	150,000 (UK, FR, BEL, NE)
Greece		3,470	
Iceland		3,110	
Italy		13,920	
Netherlands		2,120	
Norway		210	some UK military personnel
Portugal		1,670	
Turkey		5,310	
United Kingdom		28,540	
Spain		8,540	
Greenland		320	
Gibraltar			2,100 UK troops
TOTAL		327,580	ca. 152,500

(Figures from Ruth Leger Sivard. World Military and Social Expenditures, 1983. Washington, D.C., World Priorities, 1983, p. 9.)

There have only been two armed conflicts with major loss of lives in postwar Europe (in Greece and Hungary), and both were basically civil wars with intrabloc outside intervention. However, both these conflicts were shaped by interbloc conflict behaviour.

In the following pages and in the case studies a number of East-West confrontations in and outside Europe will be presented, accompanied by some more general observations on the Cold War.

The Russian export of its social system in its sphere of influence after 1945 was not altogether without parallel. American postwar leaders, fearing a return to prewar depression, felt that securing world markets was vital for maintaining prosperity and that it was therefore mandatory to oppose state-regimented economic systems. President Truman held in 1947 that the American economic system could not survive in a shrinking economy and he demanded that the whole world should adopt the American system since free enterprise could survive in the United States only if it became a world system (1). The "open door" expansionism of American capitalism implied control over markets, not directly over politics in the nations in its sphere of influence. On the other hand, political control was central to Soviet expansionism.

This different quality of control required by the Soviet system is reflected in the treatment of defeated Germany. Hundreds of thousands of prisoners-of-war were locked up for years in Soviet labour camps after the war. Tens of thousands of German civilian citizens were deported to the Soviet Union and from the new Polish territories (formerly German). Altogether the relocations in eastern Central Europe involved twelve million Germans alone. Almost five million Germans had already fled westwards before the advancing Red Army (2). Compared to this treatment, the ability to attract people as manifested in the stream of fugitives, heading westwards in 1945 and thereafter, has been an essential quality of the "open" Western democracies. The Soviet system imposed by Stalin was one which needed an "Iron Curtain" for the implementation of policies.

In the immediate postwar years a process of polarization led to a "Cold War" (a 14th century term, originally referring to the conflict between Christians and Muhammedans in Spain, popularized in 1947 by the American journalist W. Lippmann). At one time or another both leaders of the emerging two power blocs felt that they were close to a "hot" or "shooting war". Harry S. Truman wrote in March 1948 in a letter to his daughter that "... now we are faced with exactly the same situation with which Britain and France were faced in 1938-39 with Hitler. (...) I went to Potsdam with the kindliest feelings towards Russia - in a year and a half they cured me of it" (3). Less than three years later it was Stalin who thought that war was imminent. His daughter Svetlana noted that an intense war atmosphere was prevalent in Soviet military circles (4).

The Spectre of a Soviet Invasion of Western Europe

Western analysis of Soviet behaviour is based on an assessment of military capabilities and political intentions. While the first can be assessed with increasing accuracy, Soviet intentions - apart form general ideological statements like Khrushchev's "We shall bury you", which contain no direct military significance - have been less clear. Soviet military doctrine places great stress on a fast decisive offensive. This alone, however, cannot be regarded as indicative of intent (5). While it is often taken for granted that but for the atomic bomb Western Europe would be Communist, we have in fact only one piece of credible evidence which indicates that the usually cautious Stalin considered a military attack on Western Europe. This evidence comes from the dossiers of a Czech historian, Karel Kaplan, who brought them to the West in 1977. In the Dubček era he had been allowed to go through the Czechoslovakian Communist party archive and there he reportedly found records of a meeting in the Kremlin in January 1951. Stalin had invited fifty leading Red Army generals and the ministers of Defence and the party secretaries of Poland, East Germany, Hungary, Czechoslovakia, Romania and Bulgaria:

> "The topic of discussion was the possibility of launching an invasion of Western Europe up to the shores of the Atlantic. (...) On the second day he [Stalin] explained to his satraps why he felt the time had come for the final onslaught. Contrary to hopes previously indulged, Western Europe had survived the postwar economic crisis and, thanks largely to the Marshall Aid Plan and the establishment of the NATO pact in April 1949, appeared to be increasing in stability and strength. The United States was beginning a massive increase in defence spending, and the Soviet Union had to act swiftly before the Americans established air force bases capable of launching nuclear strikes against Moscow.
> All present concurred with Stalin's analysis and it was agreed that the attack must be made within three, or at most four, years. There was much to encourage a mood of optimism. The masses would rise to assist their Red Army liberators. Deprived of her Western European markets, the United States would be isolated, impotent and poverty-stricken, to the far confines of the Atlantic." 6)

Assuming the veracity of this account of Soviet intentions in the late days of Stalin, it would point to a certain blindness to reality on the side of the Soviet dictator. For one thing, the rising of the masses in Western Europe would have been limited at best to the members of shrinking communist parties. Secondly, the reliability of the East European armies for offensive purposes was also not to be taken for granted (7). Thirdly, the American capacity to threaten Moscow was not, as Stalin implied, a thing of the future. The U.S. military had briefed president Truman on "bases, bombs, Moscow, Leningrad, etc." already in September 1948 (8). The Soviet Union had few nuclear weapons in its military arsenal before 1953 while the United States had about 1,000 such weapons in 1953/54. The American preponderance was such that President Eisenhower was asked by his advisers no less than five times to use the atomic bomb in 1954. In 1950 Stalin had begun to expand and improve the Red Army again. In 1951, military expenditures of the Soviet Union and its allies climbed sharply, reaching up to 40 percent of state budgets. Yet that was not a definite indication of a design to attack Western Europe. Richard

Lowenthal has noted that "In the closing years of his life Stalin vacillated between halfhearted attempts to establish a détente and frenzied efforts to rearm" (9).

When it came to assess comparative military strength, most Western sources consistently downplayed Western strength and overestimated Soviet capabilities. They conjured up a picture of 20 or less NATO divisions facing 175 Soviet-bloc divisions. In fact, even with the overseas deployments of French, British and Dutch troops, there was enough Western manpower to match the East even before NATO came into existence. After the victory over the Axis powers the Soviet Union had demobilized its 11,365,000 troops to a level of 2,874,000 men. Of these, an estimated 700,000 - 800,000 were, according to the U.S. Joint Chiefs of Staff, immediately available for an invasion of Western Europe in 1947/48. Western strength in Europe was, at that time, 829,400 troops if the home armies are counted. Such a rough numerical parity of conventional forces still exists in the mid-1980s if France is not excluded (10).

If the expectation of success of a Soviet attack on Western Europe was unrealistic between 1945 and 1953, it has not become more realistic since, especially in the light of escalatory risks to nuclear war with the concommitant environmental risks for Eastern Europe and the health risks for occupation forces in Western Europe. In economic terms, little would be gained due to the destructiveness of even short conventional wars in industrial environments. In political terms, the addition of some 250 million dissidents would do little good to the Soviet system. In international terms, the reaction of the United States, China and the rest of the world to such a Soviet venture would be unfavourable, to say the least. It has been difficult to portray credible scenarios for a Soviet attack on Western Europe and propagandists of a Soviet threat generally concede that an all-out conquest of Western Europe is unlikely. Their solution to the problem of high Soviet capabilities combined with apparently low intent for downright invasion is to postulate the Finlandization thesis. By this they imply that preponderant Soviet military power can be translated into political accommodation to Soviet policies without a shot being fired (11). We will turn to this aspect in the final chapter. In the following pages, the key episodes of East-West military confrontation will be discussed.

Early Cold War Conflicts (1946-1949)

The post-1945 Cold War between East and West had been preceeded by several hot wars. The first engagements had taken place in the years between 1918 and 1921 when German, British, French, Japanese, American, Czechoslovakian, Polish, Finnish, Hungarian, Italian, Serbian, Greek, Turkish, Romanian, Estonian, Lithuanian and Latvian forces fought against the new Soviet state or at least helped the White counterrevolutionairies with their presence on Russian soil in the attempt to overthrow the Bolsheviks (12). The biggest Western attack on the Soviet Union occurred in 1941 when German, Austrian, Hungarian, Slovakian, Romanian, Bulgarian and Italian troops invaded Russia, fortified by Spanish, French, Belgian and Dutch SS contingents (13). In 1945 Stalin was again apprehensive that the Western allies would join forces with the Germans and conclude a separate peace treaty directed against the Soviet Union. In late 1944 and early 1945 there was a race between the Red Army on the one hand and the British on the other for the control of Vienna, Warsaw, Prague, Hamburg and Berlin. The American military commanders had no eye for this kind of territorial acquisition. The British were less than successful and only managed to prevent a Soviet advance into Denmark (14). As far as Great Britain was concerned the postwar confrontation with the Soviet Union had already started during the war. For the United States the year 1947 was a turning point in its relationship with the Soviet Union. For the Soviet Union the antagonism with the West had only be slightly under the surface. The first clash between these three powers occurred over Iran.

During the war Iran had been occupied jointly by Soviet and British troops following an impending pro-Nazi coup in the early phase of the war. In an Anglo-Soviet treaty with Iran in 1942, the two foreign powers promised to end the occupation within half a year upon the termination of the war. Until 1945 Iran had served as a gate to Russia for Lend-Lease aid from the United States. By the end of the war, a separatist regime had been established in the northern Iranian province of Azerbaijan, the breadbasket of the whole country. This new regime enjoyed the backing of the Soviet Union.
Iran brought the issue of the continuing postwar Soviet occupation before the United Nations six weeks before the deadline for the withdrawal of foreign troops was expiring. The British withdrew before the March 2, 1946, deadline but the Soviet Union not only stayed but also engaged in ominous large-scale troop movements (15). While the Iranian premier was negotiating for weeks in Moscow, the United States brought pressure on the Soviet Union by raising the issue in the Security Council of the United Nations. The Soviet leaders backed down after having obtained an agreement with Iran for the joint running of an oil company and finally withdrew their troops in May 1946. The oil agreement which premier Ahmad Qavam had signed was, however, subject to parliamentary ratification and this never occurred after the Russians had left the country (see case study VI).

The Iranian crisis was soon to be followed by the Greek crisis. In July 1946 Soviet troops closed the Bulgarian frontiers with Greece which - somewhat paradoxically - has been interpreted as a sign of support for the Greek communist-led insurgents (16). There were no Soviet troops on Greek soil, only limited numbers of British forces. In a way the Greek situation resembled the one in China, where there were limited numbers of American troops present while a civil war was going on. In both cases Russian involvement was assumed as the insurgents were predominantly communist. It was the difference in scale between China and Greece which made Western intervention effective in one case but not the other.
The Truman Doctrine - "the policy of the United States to support free people who are resisting attempted subjugation by armed

minorities or by outside pressures" - was formulated in 1947 primarily with Greece in mind. Truman's rhetoric on free and unfree, democratic and totalitarian societies was actually ill-fitted to the Greek case. The speech-writer who wrote the first draft of the Truman address of March 13, 1947, admitted that "It was not a choice between black and white, but between black and a rather dirty grey" (17). The "dirty grey" was the reactionary Greek government and the "blacks" were the 20,000 guerrillas who fought against it. The British, facing financial difficulties at home, decided to stop underwriting the corrupt right-wing regime in early 1947 and invited the United States to take over the burden. The American government subsequently poured $ 400 million in military and $ 300 million in economic aid into Greece between March 1947 and June 1949 (18), with the containment of communism as the declared goal. However, the communist-led rebels under general Markos Vafiades were essentially fighting their own war and not Stalin's war. They were fighting against his advice though with the support of Yugoslavia and to a lesser extent Albania and Bulgaria. Stalin had not recognized the Greek rebel government in 1947 and told a Yugoslavian delegation in February 1948 that "The uprising in Greece must be stopped, and as quickly as possible" (19). Perhaps he was apprehensive that the Americans would create a stronghold in the Balkans during their counterinsurgency campaign in Greece which might subsequently endanger the Soviet hegemonial position in the region (20). As it was, the uprising was to continue for another year and a half after Stalin's admonition to Yugoslavia in early 1948. This time-lag was indicative for the decreasing monocentrism of Communism; support for local revolts as well as the cause of local revolts against Western interests were not automatically an outflow of Soviet policies as was widely assumed in the West (see case study VII).

The third early Cold War crisis evolved around Berlin and here the Soviet Union was fully involved. The wider issue behind the Berlin blockade of 1948 was the fate of Germany. Two years of indecision had produced feelings of hopelessness, cynicism and also defiance in the German population. Strikes, mass demonstrations and protest meeting necessitated the strengthening of armed control (21). The rampant inflation made a currency reform long overdue, but this reform measure had been delayed by the Soviet representatives in the Allied Control Council. The monetary question was interwoven with the question of Marshall Aid and the integration of Germany's Western zones into the Western economic system. When the three Western occupation powers announced a currency reform for their zones (but not for West Berlin) on June 18, 1948, the Soviet Union reacted with an announcement that the whole of Berlin would be included in a currency reform for the East German occupation zone. The Western reaction in turn, was an announcement that the West mark would be circulated in West Berlin as well. Thereupon, on June 25, 1948, the Soviet Union cut off the overland routes which linked Berlin to the Western occupation zones (22). The subsequent purpose of the Berlin blockade was obviously to drive the Western allies out of the former German capital. Without the disturbing factor of a Western presence in the Soviet occupation zone, the sovietization of East Germany would have been greatly facilitated.

Public opinion in the West was not in a war mood and the fact that a presidential election was coming up in the United States also cautioned president Truman against breaking the blockade by military means. The solution to the isolation attempt of a city of more than two million inhabitants was an airlift operation involving 277,264 flights. 79 pilots died in air crashes (23). The toll of an armed breaking of the blockade would probably have been higher. In the meantime, West Germany was formed out of the three Western zones against the wishes of the Soviet Union. The blockade itself not only strengthened Western resolution to offer a stand to Soviet pressure but also rallied international public support against "a power which used starvation as an instrument of policy". (24). Once the foundation of the Federal Republic of Germany (FRG) had become a fact in May 1949, the blockade was lifted and the Soviet Union reciprocated by setting up the German Democratic Republic (GDR) in October 1949.

From the Korean War to the Cuban Missile Crisis

The most significant postwar theatre of the East-West conflict was not on the European front but on the Pacific rim, in Korea. Originally a Chinese vassal, Korea was occupied by Japan during the war with Russia in the early twentieth century. The Czarist empire had tried in vain to have Korea divided with Japan along the 38th parallel both before and after the Russian defeat of 1905. Soviet troops finally entered Korea on August 8, 1945, following the declaration of war against Japan. The country was divided for purposes of occupation along the 38th parallel, with the United States stationing troops in the south. Two client states emerged, each eager to unite the country on its own terms. The North Korean Army's surprise attack on South Korea, on 25 June, 1950, was interpreted in the West as a Soviet attack on a free country and the Truman Doctrine was invoked and implemented under the auspices of the United Nations at a time when the Soviet representative in the Security Council, Malik, was absent. American troops, assisted by lesser contingents from Thailand, Australia, Ethiopia, New Zealand, the Philippines and other states linked to the United States, almost managed to reunite the country after a counterattack. However, they were pushed back by increasing numbers of Chinese "volunteers", until fighting stabilized roughly on the 38th parallel.

The role of the Soviet Union in the North Korean attack and, subsequently, in the Chinese participation, is still open to different interpretations due to the absence of reliable historical evidence. Adam Ulam wrote that "... it would be superfluous to discuss the contention that the North Koreans attacked without explicit Soviet permission or orders..." as "No sane person could doubt the ultimate Soviet responsibility for the attack" (25). Khrushchev offered an interpretation in his memoirs according to which the North Korean leader Kim Il Sung convinced Stalin that the invasion was a low-risk, internal affair of short duration with no danger of outside intervention, whereupon he received from Stalin the permission to go ahead (26). The theses that Stalin ordered the attack alone, or that he jointly with Mao Zedong decided on it when the Chinese leader was in Moscow in the spring of 1950, have not been substantiated by historical evidence.

The entry of Chinese "volunteers" into the war had been threatened when the U.N. troops pushing northwards crossed the 38th parallel and voices in the United States pleaded for a reunification of Korea on Western terms. The Chinese intervention began in mid-October, and it was supported by Soviet arms, as had been the initial North Korean trust. While Stalin could hardly have ordered Chinese intervention, the Chinese nevertheless saw themselves to some extent as Soviet proxies. In 1963 a Chinese statement referred to a division of labour between them. It spoke of the "Korean War against U.S. aggression in which we fought side by side with the Korean comrades" in these terms:

> "We ourselves preferred to shoulder the heavy sacrifices necessary and stood in the first line of defense of the Socialist Camp so that the Soviet Union might stay in the second line." 27)

However, it would be wrong to see the People's Republic of China as a kind of mercenary power. After all, they were not paid by the Soviet Union. On the contrary, China had to reimburse the Soviet Union for the weapons it received (28). Russia and China had parallel interests and China might have hoped that the Soviet Union would come to its assistance when the time was ripe to liberate Taiwan. The Chinese decision to intervene in the Korean war in the face of the deteriorating position of North Korea was taken jointly by the USSR and the PRC in late August and the role assigned to Soviet troops was principally to back up the Chinese in order to deter reprisals on the People's Republic of China. For this purpose, Soviet pilots were guarding the skies and became involved in direct, though limited fights with American pilots (29). American planes in turn also crossed borders and on one occasion bombed an airfield eighteen miles south of Vladiwostok. However, such trespassing was either downplayed or not publicly disclosed as both the Soviet Union and the United States were anxious not to become involved in open hostilities. Soviet air and ground forces effectively deterred an American attack on Chinese territory and, later in the war, stabilized North Korea. The American analyst S.S. Kaplan concluded:

> "Had American troops gone across the Yalu to China, Soviet troops would have crossed the Tumen in force. Stalin was evidently willing to sacrifice some Russian lives to reduce the danger that North Korea would collapse. After the front in Korea had been stabilized, the Soviet Union reintroduced enough military personnel into North Korea to affect the waging and the outcome of the war at very little risk to itself since the United States was no longer disposed to seek total victory in Korea. By September 1951, according to U.S. intelligence estimates, 20,000 to 25,000 Soviet troops were in North Korea, including roughly 5,000 ground air troops, a 5,000 man artillery division, 2,000 military advisers, and 1,500 engineers. The effect was to reinforce the American disposition to settle for the restauration

of the prewar status quo. Since the United States was deterred by its clash with the Chinese when American forces had approached the Yalu, there was almost no risk to Soviet security in implanting troops in North Korea after the front had stabilized. (...) Ultimately, therefore, Soviet troops did cross the Tumen but only after the Chinese had crossed the Yalu, when the prospects that the war might again come close to the Soviet border had become remote." 30)

Not before July 1953, after the death of Stalin, was an armistice concluded. Stalin's successors, were apparently less willing to provide China with credible counter threats in the face of stepped up American pressure under president Eisenhower who was apparently prepared to "go nuclear" (see case study VIII).

In the West, the Korean War was widely interpreted as a sign of a Soviet quest for world domination. It led to the establishment of great standing armies in both blocs. American military expenditures trippled in the early 1950s and military force strength was increased from 1,460,000 to 3,640,000 men. The Soviet Union increased its troop strength by possibly as much as three million men with the high point being reached in 1955 at a level of 5,763,000 men (31).

A sign of change in Soviet conflict waging with the West after Stalin's death was the handling of the Austrian question. Unlike Germany, Austria had been treated more like a liberated than like a defeated country by the Allies in 1945. The pattern of occupation, however, was modelled on the German formula with four occupation zones both for the countryside and the capital. Contrary to the situation in the Soviet-occupied parts of East Germany, there were no important Moscow-trained Austrian communists who could be counted on to take over civilian control in the footsteps of the Red Army. Political parties were brought back into play early. In the elections of November 25, 1945, the Austrian communists received only 5 percent of the total vote, a situation that remained unchanged in the subsequent elections of 1949 and 1953. This lack of support for communism and the fact that the Soviet-occupied part was too small to form a viable state, were probably major reasons for the final Soviet decision to release the country from Russian control (32). Soviet attempts to use the Austrian state treaty as a bargaining element to prevent the rearmament of West Germany were unsuccessful (33). However, an armed neutrality of Austria was in itself already a desirable goal. The neutralization of Austria on the Swiss pattern put a geographic bar between Nato's southern and middle flanks in Europe. Through the formation of the Warsaw Pact on May 14, 1955, the presence of Soviet troops in Hungary and Romania had no longer to be justified in terms of liaison with Soviet occupation forces in Austria (34) (see case study IX).

The release of Austria from Soviet occupation was a break with the Stalinist tradition. It was rather unexpectedly (for the Austrians) decided in early 1955 by the Soviet Politburo in the same session that also authorized the return of the leased naval bases of Port Arthur and Prokkala to China and Finland respectively. Khrushchev did not fail to use it as an example for propagating the possibilities of a policy of "peaceful coexistence" with the West. However, the events

in Hungary and Poland in the following year underlined the danger of
a decrease in tensions for the stability of the Soviet empire and the
post-Stalin "Thaw" was frozen in again.

The Austrian State Treaty left only one issue undecided along the
European frontier between East and West and that was Berlin. Like
Austria, Berlin provided insufficient leverage for the Soviet Union to
change the course of events in West Germany. With the building of
the Berlin Wall in August 1961, the possibility of military conflict in
Europe became remote, especially after the Cuban missile crisis.

The Cuban missile crisis was in fact an outflow of the Berlin crisis
which had begun on November 27, 1958, with a Soviet diplomatic note
to the other occupation powers of the former German capital.
Therein Khrushchev made it known that a separate peace treaty with
the German Democratic Republic would be concluded unless the
Western powers agreed to enter negotiations within six months with
the goal of turning Berlin into a demilitarized "free city". The six
months' deadline passed without this threat being effectuated. In
1960, however, Khrushchev returned to his Berlin proposal at the
Vienna summit meeting with the soft and inexperienced (so the Soviet
leader thought) new American president. J.F. Kennedy rejected the
idea of a "free city" with the access controlled by the German
Democratic Republic. One week after a new nuclear threat had been
issued by Khrushchev over Berlin (an earlier such threat had been
issued in 1959), the Berlin Wall was built. The Soviet threat had
obviously not been credible and effective. Thereupon the Soviet
Union, lacking non-experimental intercontinental missiles, decided to
place 42 SS-4 and between 24 and 32 SS-5 missiles on Cuba. Michel
Tatu, a French analyst, noted:

> "The object of the manoeuvre was clearly Berlin. Ever since
> Khrushchev had raised the issue in 1958, the Russians had tried
> all possible tactics: first pressure (the six-month ultimatum), then
> smiles (at Camp David), then pressure again and even the
> fist-banging session (during Khrushchev's summer offensive of
> 1961). Everything had been in vain. In the spring of 1962 an
> entirely fresh approach was needed. Khrushchev's prestige was at
> stake and his adversaries in the communist camp were using the
> issue as a weapon against him." (35)

The outcome of this crisis is well known: on November 20, 1962, the
missiles brought to Cuba in September and October were withdrawn
after the two superpowers had been dangerously close to a nuclear
showdown. From then on, the theatre of conflict between East and
West shifted to the southern hemisphere, to Latin America, Africa
and Asia. Only in the Middle East *) and Vietnam was there a
possibility of direct confrontation between East and West.

----

*) The Middle East confrontations will be treated in Chapter 3. Here,
   only two minor incidents involving NATO will be recalled. Both
   were accompanied by vague Soviet threats of nuclear escalation.
   The first incident took place in September 1957 over Syria. Turkey
   had, on American instigation, amassed troops on its Eastern   >>

The USSR and Vietnam

In the immediate postwar period Stalin had refused to support Ho Chi Minh's war of national liberation against France as the French Communists, then still in government, were co-responsible for the return of colonialism to Indochina after the defeat of Japan. At the Geneva conference of 1954, the Soviet Union was co-chairman, presiding over the end of French colonialism in Asia and the creation of two Vietnams. Until the mid-sixties it was the People's Republic of China rather than the Soviet Union which was more receptive to North Vietnamese aid requests. In late 1962 and early 1963 North Vietnamese aid requests had been turned down by the Soviet Union. However, not all aid was refused. Between 1961 and 1965 the USSR had provided air transport services to both the National Liberation Front of South Vietnam and the Pathet Lao. The initiation of regular air warfare against North Vietnam in February 1965 coincided with the arrival of Premier Kosygin in Hanoi. However, the Soviet contributions to the strengthening of the North Vietnamese air defence system were by no means commensurate to the degree of American escalation. In the period 1965-1971 the Soviet Union, according to one count, provided military aid to the amount of $ 1,660 million to North Vietnam while the Chinese contribution was $ 670 million. Another count puts Soviet military aid to North Vietnam at over $ 3 billion for the period 1965-1972. Economic aid in the two decades preceeding the fall of Saigon was of the same order (37). These sums dwarf when compared to the American expenditures for the Vietnam war which are estimated to amount to $ 112 billion. The number of Soviet military advisers and personnel increased from well under one thousand before 1965 to about 3000 men in 1968 - which was ten times less than the number of Chinese serving in Vietnam (not to speak of the American presence of 550,000 troops) (38).
Soviet commitments to Vietnam were clearly more limited than in the case of Korea. Soviet military personnel did not lay sea mines or fly combat missions in Vietnam as happened between 1950 and 1953.

>> border, following American displeasure with Syrian arms acquisition from the Soviet Union. To make the show of force more impressive, the U.S. Sixth Fleet was also ordered into the Eastern Mediterranean. The Soviet answer consisted of conspicuously conducted military manoeuvres on its southern border. The second incident occurred in July 1958 and involved Iraq. The Soviet Union was concerned that the U.S. military intervention in Lebanon might be tempted to advance to Baghdad where a pro-American regime had been toppled. The Soviet answer consisted of manoeuvres on the borders of Turkey. However, the friction was temporary and since the 1960s the Soviet Union and Turkey became, as a consequence of Western policy over Cyprus, more friendly towards each other. In fact, Turkey, together with Morocco, became the most favoured Soviet economic aid recipients, receiving more than India, Egypt or Afghanistan in the quarter of a century since 1954 (36).

However, Soviet personnel manned air defence sites around Hanoi in 1965 and 1966, while native crews received training in the Soviet Union for these tasks. Soviet leaders made occasional references that "volunteers" might be sent to North Vietnam but it remained rhetoric like in the Arab-Israeli confrontations of 1956 and 1967 (39). The obligations of "proletarian internationalism" evoked by North Vietnam and the rivalry with China for the favours of Third World nations were probably more important factors for Soviet involvement in Vietnam than a desire for confrontation with the United States. In 1972, a visit of president Nixon to the Soviet Union was not cancelled despite the fact that U.S. bombing attacks in the vicinity of Hanoi and Haiphong reached new peaks of intensity, damaging Soviet ships and killing Soviet sailors. The American rapprochement to the USSR which found its expression in the Nixon visit was, ironically, based on the premise that the Soviet Union had a high measure of influence over North Vietnam, that Hanoi was merely a proxy of Moscow. R.J. Barnet writes:

> "...Nixon believed that the Soviet Union would help him to end the Vietnam War. Indeed, his original interest in détente grew out of that hope. Helmut Sonnenfeldt believes that the Soviet Union went as far as it could in exerting pressure on the Vietnamese to settle with the Americans on something close to Nixon's terms, but he thinks that Kissinger overestimated the power the Kremlin had over Hanoi." 40)

Conclusion

The Cold War between the Eastern bloc and the Western bloc began in Europe when the one power possessing the "absolute weapon" was unable to check the territorial expansion of the Soviet Union despite the latter's nuclear powerlessness. The Western inability to translate nuclear power into greater political leverage in a monopoly situation remains a historical riddle. One Russian scholar, when asked why the United States did not use the atomic bomb against the Soviet Union, in the period when retaliation was not possible held that "American public opinion wouldn't allow it" (41). This begs another question: how was it possible that the crimes of Stalin, resulting in millions of victims in the postwar period alone, did not produce a greater public outcry in the West, with demands for more offensive actions against a system of government which made the Czarist system - with its 14,000 execution of political opponents in the last half century of its rule - look decent in comparison? The horrors of World War II, the war weariness resulting from it, provide parts of the answer why the Cold War did not turn hot, for instance during the Berlin Blockade.
East-West relations in the postwar period have gone through several phases of frost and thaw, of tension and détente. Zbigniew Brzezinski has offered a cyclical theory of how the Cold War was played. He sees alternating periods and degrees of assertiveness on the side of the antagonists at work and distinguishes six phases to which one might now add a seventh (see Table II which condenses Brzezinski's scheme).

Table II: How the Cold War Was Played, According to Brzezinski (42)

Phase I: 1945-1948: Both sides demobilized. (The United States had fewer than 100 atomic bombs). Both sides were skirmishing for position. The USSR had an advantage in ground troops while the USA had a nuclear monopoly. Soviet attempts to expand its power in the Pacific and the Mediterranean did not produce results, but the Soviet position was strong in Europe.

Phase II: 1948-1952: The USA became overtly anti-communist as witnessed in the Truman Doctrine, the counterinsurgency in Greece and the bipartisan Congressional support for "containment". The USSR, despite its economic weakness - only in 1953 was the prewar production level reached - remained assertive, as witnessed by the Czechoslovakian coup, the Berlin blockade, the consolidation of its East European empire and its role in the Korean war.

Phase III: 1953-1957: A period of U.S. initiative. A rearmament programme precipitated by the Korean war and a nuclear build-up with plans for forward deployment of nuclear warheads in Europe. In the USSR, the new leaders lacked Stalin's nerve for brinkmanship and proposed "peaceful coexistence" which took the place of the "inevitability of war" thesis. The "rollback" policy of Dulles proved to be rhetoric in the Hungarian crisis in 1956 but interventions elsewhere (Guatemala and Iran, 1954) showed U.S. assertiveness.

Phase IV: 1958-1963: A period of "premature Soviet globalism", with Soviet commitments in Indonesia and Cuba and pressures on Berlin. Support for "wars of national liberation". Due to inadequate economic foundation and insufficiently developed military technology the USSR could not realize its goals.

Phase V: 1963-1968: A period of "cresting American globalism". Pro-Soviet leaders in Brazil, Greece, Algeria, Indonesia, Ghana were removed, sometimes with the aid of the CIA. The Soviet Union had "lost the quantitative race" (McNamara) in the military field and played a very modest role in Vietnam.

Phase VI: 1969-1978: While the USA was bogged in Vietnam, the USSR built up military strength and surpassed the USA in the early 1970s in numbers of missile launchers. The rough equality in destructive power between the superpowers led to a new "correlation of forces" which made détente possible.

Phase VII: 1979-present: The "Second Cold War": United States loose ground in Central America, Southern Africa, and Iran while the Soviet Union invades Afghanistan and achieve parity or superiority in many military weapon system categories. The USA refuse to sign the SALT II agreement, rearm on a massive scale and become more interventionist, with some voices advocating a policy of "global unilateralism".

Brzezinski's scenario, however, leaves out many important features, especially on the Soviet side, which have influenced the postwar course of East-West relations. There were several periods of relaxations of tensions once the most repulsive features of the Soviet system were dismantled after Stalin's death. One such period, the "Thaw" saw the Soviet Union in Geneva negotiating over a Vietnam conflict solution and in the same period Austria and Finland were given back control over occupied territories. In 1959 Khrushchev ventured to travel to the United States. After the Cuban Missile crisis the Hot Line Agreement and the Partial Test Ban Treaty were signed in 1963. In the late 1960s when Soviet relations with China deteriorated into a border conflict, relations with West Germany were improved in response to Chancellor Brandt's new 'Ostpolitik'. This initiated the most prolonged period of détente wherein the status of Berlin was settled in 1971 in a Four Power Agreement. A series of treaties between West Germany and East Germany, Poland and the Soviet Union normalized interstate relations in Central Europe.

However, while these developments led to the Helsinki Agreement of 1975 in Europe, Soviet relations with the United States began to decline. The Arab-Israeli War of 1973 in the Middle East saw both superpowers support their local clients to the level of alerts for airborne divisions and strategic nuclear forces. With the Jewish lobby in the United States mobilized by the Yom Kippur War, the trade agreement between the United States and the Soviet Union was abrogated by the latter when the Jackson amendment made a Most-Favored-Nation trading status for the Soviet Union conditional upon increases in Jewish emigration from the Soviet Union. Brezhnev's expectations of full access to Western credits, technology and trade were gone and his power position was affected. While détente had led to a stable situation on the Soviet Union's Western front due to the Helsinki Agreement, the Soviet leaders could obtain no assurances that the United States shared Russian concern about China and would jointly isolate the new Soviet rival. The United States, on the other hand, saw its hope gone that detente would reduce Soviet interference in the Third World. With a Soviet intervention in Angola, the fall of South Vietnam and another Soviet intervention in the Horn of Africa, détente was no insurance against more "Vietnams". After China had intervened in Vietnam in 1979 it "earned" the Most-Favored-Nation status which the Soviet Union could have got only for the prize of the potential loss of its Jewish population (some 3 percent of the total Soviet population).

While the Soviet Union was punished for Afghanistan by economic sanctions in 1980, China was receiving military technology from the United States. In addition to the United States, Japan also played the "China card" after the inflexibility of the Soviet Union over the restitution of the Kuril islands blocked any alliance with Japan, which would have given it the high technology needed for the rejuvenation of the Soviet economy. In 1978 the Japanese-Chinese Treaty of Peace and Friendship had been concluded and with both China and Japan linked to the United States, a powerful hostile combination emerged on the Soviet Eastern flank. When in 1980 and 1981 the Polish people massively rallied behind the independent trade union movement Solidarity and warm signs of support were conveyed to it by Western powers, the Soviet Western front appeared endangered as well. In addition to this intrabloc threat to its security, the massive rearmament of the Western powers after the shelving of the SALT II treaty and the prospect of a new high-technology arms race froze the Soviet Union again into a Cold War posture. A 'second' Cold War had apparently begun (43).

Case Study VI

THE IRANIAN CRISIS (1945-1946)

On August 25, 1941, the Prime Minister of Iran was notified by the
United Kingdom and the Soviet Union that their forces had invaded
Iran. The Iranian army soon collapsed after offering feeble resistance
(1), and Reza Shah was forced to abdicate in favour of his son. Iran's
northern provinces, which had traditionally been a Russian sphere of
interest, were occupied by the Soviet Union. The British controlled
the much larger southern and central part of the country, while a
small area around Tehran formed a neutral zone in between.
Negotiations started in September 1941 and on January 29, 1942, a
treaty was concluded between Iran, the United Kingdom and the
Soviet Union. The latter two acquired the right to maintain forces in
Iran but this was not to be understood as a military occupation (2).
They promised to withdraw their forces no later than six months
after the ending of the Second World War. Great Britain and the
Soviet Union pledged to avoid disturbing the internal affairs of Iran
as far as possible and they guaranteed the territorial integrity,
sovereignty and political independence of Iran. Iranian forces were
only to be deployed to maintain internal security. The United States
later stationed troops in Iran as well but officially never entered the
tripartite treaty of January 1942. It seemed to be tacitly understood
that the American presence was covered by the same terms as those
applying to the British.
By their action, the Allied powers aimed to prevent a further
strengthening of the relationship between Germany and an officially
neutral Iran, to protect the oil fields vital to the war effort and to
shield the southern supply route to the Soviet Union. Besides, there
were various other reasons to be interested in Iran. The oil fields
around Baku in the Soviet republic of Azerbaijan were situated close
to the Iranian border, and the Soviet Union made reference to its
1921 defence treaty with Iran. According to this treaty the Soviet
Union was permitted to move troops into Iran if the latter was unable
to defend itself or could not prevent an attack on a Soviet republic
from within its borders. Moreover, the Soviets were pressuring Iran
for oil concessions throughout the war. The United States, which
apparently wanted to block Soviet expansionism and to protect
American interest in the Middle East (notably in Saudi Arabia),
seemed to take an interest in Iranian oil concessions as well. At the
end of the Second World War it was commonly thought that America's
oil reserves were running out (3). The British evidently tried to
protect their position in this part of the world for strategic motives
connected with their interests in the Middle East and India. There
were equally strong economic reasons since the United Kingdom held
large and profitable oil concessions in the south of Iran. The Iranian
government distrusted both the British and the Soviets and might well
have feared a division of the country. With American military
assistance the Iranians reorganized their army and gendarmerie into

an efficient force which was generally loyal to the monarchy. This foreshadowed the Shah's close relationship with the United States after the war. The Iranian army, however, was outnumbered by the foreign troops in the country and its equipment was inferior.

Disregarding the stipulations of the 1942 treaty, the Soviets were quick to exert pressure on internal Iranian affairs. They sealed off northern Iran from the rest of the country, blocked the free flow of goods and sent much of the agricultural surplus to the Soviet Union. Reportedly, Anglo-American relief measures were necessary as a consequence (4). The Soviet propaganda was extensive and well organized. During the early stages of their presence the Soviets did not appear to have interfered directly with the administration of northern Iran, but subsequently other parties than the communist Tudeh party came to be prohibited and government officials were prevented from carrying out their duties unless they were Tudeh members. Thus, in the Soviet zone the Tudeh party dominated political life though it formed a minor faction in the Majlis, the national parliament of Iran. In the British zone parties came into existence that were favouring the British, like the Mehan party.

Oil was an important motive for the foreign involvement in Iran. The Soviet Union, claiming to be neutral towards western oil concessions in the south of the country, pushed for concessions of its own in the north. The United States, for obvious reasons, was opposed to such concessions, while Great Britain took a lenient position towards the Soviet requests. In October 1944, however, the Iranian government informed the Allied powers that negotiations on oil concessions would be postponed until after the war. Following this statement massive demonstrations broke out in the Soviet zone in favour of oil concessions for the Soviet Union.

As far as Iran's position in the Second World War was concerned, the presence of foreign troops was a major determining factor. On September 9, 1943, Iran declared war on Germany, and at the Tehran Conference at the end of that year the Allied powers reaffirmed Iran's independence, sovereignty and territorial integrity.

In accordance with the tripartite treaty of 1942, the foreign troops had to be withdrawn from Iran before March 2, 1946. The Soviet Union and Britain evacuated the jointly controlled Tehran area and the British started to withdraw their forces from the southern zone during the spring of 1945. Although negotiations on the question of troop withdrawal at the London Big Four Minister's Meeting (September-October 1945) and the Moscow Foreign Minister's Conference (December 1945) remained fruitless, Britain completed the withdrawal of its troops by March 1946. All American forces were evacuated by New Year, 1946. However, the Soviet Union sent new divisions to Iran in October 1945 (5).

On December 12, 1945, the Autonomous Republic of Azerbaijan was proclaimed in Tabriz, the capital of the Soviet-controlled zone. The communist Tudeh party (in Azerbaijan renamed as 'Democratic Party') had played a major role in the course of events and the rebels had reportedly used Russian weapons. An earlier coup in August 1945, had proved to be unsuccessful despite Soviet assistance. Now, the Soviets effectively protected the rebels, intimidated the population and obstructed all movements of the forces which the Iranian central government deployed against the insurgency. The Azerbaijani government consolidated its control over the province, and the administration and the police were organized upon the Soviet model. The Soviets developed the Azerbaijani army and exerted strong pressure on the Iranian government, including economic pressure. Azerbaijan was a major wheat-producing area of Iran. Its two million inhabitants, about one fifth of Iran's entire population, spoke a dialect identical to that of Soviet Azerbaijan. The Soviets also sponsored the Kurdish People's Republic of Mahabad in western Azerbaijan which had proclaimed its independence in December 1945, though they did not render material assistance (6).

By the end of 1945 the continued presence of Soviet forces in Iran and the separatist regimes under Russian protection in the north had shaped the Soviet-Iranian conflict. After Iranian complaints, the Security Council of the United Nations endorsed talks between Iran and the Soviet Union in January 1946. However, the negotiations during the following two months remained unsuccessful. The Soviet Union demanded - among other things - the continued presence of Soviet troops in parts of Iran for an indefinite period ('dependent on Soviet relations with the central Iranian government') and a 51 per cent Soviet-owned Iranian-Soviet joint stock oil company (7).

One or two days before the Soviet Union had to withdraw under the 1942 treaty obligations, it announced that it would evacuate some troops from Iran on March 2 and after (which in some districts appears to have been carried out (8), but that it would keep forces in the region until the situation had 'clarified' (9). At the same time, the Soviet Union reportedly began a massive build-up of its offensive forces in the province. During the same period, it deployed another armoured force in Bulgaria along the border with Turkey. The Kurdish People's Republic of Mahabad proclaimed the right of sovereignty over the Turkish Kurds.

Great Britain and the United States were hereby drawn into the Soviet-Iranian conflict and Iran received assurances of their support. Since British and American protests proved to be of no avail, Iran appealed to the Security Council. However, the UN debate, while publicizing the problem, did not solve it. On March 21, 1946, President Truman threatened to send US naval forces into the Persian Gulf and to land troops in Iran unless the Soviet Union withdrew its forces, and he apparently ordered the US military chiefs to prepare for deployment of ground, sea and air forces (10).

On March 24, 1946, the Soviet Union announced that it would withdraw its forces completely from Iran within six weeks if nothing unforeseen occurred. This was confirmed on April 4, when Iranian Prime Minister Qavam signed an agreement with the Soviet Union. Therein it was agreed to establish a joint Iranian-Soviet oil company to be ratified by the next Majlis. In addition, it contained a pledge for peaceful settlement of the Azerbaijan question, which was declared to be an internal Iranian affair. The agreement thus met the aims of the Soviet Union as well as Iran regarding both provisions on oil concessions, Azerbaijan, and the troop withdrawal. Following the signing of the agreement, however, tension rose almost immediately.

The Soviet Union put strong pressure on the Iranian government. Soviet troop movements increased and Azerbaijani forces started to move in the direction of Tehran. Some local fighting was reported (11). Though Iran withdrew its complaint at the United Nations, possibly under Soviet pressure, the Security Council continued to pay attention to the Iranian question without the Soviet members.

The evacuation of 60,000 Soviet troops was completed within the agreed time limit in the first half of May 1946. Around the same period the Soviet occupation forces were also withdrawn from Manchuria. The Security Council decided to retain Iran on its agenda without discussing the conflict again. In June 1946, Prime Minister Qavam concluded an agreement with the Azerbaijani government, which granted Azerbaijan important concessions though Tehran held nominal authority over the province. Ultimately the Azerbaijani army had to be incorporated into the national army, but for the immediate future the Azerbaijans retained their army and a de facto control over the province of Azerbaijan.

After the withdrawal of their forces, the Soviets vigorously pursued their objectives in Iran through non-military means, notably by efforts to gain control of the Iranian government. Violent Tudeh-provoked riots and strikes broke out in Khuzistan. On August 2, 1946, Qavam reshuffled his cabinet to include three Tudeh members. The next day British troops, which were stationed in Iraq, moved to the border with Iran 'to protect British interests' (12). Soviet troop concentrations were reported near the border with Iranian Azerbaijan. Since Tudeh-instigated unrest spread to the south as well, martial law was declared in the surroundings of the British-Iranian oil fields. British cruisers took up position in the Persian Gulf and anti-Tudeh tribal risings developed, possibly on the instigation and certainly with the tacit support of the British. The Iranian army was unable to handle the situation. In mid-October the central government had to sign an agreement with the tribes, by which it met most of their demands. On October 19, Qavam again reshuffled his cabinet. The Tudeh members were dropped and the new cabinet appeared to be centrist. A major reversal of the policy towards the Communist movement followed.

The contract of the Soviet-Iranian oil company could not become law until ratified by the 15th Majlis, and general elections for the Majlis could only be held after the situation was normalized throughout the country, including Azerbaijan. Whether Qavam had been flirting with the Soviet Union or had just been cleverly diplomatic is uncertain, but the outcome proved to be very favourable for Iran. National elections were fixed to begin on December 7, 1946, on the condition that the central government could supervise them in all areas of the country. On November 22, the central government sent troops to Zanjan and Azerbaijan, while local tribes were at the same time encouraged to revolt. Tehran's policy was opposed by the Soviet Union but the Iranian government received public assurances of American support. The Zanjani communist leaders escaped before the government troops arrived. The border of Azerbaijan was crossed in December 12, 1946. Minor hostilities broke out, and within a few days the Azerbaijani and Kurdish autonomous regimes collapsed. According to American and British correspondents the Iranian troops were greeted as liberators (13). The Soviet Union criticized the Azerbaijani leaders for not having compromised with the central government. Moscow increased its diplomatic pressure for ratification of the oil concessions and 3,000 Soviet troops were reportedly deployed onwards the border with Iran (14). However, the Soviet position in Iran was a lost one. Subsequent Soviet-initiated border incidents and military exercises could not intimidate the government in Tehran.

By the end of June 1947 the delayed parliamentary elections were finally completed, securing an absolute majority for the Democratic Party of Prime Minister Qavam. On October 22, 1947, the Majlis, by a 102 to 2 majority, declared Qavam's earlier oil agreements with the Soviet Union null and void. The bill had been sponsored by Qavam himself. After the reunification of the country the position of the Shah and the army had been strengthened, and American influence increased. The new pro-western government took action against Iranian Communists, who repeatedly provoked unrest in various parts of the country during the following years. These incidents strained the relationship between Iran and the Soviet Union. In 1947, Iran requested the Soviet Union to make compensation payments for its earlier occupation.

The Iranian crisis of 1945-46 has to be considered within the context of the Cold War. Though events never developed into an outright East-West confrontation, they fueled the general polarization which was growing during the same period of time which in turn must have influenced the Soviet Union in its decision to delay the withdrawal of its forces. The dispute over Iran "opened to the Soviet-American competition a new arena - one that would later be called the Third World. As polarization increased, each side saw the other engaged in provocative action" (15).

Case Study VII

THE GREEK CIVIL WAR (1944-1949) - A CASE OF SOVIET NON-INTERVENTION

In October 1940 the Italian forces had invaded Greece but were
defeated. This led to an invasion by German forces in April 1941.
They overran the country. A British military effort to counter the
Nazi occupation failed. British forces returned to Greece only in
October 1944 when the Germans were already retreating.
Various resistance movements had opposed the fascist forces in the
war. The Greek Communist Party (KKE) organized a National
Liberation Committee (EAM) which also included other left-of-center
forces. It counted about 700,000 active members. EAM's military
wing, ELAS, controlled about one third of the Greek mainland by the
middle of 1943. Another resistance movement fighting the Germans
was the much smaller National Republican Greek League, EDES,
which was favoured by the British despite its lesser significance. In
addition to fighting the Germans, ELAS and EDES fought each other
so that an Allied Military Mission had to negotiate an armistice on
February 29, 1943, in Plaka. The following month ELAS, dominated by
the KKE, formed the Political Committee of National Liberation,
which was a direct challenge to the Greek exile government and to
King George II who was residing in London. The king was associated
with the Metaxas dictatorship which had brought the monarch to
power in 1936 after more than a decade of republican rule in Greece.
George II's return to Greece in 1944 was therefore opposed by broad
sections of the Greek population. In September 1944 a compromise of
sorts was reached in the form of a Government of National Unity
under Papandreou in which EAM was to be given six ministerial posts.
When British forces (some 20,000 at the beginning) landed in October
1944 and took control of the capital (accompanied by insignificant
forces of the exile government) many members of EAM feared that a
reactionary monarchy would be restored after the demobilization of
ELAS and EDES . EAM resigned from the Papandreou government and
issued a call for a general strike and a mass demonstration on 3
December 1944. Fighting broke out between the demonstrators and
the police and a month of bloody hostilities followed in which British
and ELAS forces clashed. Churchill instructed the British Commander
in Chief, General Scobie, to treat ELAS as a rebel force and to
occupy the capital. The open fight between the British troops and the
main resistance movement against the Nazis placed British policy in
an unfavourable light, especially with American public opinion.
Churchill attempted to improve this image by personally going to
Athens in order to discuss Greece's future with the main
protagonists.
This visit to Athens in late December 1944 had been preceeded by
one to Moscow in October 1944. On that occasion Churchill had
proposed a sphere-of-influence-deal to Stalin for the Balkan and
Eastern Europe. For Yugoslavia this deal came down to a 50% - 50%

influence for the Soviet Union and the West, for Rumania a 90% Soviet and a 10% Western influence was proposed. For Greece, it was agreed that Great Britain, in accord with the United States, should get a 90% and the Soviet Union a 10% influence (1). At that time the Greek communist party, KKE, which was the leading force in ELAS, knew nothing of this deal and had not been consulted. At least with regard to Greece Stalin adhered to this sphere-of-influence-deal throughout the Greek Civil War which, with an interruption of about one year in 1945, would go on until the fall of 1949.

After the bloody December fighting of 1944 a cease-fire was reached and on 12 February, 1945, the Agreement of Varkiza was signed. ELAS which had not only fought the British but also EDES, surrendered its arms (though not all of them) and most of the fighting stopped although some guerrilla groups took to the mountains to harass British forces (some 75,000 in the meantime) and the Greek government from there.

The Varkiza Agreement stipulated that King George II would return from London only if a plebiscite affirmed the support of a majority for a restitution of the monarchy. Additional clauses in the agreement dealt with an amnesty for political acts, guarantees of civil rights and the election of a new constitutional assembly. The various Greek administrations which ruled the country following the Varkiza Agreement took little notice of the civil rights provisions. The police, the gendarmerie and the civil service contained many reactionary elements associated with the Metaxas dictatorship and the fascist occupation forces. Consequently tens of thousands ELAS/EAM members were arrested and hundreds of them assassinated (2). The repression provoked resistance and many former ELAS and EAM members took to the mountains again.

The Greek post-war governments had not only alienated the wartime resistance forces but also alarmed its neighbours in the north by making territorial claims on them. These countries had become Communist and with the leading role the Greek Communist Party played in ELAS, the latter saw in them natural allies. In December 1945 KKE members met in Bulgaria with Bulgarian and Yugoslavian general staff members and a promise of support for the establishment of a Democratic Army of Greece (DAG) was apparently reached (3). The DAG was a reincarnation of the ELAS although the number of noncommunists in it was smaller than in the wartime resistance coalition. It was led, for most of the time in the coming three years, by General Markos Vafiades, a nationalist communist like Tito, his Yugoslavian friend and backer.

In March 1946 governmental elections took place in Greece, but EAM had appealed for a boycott. The elections brought no surprises except that some 60 percent of the electorate nevertheless decided to cast a vote. In the same month the guerrilla war begun in earnest. In September 1946 the plebiscite on the monarchy took place prematurely on the urging of the British and produced the result the government desired and helped to bring about. With the return of the King the guerrilla operations intensified to a civil war.

The Greek government was hard pressed and could get only insufficient support from the British government. The British had no desire to get involved in the civil war. They were also put off by Greek government's corruption and repression. The Greek government conjured up a "Red Spectre" in its dealing with the Western powers, making much of a series of border incidents with its communist neighbours. That Yugoslavia, Albania and Bulgaria supported the DAG with arms, food, supplies, training and sanctuaries was true. Some of these arms must have originally been provided by the Soviet Union. However, they did this apparently not because Moscow ordered them to do so but more out of nationalist considerations and in settlement of older bills of Balkan rivalry. That the Soviet Union disapproved of the rebellion of the DAG and that it urged the Greek Communists to resort to other tactics was certainly known to the Greek government by 1948 and probably from the outset of the conflict (4). Nevertheless the Greek government portrayed its fight as one against Soviet expansionism and managed to convince the United States' government of its interpretation without much effort. When the British government in February 1947 announced that it could no longer shoulder the burden of supporting the Greek government, the Truman administration was eager to utilize the Greek case for a reorientation of its postwar foreign policy.

The British withdrew most of their troops in April 1947, leaving behind only one brigade as a kind of counterweight to the Russian military presence in Bulgaria. The British also retained a sizeable military advisory group in Greece to provide staff assistance in military planning. The United States, however, took over many functions of the British. The Mediterranean Fleet had been making a show of force on the request of the U.S. ambassador already in September 1946 and demonstrated its presence throughout the civil war. The consequences of a loss of Greece to communist-dominated local forces were already perceived by president Truman in the fall of 1945. The "loss" of Greece, it was feared, would make Turkey untenable as well and extend the Iron Curtain across the Eastern Mediterranean. The Truman Doctrine was proclaimed on March 12, 1947, and while its immediate cause were Greece's and Turkey's difficulties, it postulated a worldwide containment policy of Russian expansionism. Ironically, Greece was the case where the Russian record was clean and the charge of expansionism was unfounded.

The American intervention in Greece, which begun in 1947, took not the form of a military fighting force, although that possibility was not ruled out and in fact considered in late 1947 when the situation looked bleak for the Greek government (5). The American military support consisted of large quantities of arms and a sizeable military mission of 250 officers, headed by General Van Fleet. Some members of this mission worked as instructors in training camps. More than fifty of them were attached to the Greek General Staff and took an active role in the planning and supervision of operations. They did, however, not directly command Greek units (6). Apart from providing military assistance, the United States prevented the Greek economy from collapsing with a massive loan of 300 million dollars. Through the British and American support, the Greek armed forces ultimately grew to more than 200,000 troops - eight times as many as the DAG (7). The superiority in manpower, equipment and resources began to pay off on the battlefield in the course of 1948. The DAG wavered between guerrilla operations and conventional warfare. On the whole DAG was effective with the former and suffered setbacks with the latter strategy. It seems that political pressures from the KKE (which wanted to see a liberated part of the country) pushed the DAG in the direction of regular warfare. The rebels had announced the creation of a rival Provisional Democratic Government of Greece in late 1947 but neither Yugoslavia nor the Soviet Union nor any other nation recognized it as the legitimate government of Greece.

When, in 1948, the confrontation between Tito and Stalin forced Communist movements everywhere to make a choice against Tito, the Greek Communists could ill afford to loose Tito's support. Tito, however, pressed hard by Stalin on the economic as well as other fronts, had to make some opening to the West in order for Yugoslavia to survive. A discontinuation of support for the Greek Communists could serve as a ticket to Western assistance. It seems that this was one reason why he decreased his aid and closed the Yugoslavian border to Greek insurgents by July 1949 (8). Yet a continuation of Yugoslavian assistance would not have saved the DAG. The Greek government had in fact defeated the DAG by taking its mountain strongholds and by driving the guerrillas into Albania. Bulgaria's increase of support after the Yugoslavian volte-face was insufficient and alienated many sympathizers of DAG because the price the KKE seemed willing to pay was the detachment of Macedonia from Greece. On 16 October 1949, the Provisional Government, after having made several unanswered peace proposals to the Athens government in the preceeding year, announced that it would put aside its arms.

With the help of Great Britain and the United States the Greek national government in Athens had achieved victory after almost five years of fighting. Except for some Albanian soldiers in the very last phase of the conflict and the British troops in the beginning, no foreign combat troops had participated in the fighting on Greek soil (9). However through the support of five nations the local conflict had become internationalized, thereby lasting longer and probably costing more Greek lives than would have been the case if the struggle had remained a Greek affair.

Case Study VIII

THE KOREAN WAR (1950-1953)

During August and September 1945 Soviet forces occupied the north of Korea and American forces occupied the south in order to accept the surrender of the Japanese government of Korea. The line of division between the occupation zones was marked by the 38th parallel of latitude. From 1945 to 1947, a joint Soviet-American commission attempted to create a Provisional Government for the establishment of an interim trusteeship by the Soviet Union, the United States, Great Britain and China as a preliminary to an independent Korea. Yet nothing came of this. The United States finally called in the aid of the General Assembly of the United Nations, which recommended elections throughout Korea under UN supervision. However, since the UN representatives were denied admission to the north of Korea, elections were held in the south only. The proclaimed Republic of Korea (South Korea), with Seoul as capital, was recognized by the UN General Assembly as the only legal government of Korea. The Soviet Union repeatedly vetoed its UN membership. The division of Korea became complete when in September 1948 the Democratic People's Republic of Korea (North Korea), with Pyongyang as capital, was proclaimed. It was recognized by the Communist bloc as the only legal government of Korea. Some 9 million people lived north of the 38th parallel, and more than twice as many lived in the south.

The first Prime Minister of North Korea was Kim Il Sung, a central figure in the militant wing of the resistance movement against the Japanese. Korea had been dominated by the Japanese since the beginning of the century. The Korean partisans had operated mainly out of Manchuria and Siberia and had gradually become overtly leftist. In this way there had been some exposure to Communist ideology in North Korea before the Soviet occupation. The Soviets, moreover, had established a pro-Soviet regime, had set up people's committees and introduced reforms along Soviet lines. They had also built up a strong North Korean army. Syngman Rhee became President of the Republic of South Korea. He had been a major representative of the non-militant right wing of the Korean independence movement, which had stronger roots in the south of the country. Syngman Rhee had been the first President of the Korean Provisional Government in Exile. His regime joined forces with the American Military Government, which had relied heavily on the conservative, wealthier Koreans during the occupation. The Communist party was banned. The Americans had not supplied the South Korean army with heavy weapons, aircraft or tanks, but had instead prepared it for defensive tasks. They feared that Rhee might otherwise attack the North.

The Soviet Union withdrew its forces from Korea at the end of 1948, while the Americans evacuated theirs in May-June 1949. Once all occupation forces were withdrawn, border incidents increased. Both North and South Korea refused to recognize the division and claimed to represent the entire country. The tasks of the United Nations' Commission on Korea, which had been established with the purpose of continuing reunification efforts, were expanded in the autumn of 1949 to include reporting of events that might escalate to military conflict. By the spring of 1950 border incidents were up to several dozen a week (1) and the relations between the two countries became increasingly bitter. Nevertheless the North Korean invasion took everybody by surprise.

At four o'clock in the morning of June 25, 1950, local time (2), about 100,000 North Korean troops crossed the 38th parallel and marched into South Korea. The South Korean army offered little resistance and quickly found itself in a condition of complete disarray. Within a short period of time the North Koreans advanced deep into the south, while a flood of refugees was moving in the same direction. The North Korean claim that they were reacting to a South Korean invasion is hard to believe, although the South Koreans might well have provoked an incident.

The Security Council of the United Nations met in New York immediately and adopted American resolutions on June 25 and 27 calling upon North Korea to cease hostilities and to withdraw its troops. In addition, the UN members were urged to render such assistance to South Korea as was necessary to repel the armed attack and to restore international peace and security. It was the first time the United Nations had called for military assistance for a country under attack (3). 53 members of the United Nations assented to the request for assistance for South Korea. Most of them rendered medical aid, food supplies and the like. Sixteen members provided military assistance, i.e. the United States, Canada, Great Britain, France, the Benelux countries, Greece, Turkey, Thailand, the Philippines, Australia, New Zealand, Ethiopia, South Africa and Colombia. Compared with the preponderant contribution of the United States, the assistance of the other fifteen UN members was small (at the peak, the ratio was more than 300,000 troops to 44,000 troops) (4) and had political rather than military significance. While military operations were to be carried out under the UN flag, the United Nations were little more than an instrument of American policy with regard to the Korean War.

Before the American resolution had been adopted by the Security Council, the United States had already decided to evacuate American citizens from South Korea, to supply South Korea with military equipment and to render naval and air support. The latter were to amount to more than 85 to 93 per cent of the total naval and air forces deployed against the North (5). A naval blockade was established, and on the advice of US general Douglas MacArthur ground units from the American forces in Japan were committed as well a few days after the decision of the Security Council. The United States was eventually to contribute about half of the ground forces deployed against North Korea. In the beginning of July 1950, the Security Council established a Unified Command of the UN forces under the leadership of the United States. General MacArthur was appointed Supreme Commander but he retained his function of Commander-in-Chief of US forces in the Far East and received his instructions directly from the President of the United States, Harry S. Truman.

The North Koreans quickly occupied the entire country except for a small area in the south-east, and they were not effectively driven back until after a successful landing of MacArthur's forces at Inchon in mid-September. Two weeks later the UN forces reached the 38th parallel and the North Korean aggression had thereby been repelled. On October 7, 1950 the General Assembly of the United Nations adopted an American resolution calling for appropriate steps to insure stability throughout Korea and to establish a unified, independent and democratic government. The General Assembly therefore permitted South Korean forces to cross the 38th parallel. However, the South Koreans had already done so a few days before, and immediately after the UN resolution American forces penetrated into North Korea as well. The Joint Chiefs of Staff approved of the American advance on condition that US forces would stay at ample distance from the Yalu river which constituted the border with China. Yet the armies rapidly penetrated deep into the north.

The People's Republic of China had repeatedly warned that it would take action if the US forces crossed the 38th parallel. In late October and November "volunteer" troops from China intervened in the Korean war by launching large-scale attacks on the South Korean and American forces, which had almost advanced to the Yalu river. Both sides suffered heavy casualties and the front moved to the south again. A western resolution demanding that China withdraw its forces from Korea was vetoed by the Soviet Union in the Security Council. The Chinese had received weaponry from the Soviet Union, with which they were formally allied since February 1950 by a treaty of Friendship and Mutual Assistance. In the autumn of 1950, Soviet armed forces were stationed in Manchuria for the apparent purpose of backing up the Chinese forces and deterring American reprisals on China. In addition, the Soviet Union held five divisions in readiness to assist in repelling 'American aggression' if the situation in Korea grew worse (6). General MacArthur, who on several occasions had underestimated the Chinese warnings and tactics (7), favoured a hard-line policy towards China. President Truman, foreseeing only limited gains from the expulsion of Communists from Korea, was inclined to avoid any further confrontation with China. Disagreements between MacArthur and the American president had occurred on earlier occasions. During the Korean War, various decisions taken by MacArthur had been ratified in retrospect. The general's open deviations from his instructions had been tolerated because of his high standing and his impressive military record. After the setbacks caused by the Chinese intervention, MacArthur publicly advocated a deployment of Taiwanese troops and an expansion of the war into China. This led to his dismissal of all his functions. He was replaced by lieutenant-general Matthew B. Ridgway on April 11, 1951. Truman's decision to dismiss MacArthur was taken after consultation with the Joint Chiefs of Staff, but it was met with strong opposition in the Congress. On his return to the States MacArthur was greeted as a hero, but his tremendous popularity soon faded away. His dark horse candidature for presidential nomination by the Republican party in 1952 was unsuccessful.

At the beginning of January 1951 the North Korean and Chinese forces approached the 38th parallel, and from spring 1951 onwards, fighting stabilized around this line of demarcation. The war turned into static trench warfare, with mine fields and air activity. The UN and South Korean forces achieved modest gains in the ensuing years at the expense of the Chinese and North Koreans. Negotiations started in July 1951, but for a long time were unsuccessful. A major issue was the fate of the numerous prisoners of war. Several tens of thousands of North Korean and Chinese captives were reported to be unwilling to return home. In March 1953 Stalin died. By May 1953 the American government of President Dwight D. Eisenhower was threatening to escalate the war by no longer excluding the use of nuclear weapons and by carrying the war onto Chinese soil (8). Negotiations were resumed in June and on July 27, 1953, an armistice agreement was signed in Panmunjom. At the Conference in Geneva in April 1954 the Korean question was discussed without result. A peace treaty was never concluded. The issue of the prisoners of war was finally resolved in January 1954 when 14,000 Chinese and 7,500 North Koreans voted to remain in South Korea or to move to Taiwan (9).

The line of contact between the belligerents was established as cease-fire line, and on either side of the line a demilitarized zone of two kilometres was created. This new border line between North and South Korea involved minor changes compared to the pre-war frontier. All in all, the South slightly enlarged its territory. During the summer of 1953, the United States and South Korea concluded a Defence Alliance. The UN members who had intervened militarily declared their willingness to render renewed assistance to South Korea in case of a new attack. Gradually, various nations withdrew their forces from Korea. From 1971 onwards, only American troops represented the United Nations in the demilitarized zone. In 1983, the US forces along the demarcation line numbered 40,000 (10). Until 1971, the UN General Assembly had discussed the Korean question and the problems of unification year after year. After that date, a few major incidents occurred, and in 1974 tunnels were discovered under the demilitarized zone running from the North to the South. Nowadays, the army of South Korea is the seventh largest in the world in absolute numbers. The North Korean army is sixth, but in relation to the size of the civilian population it is unmatched by any other army in the world (11).

The Korean War is generally considered to have been a major episode of the Cold War. After the Communist takeovers in Czechoslovakia and China and during a period of tension in international politics, the West was not inclined to perceive the North Korean invasion as an internal Korean affair or as just another war between two neighbouring countries. Moreover, it was hard to imagine that North Korea would have taken the decision to invade independently and without the approval of the Soviet Union and/or China. The Truman administration therefore did not hesitate to consider the North Korean aggression as another proof of red imperialism which ought to be contained. On the other side, North Korea did not expect a large scale American intervention. After all, only in January 1950 the US Secretary of State Dean Acheson had declared that Korea did not belong to the defence perimeter of the United States (12).

When the United States initially decided to repel the North Korean invasion of South Korea, it is probable that neither Truman nor MacArthur thought of intervening in North Korea. Yet temptation beckoned when the tide of the battle had turned after the Inchon landing. The wisdom of the UN resolution to cross the 38th parallel proved to be dubious, and the decision to advance to the Yalu river proved to be disastrous when China intervened, thereby prolonging the war by two years (13).

Although the Truman administration tried to prevent a conflict with the People's Republic of China by declining Taiwanese offers of troop assistance, it protected Chiang Kai Shek and shielded Taiwan with the Seventh Fleet. Apart from demanding the withdrawal of all foreign forces from Korea, China demanded the removal of US forces from the area of Taiwan during the negotiations. China also called for the expulsion of Taiwan from the United Nations and its own acceptance as a member of the world body. However, in what proved to be a dubious resolution, the UN General Assembly depicted China as an aggressor and China was not admitted as a UN member until 1971.

In June 1950 the Soviet Union had failed to veto the Security Council's resolution to intervene in Korea, as its representative Ya.A. Malik was still boycotting the meetings as a protest against the occupation of China's permanent seat in the Council by Nationalist China instead of Communist China. Apparently, Malik did not receive new instructions from Moscow in time. The Soviet Union resumed attendance and took the rotating chairmanship of the Security Council upon itself on August 1, 1950. It subsequently vetoed the American resolution which called for intervention throughout Korea after the south of Korea had been freed from North Korean troops. The resolution was then adopted by the western dominated General Assembly, in which only the Soviet bloc opposed it. On November 3, 1950, the General Assembly was to adopt the 'Uniting for Peace' resolution by which it received important powers if the Security Council was paralyzed by a veto. This signified a major amendment to the United Nations' Charter.

The Soviet Union evaded direct involvement in the Korean War. It had made large deliveries of tanks, trucks and heavy artillery to the North Korean army in April and May 1950, yet well before the invasion materialized it sharply reduced the number of its military advisers in North Korea (14). During the spring of 1950 China redeployed large numbers of troops to Manchuria (15). The first Soviet reaction to the Korean hostilities in the summer of 1950 was diplomatic in nature. According to American intelligence estimates the Soviet Union introduced some 20-25,000 troops into North Korea only after the front had stabilized, and they did apparently not participate in serious fighting (16).

The number of casualties caused by the Korean War ran into millions. It is estimated that South Korea had some 800,000 casualties, North Korea over 500,000, and China about 900,000. The number of Korean

War fatalities must have reached a million. Of the UN forces, the Dutch contingent, for instance, lost 120 men with 496 wounded and 3 missing; the United States had about 34,000 fatalities with some 105,000 wounded. With the frontlines having moved almost throughout South and North Korea, it is commonly held that the proportion of civilians in the Korean casualty figures is very high (17). In addition, as a result of the war more than one third of all Koreans had been separated from their relatives (18).

Case Study IX

THE SOVIET ROLE IN THE ALLIED OCCUPATION OF AUSTRIA
(1945-1955)

At the end of the Second World War, Austria was occupied by Soviet, American, British and French troops (1). The Russians were the first to enter Vienna in April 1945. After four months, the western Allies were permitted to transfer their headquarters to the capital as well. The town was divided among the Allied powers into four zones and one jointly occupied sector. The division of the country followed the provincial boundaries of 1937. The Soviet Union controlled the north-east (Lower Austria around Vienna), the British the south (Styria, East Tirol and Carinthia), and the Americans the central-northern part (Salzburg and Upper Austria). The French, who wished to participate in the occupation, were given control over Tyrol and Vorarlberg in the west. The first period of occupation has been described as one of "four elephants in a rowboat": for every twenty Austrians there was approximately one member of the occupying forces (2). Gradually the number of Allied forces was reduced. In 1949 the United States maintained some 9,000 troops in Austria. This number was raised to about 15,000-17,000 in 1954-55 in connection with the considerable troop reductions by Great Britain and France (in reality France had started its troop reductions well before 1953). Henceforth the United States stationed a small number of their forces in the French sector. Except for the first period, the Soviet Union maintained some 40,000 troops in Austria. Altogether the Allied occupying forces in Austria numbered 60,000 men (3).

The occupation was to be ended by a State Treaty, which was also to determine the future of Austria. Since Austria had been incorporated into the German empire by the Anschluss in 1938, no separate peace treaty with Austria was necessary. In September 1945 the Allied Control Commission for Austria, consisting of an Allied Council and an Executive Council, was set up to solve the Austrian question. The Allied Council had to meet 249 times before the occupation was lifted in 1955.

Shortly after their arrival in Vienna - Germany had not yet capitulated - the Soviets set up a Provisional Government. The right-wing socialist Karl Renner presided it and Communists were strongly represented in this government. At the end of April 1945, the Second Austrian Republic was proclaimed and in November 1945 national elections were held. The Austrian Socialist Party and the People's Party of Austria won by an overwhelming majority of votes and formed a coalition government under Chancellor Leopold Figl. On June 28, 1946, a new Austrian Control Agreement was signed. The Soviet Union voluntarily gave up its right to veto any Austrian legislative action; since then all laws (except constitutional laws) became binding, unless they were unanimously rejected by the Allied Council after having been passed. The bulk of the Austrian administrative and legislative buildings were situated in the

international zone in Vienna. Unlike Germany, Austria thus had a
civilian government with a rather high degree of political
independence. Control by the occupation authorities gradually became
indirect.

The Provisional Government, the elections, the Second Control
Agreement and other measures to arrange affairs under occupation
conditions, had been finalized before East-West relations deteriorated
from the spring of 1947 onwards. Moreover, during the earliest period
of occupation, both the Soviets and the Austrian Communists had high
hopes of a peaceful transition towards socialism (4); therefore they
had strongly favoured the November 1945 elections. These elections
proved to be a watershed in Austrian post-war history. In November
1945 the Communist party polled only 5.42 per cent and in subsequent
elections Communist votes remained roughly on the same level. After
the spring of 1947 the tolerant attitude of the former Allies with
regard to the Austrian question disappeared and the future of the
country increasingly depended on the international situation - the
early Cold War and the 'Thaw' following Stalin's death. By late 1947,
neither the Soviet Union nor the Western powers were willing to
withdraw from Austria. After the spring of 1948, major initiatives for
a settlement were launched by the Western Allies, but the Soviets
became more obstructive as the division of Germany was consolidated
in the course of 1949.

At the Potsdam Conference in 1945, the Soviet Union had been
granted the German assets in the Russian sector. The Soviets
interpreted these broadly as including properties seized by the
Germans after 1938, and quickly exploited the economic advantage of
the occupation (5). The Soviet interpretation of what constituted
German assets was opposed by the Austrian government as well as by
the Western Allies. The latter also supported Austria's claim to
retain its 1938 frontiers while the Soviet Union strongly supported
Yugoslavia's claims for parts of Austrian territory. In general, the
Soviet Union linked the Austrian question to other Cold War issues
like Germany's reunification and rearmament. It apparently saw no
advantage in a permanent division of Austria along the German
model. This would have deprived the Soviet zone of the industrial raw
materials and electric power from western Austria (6). In the Soviet
vision, Austria was to adopt neutrality once the occupation was
lifted. This also implied Austria's abstention from membership of
supra-national organizations.

The western occupying powers hardened their stance in the
negotiations as well, notably after the Communist coup in
Czechoslovakia in 1948. In the view of the Western powers, there
could be no settlement until Austria had economically recovered by
means of the Marshall Plan, which Austria had joined notwithstanding
strong Soviet opposition. The United States, in particular, disliked the
prospect of a neutral Austria and wished to include the country into
the western defence system. After the withdrawal of Allied troops, a
Western-trained military force would, in the American vision, have to
replace the occupying troops. At this time, the United States paid a
large proportion of the formation costs of the Austrian reserve
gendarmerie, and they supplied weapons and financial aid. Moreover,

there is little doubt that the western powers supported the Austrian government in 1949-1950 in creating elite groups within the gendarmerie (Alarmbataillone) that effectively put an end to Communist-instigated strikes and demonstrations in the Western zones (7).

Negotiations between the occupying powers dragged on without result. In Austria discontent with the situation was growing. In December 1952, the United Nations' General Assembly, by 48 to 0 votes, called on the governments involved to make a new attempt to conclude the Austrian State Treaty.

A new period of hope began when the Soviet leadership directed a peace offensive at the West shortly after Stalin's death in March 1953. The Soviet Union softened the rules in its occupation zone, which up till then had been very strict in comparison with the western sectors. Controls at the demarcation line were lifted and so was censorship. Soviet troops were given more liberty to leave the barracks and to get into contact with the Austrian population. The Soviet Union also decided to pay occupation costs itself. This example was followed by the Western Allies (8). In Austria expectations were raised and the government was keen to counter anti-Soviet sentiments. At the Berlin Conference in early 1954, Soviet Secretary of Foreign Affairs Viacheslav Molotov still linked the future State Treaty with a neutral Austria and a peace treaty with Germany. Only in a speech to the Supreme Soviet on February 8, 1955, did Molotov officially declare that troop withdrawal from Austria was possible without a prior peace treaty with Germany.

During subsequent negotiations in Moscow between the Soviet and the Austrian leadership, it was agreed that Austria would adopt military neutrality along the lines of Switzerland. Austria wished to choose for neutrality independently and on its own free will by amending the Austrian constitution. The neutral status of Austria therefore should not be guaranteed but recognized by the Allied powers. Consensus was also reached on the withdrawal of troops and the German assets. The Soviet-Austrian agreements were laid down in the Moscow Memorandum of April 1955. The reserve gendarmerie program had already been enlarged in connection with troop reductions of Great Britain and France in 1953. From the moment it was decided that Austria would adopt neutrality after the Swiss example, the reserve gendarmerie held a key position in the formation of Austria's military defence (9). The nucleus of the Austrian army was formed from gendarmerie officers (10). The United States supplied equipment for 28,000 troops and the other occupying powers also provided army equipment and weapons (11).

On May 15, 1955, the Austrian State Treaty was signed. It was ratified by all parties involved by the end of June. The treaty granted the Soviet Union cash payments, temporary oil concessions and assets of the Danube Shipping Company. In return, the Soviet Union transferred former German properties to Austria. The United States, Great Britain and France returned former German assets without recompensation. At the very last moment Austria's co-responsibility for the Second World War had been expunged from the treaty (12). Austria's borders remained unchanged and an

Austro-German political or economic union was prohibited. All foreign troops had to be withdrawn within 90 days and no later than December 31, 1955. The British were the last Allied soldiers who left Austria. They crossed the border at Thörl-Maglern on October 25, 1955. The last Soviet troops had left Austria on September 19 (13). Austria adopted a permanent neutral status in world politics. Bruno Kreisky, Austria's Chancellor from 1970 to 1983, would later define one of the benefits of Austria's neutralism as "the gaining of as much trust from the West as possible, and as little distrust from the East as possible" (14).

The Austrian State Treaty marked the first and only occasion that the Soviet Union agreed to a major readjustment of the demarcation line which had been established in Europe at the end of the Second World War. According to Khrushchev, this did not imply a weakening of the position of the socialist bloc, because the Communists had never been in control of the Soviet zone in Austria (15). During the occupation, the Soviet zone had not, like other East European countries, been sovietized. For the Soviet Union, the economic advantage of occupying parts of Austria had gradually decreased, while the strategic and political necessity had also largely disappeared. Western Europe had become a military unity and was politically pacified. On May 14, 1955, one day before the Austrian State Treaty was signed, the Warsaw Pact Treaty had been concluded. The Soviet Union thereby obtained the right to maintain troops in Hungary and Romania. Up till then treaties with Hungary and Romania, which both had been allied with Germany during the Second World War, had permitted the Soviet Union to station troops in these countries in order to maintain lines of communication with the Soviet occupation forces in Austria. As a consequence of its neutrality, Austria came to represent more or less a military vacuum between East and West. The lines of communication between NATO members Italy and West Germany, moreover, had to pass through France. The Soviet Union therefore considered the Austrian neutrality to be an attractive option and a good example to follow for other West European countries (16). However, it would not appear that the Soviet Union had great respect for Austria's neutrality. A military plan which surfaced in 1974 showed that in case of war, Soviet armed forces would push through a weakly defended Austria into Western Europe (17).

Chapter III

EXTRA-BLOC CONFLICTS: SOVIET MILITARY INVOLVEMENT IN THIRD WORLD CONFLICTS

Introduction

The five permanent members of the UN Security Council - the United States, the United Kingdom, France, the Soviet Union and China - have all intervened militarily in Third World nations in the post-war period. China's punitive expedition into Vietnam in 1979 and the Soviet invasion of Afghanistan are recent examples. Great Britain has been heavily involved as a colonial power and so has France, though in contrast to the British the French are still very active in their ex-colonies. The United States, a global power since World War II, has intervened militarily less frequently than the other two NATO members but more often than the Soviet Union. According to one count, Western powers have intervened roughly 13 times as often as Communist powers in the period 1945-1980 with armed forces, accounting for 79 percent of direct military interventions, in contrast to 6 percent for Communist powers and 15 percent for developing countries among themselves (1).

With the colonial links of France and Great Britain and the Monroe Doctrine of the United States in mind, the postwar and postcolonial interventions of these powers look somewhat more understandable if not more legitimate to many observers than those of the Soviet Union. The Western nations, after all, have a much higher economic stake in the Third World than the Soviet Union and its allies. This is refected in trade flow figures (see Table III).

Table III: Structure of World Trade, 1979 (2)

Trade Flow as Percentage of Total World Trade

Export to from	West (OECD)	East (Comecon)	Nonsocialist South	Total
West	43.8	2.4	15.7	61.9
East	2.3	4.0	1.2	7.5
South	18.9	1.1	7.3	27.3
Total	65.0	7.5	24.2	96.7

Compared to the Soviet Union the West is less self-sufficient in raw materials. In particular with regard to energy requirements, Japan and Western Europe, and to a lesser extent the United States, are heavily dependent on Middle Eastern oil. The Western powers' involvement in the Third World, in short, appears quite "natural", while the involvement of the Soviet Union does not. In one respect this perspective is shared by the Soviet Union, namely when it comes to providing economic aid for development. The poverty of the Third World is, in the Soviet vision, the outcome of past Western exploitation and the responsibility for improving depressed economic conditions therefore rests with the West. Soviet aid to Third World nations has been minimal, amounting to an annual average of 0.05 percent of its GNP as compared to 0.33 percent for the Western donor countries. Putting the blame for the state of the Third World at the door of the West, the Soviet Union sees its responsibility rather as one of restraining "imperialism" (3). Having been the first nation that has shaken off the yoke of capitalism, the Soviet Union sees it as its duty to come to the aid of forces in the Third World that try to do the same.

Many observers see such a definition of the 'Red Man's Burden' as ideological camouflage for imperialist motives. The Soviet constitution of 1977 contains an explicit reference to the USSR's foreign policy aim of "consolidating the position of world socialism and supporting the struggle of peoples for national liberation and social progress". In the same vein Brezhnev told Carter that "solidarity with liberation struggles is a principle of Soviet policy" (4). This principle had a long anchestry, dating back to the early days of Bolshevik rule. In September 1919, for instance, Pravda held that pushing south into Turkestan would bring Persia, Afghanistan and India within reach. This could constitute a threat to England, which in turn might be a lever to force it to discontinue its support for the White Guards (5). The usefulness of the Third World to bring pressure to bear on the West lived on in periods of peace. In 1955, for instance, a functionary of the USSR Council of Ministers declared with regard to the Middle East that "The long-term objective is to use Arab nationalism in order to cause difficulties for the oil supplies of the Europeans and thus render them more malleable" (6).

In the early postwar period Soviet interest in the Middle East was couched in terms of commercial interests. In July 1945, at Potsdam, Stalin demanded that at least one of the ex-colonies of Italy, Libya or Somaliland, be placed under Soviet trusteeship. With a naval base in the Mediterranean, the Soviet Union could "take her share" in the developing world trade. Due to its great power status obtained in the war, the Foreign Minister V.M. Molotov claimed "a right to play a more active part in the fate of the Italian Colonies than any rank and file member of the United Nations...." (7). However, this move was blocked by the Western powers who did not grant the Soviet Union an effective participation in the Allied Control Commission in Italy - as they were obtaining no such rights in Soviet-dominated occupation zones. Equally unsuccessful were Soviet-attempts to obtain the Anatolian territories of Kars and Ardahan from Turkey and a naval base at the Bosporus comparable to those of the United

States and Great Britain at the Panama and at the Suez Canals
(Soviet claims on Turkish territory were only given up in 1953,
shortly after Stalin's death) (8).
In this chapter an attempt will be made to chronicle the military
involvement of the Soviet Union in the Third World in the postwar
period. Given the limitations of the present study this effort cannot
be exhaustive and a comparison with the military policies of the
other major powers (notably the United States, Great Britain, France
and China) has also to be excluded, desirable as this would be to put
the Soviet activities in perspective.

Soviet Military Involvement in the Third World

Soviet policy in the postwar period can roughly be divided into the
Stalin, Khrushchev and Brezhnev periods. In the first period interest
in the Third World was small and so was actual involvement. In the
second period, interest was big but the logistics of military power
projection were insufficient to make a real impact and words outran
deeds under Khrushchev. In the third period the Soviet Union acquired
the necessary air- and sealift capacity to intervene decisively in
local Third World conflicts and it also had the political will to show
its muscle, taking advantage of the American foreign policy paralysis
in the wake of Vietnam and Watergate. In the following pages we will
adhere to this periodization, taking into account the time it took the
successors of Stalin to modify their foreign policies vis-à-vis the
Third World.

The Period 1945-1955

The reconstruction of the Soviet Union after the Second World War
and the consolidation of its influence in the occupied countries of
Central and Southern Europe left Stalin little time to devote to the
colonial territories and to the few (newly) independent nations in the
Third World. There was a curious change in the Soviet attitude
towards Third World leaders in 1947, when the Cold War began in
earnest. From 1945 until 1947, Lenin's assessment that nationalist
movements in the colonies had initially a bourgeois character but that
temporary cooperation with them was nevertheless tactically wise
(provided that they left room for a Communist movement) had served
as point of orientation. Consequently the independence movements in
Indonesia, India, Burma, and the Philippines were looked at
sympathetically. However, with the founding of the Cominform in
September 1947 and the advent of the "two-camp theory" - an
internationalist, democratic socialist camp versus a capitalist,
imperialist, nationalist camp -, the Nehrus and Sukarnos were no
longer placed on the side of the angels by the leaders in the Kremlin.
The infant Communist movements in the Third World were therefore
supposed to oppose the national bourgeoisie with whom they had
hitherto sided in the fight for independence. Since they received no
help from the Soviet leaders this policy spelled disaster for many of
them (9).

In this period, the Soviet Union was militarily involved in the northern provinces of Iran, where it showed a keen interest in obtainly oil concessions. This, however, was a wartime-legacy and the confrontation with Iran was terminated with the withdrawal of Soviet troops under American pressure. A less obvious military move in the Middle East at that time was the Soviet decision to support the creation of the State of Israel in 1947/48 and to provide the Haganah clandestinely with weapons from Czechoslovakia. Given the antisemitism in Russia under Stalin at this period, this move is explainable only in terms of hurting British interests. These weapon supplies (rifles, machineguns, grenades, ammunition and explosives as well as 25 Messerschmitt aircrafts) were probably quite crucial for Israel to survive the first Arab attack in the same year. Strange enough, Czech weapons were also shipped to Syria at the same time. When Jewish intelligence intercepted such a shipment at Bari, the duplicity of Soviet support became known (10). This policy of backing both sides to be sure to end up in the winning camp in a foreign conflict seems not to have been confined to Stalin. In the early 1980s, before the Soviet Union definitely sided with Iraq, the USSR seems to have supplied both Iran (indirectly through North Korea and other friendly nations) and Iraq in their border conflict (11).

The Israeli arms deal of 1948 marked the opening of a channel of influence which was to play a major role in the years to come. Providing arms to those who were denied arms from the West became an important hallmark of Soviet foreign policy in the Third World. The structure of Soviet development, with its emphasis on heavy industry, made guns and tanks one of the few Soviet articles of which there was an abundance and for which there was a demand in the Third World. At the same time the structure of the Soviet economy, with its weak agricultural sector and its relative neglect of light industry, made it an unattractive developmental model for most Third World nations. But this realization came only later, not in the period of Stalin.

The only major military involvement in a Third World nation under Stalin was of course the Korean war, where the Soviet Union provided arms, including 2,400 aircrafts, to the People's Republic of China and North Korea and provided an active air cover to the Chinese. Less well known is the fact that the Soviet Union also aided China directly in the last phase of the civil war. Following the Mutual Assistance Treaty concluded between Stalin and Mao on February 14, 1950, Soviet aviation units were participating in the civil war (12). The Democratic Republic of Vietnam, on the other hand, though recognized by the Soviet Union on January 30, 1950, apparently received little or no aid after an earlier refusal of Stalin to support Ho Chi Minh in the struggle against France (13).

The only other known cases of Soviet military support to a Third World nation in the first postwar decade were Afghanistan and Guatemala. There a reformist president, boycotted by the United States, had sent a friend to Switzerland to negotiate the purchase of 2,000 tons of Czech arms, ammunition and light artillery. These were transported on a Swedish ship in unmarked cases from Poland to Guatemala and managed to evade American attempts at interception (after an earlier shipment from Switzerland had been confiscated by the U.S. Navy) (14). Given the Soviet control over Czechoslovakia at that time, it is unthinkable that Moscow did not approve of this arms deal. Contrary to the arms sales to Israel six years earlier, the effects of these weapons were counterproductive. The U.S. National Security Council concluded that these arms served to establish a Soviet foothold in Central America and were a threat to El Salvador and Honduras. President Eisenhower consequently authorized the CIA to organize the ousting of the reformist Guatemala government (15). While local Communists had strong influence in the labour movement of Guatemala and the Communist party had been one of the four coalition parties in the overthrown Arbenz government, the historical evidence which has surfaced, has not established Communist control of this government (16). Certainly before the Cuban revolution - and in fact later on as well - Latin America has been treated with special caution by the Soviet Union, which recognized de facto the American special interest in Hispano-America. The time, early 1954, was one of transition after Stalin's death; the new Soviet leaders were anything but adventurous and bold steps in Guatemala would have been completely out of tune.

The Period 1955-1965

The outcome of the Soviet-Czech arms deal with Guatemala did not deter other potential clients of East European weapons. When Egypt concluded a principal agreement to buy East-bloc weapons to the value of $ 250 million in February 1955, it first turned to the West for arms. Since the quantity and quality of weapons President Nasser requested from the United States was considered to be upsetting the regional balance of arms, he did not obtain American weapons. With this provoked refusal in his pocket, he could play the East European card with more confidence, thus hiding the fact that a decision for Czech and Soviet arms had already been made. The barter arms package to be paid for in cotton and rice, included 100 MiG-15 and MiG-17 jet fighters, 45 Ilyushin-28 bombers, two destroyers, submarines, torpedo boats, tanks, artillery and ammunition (17). The same game Nasser played for obtaining arms from Eastern Europe was played by the Sukarno regime in Indonesia in 1956-58. The training in the use of these weapons was, in this case, provided by Egyptians (18).

Egypt, Syria, Indonesia and India became the major Third World Communist arms clients in the Khrushchev period. Khrushchev recognized the futility of Stalin's 'two camps' doctrine and saw new opportunities for the Soviet Union in the Third World as decolonization struggles intensified. The new Soviet leader developed a 'two zones' doctrine. The "zone of peace" included the peaceloving Communist countries and the nonaligned Third World nations, while the "war zone" was reserved for the Western imperialists (19). Although there was an increase of Soviet trade and, to some extent, economic aid to the Third World, the main export article were weapons. In the quarter of a century since 1955 the Soviet Union provided weapons worth more than $ 50 billion to some 45 Third

World nations (20). The USSR brought, in the same period, 52,000 officers and soldiers from these nations to the Soviet Union and Eastern Europe for training *).

Some of the military links which the Soviet Union developped in the 1950s in the Third World were an indirect consequence of the American containment policy towards the Soviet Union. By arming Pakistan and Iraq and welding them into the Baghdad Pact, the United States armed opponents of Egypt and India. Their attempts to restore regional balances of power created by the American concern for a global balance of power made them receptive to arms offers from the Soviet Union and its East European Warsaw Treaty Organization partners. In the same manner the Soviet Union also established a military link with the west African state of Guinea.

When Guinea became independent in 1958 and rejected a continued close relationship with France, (later this turned out to be the consequence of a misunderstanding) it was put under great pressure by De Gaulle who withdrew French administrators and cancelled subsidies. For its economic survival, it turned to the Soviet Union which not only provided credits and trade but also weapons. The Chinese and later the Cubans also came to the aid of the rather brutal regime of Sekou Touré and the Soviet Union managed to obtain some naval and port services in return. Together with Ghana and Mali, Guinea was for a while considered by the Kremlin as a "revolutionary democracy" showing the way for other Third World nations (22). Soviet support was only made conditional to an anti-imperialist stance in foreign affairs.

This criterion also applied to Indonesia's contacts with the Russians in the 1950s. Sukarno's nonaligned policy enervated the United States to such an extent that the American CIA conspired with some dissenting Indonesian army colonels for the overthrow of his regime in the spring of 1958 (23). It took Sukarno several months to suppress this pro-Western colonels' rebellion in West Sumatra and the Soviet Union assisted him by sending ships, aircrafts and arms (24). The Soviet Union also supported Sukarno in his conflict with the Dutch over West Irian in the early sixties. In 1961 Indonesia was offered a cruiser, a few destroyers, submarines, PT boots, missiles, torpedoes, anti-aircraft guns, fighter planes and TU-16 bombers on credit. In addition, the Soviet Union also provided Russian pilots to fly these planes and officers to command the submarines. When these secret support pledges were made known by the Indonesian government to the United States to the embarrassment of Moscow, the Dutch learned

----

*) These figures however, stay well behind the American equivalents. The United States transferred, in the period 1950-1979, military material and services to the value of $ 110 billion to more than 70 friendly other nations (not only Third World countries - which makes comparison difficult). Under its military Assistance Training Programme, initiated in 1950, 495,367 officers and men from Latin America, Asia, Africa and Europe were trained in the United States or on U.S. facilities such as those in the Panama Canal Zone as of 1979 (21).

about it. It is probably that this contributed to their loss of nerve to fight out the issue of West Irian with Indonesia (25). If the Dutch had not backed down in the Guinea question, they might have ended up fighting Soviet-piloted planes and submarines. Soviet weapon supplies to Indonesia in the periode 1958-1965 amounted to more than $ 1 billion. These arms enabled Sukarno to survive the Sumatrian rebellion of 1958 and embolded him to claim West Irian. However, the Soviet Union was resenting his "Crush Malaysia" campaign of 1963-1965 (26). While in the Dutch-Indonesian confrontation the side which the Soviet Union should take was clear, this was less so in the Sino-Indian border disputes since 1959, culminating in full-scale fighting in October 1962. After some hesitation and in the light of the fact that the United States was willing to step in as weapons supplier to India, the Soviet Union promised to send MiG-21 aircrafts to India (27). While relations with Peking were already strained, the Kremlin leaders were unwilling to either offend China or the biggest nonaligned nation, India. When the crisis had passed, India was offered surface-to-air missiles, warships and other military equipment in addition to the fighter aircrafts. In 1964 a whole factory for the production of MiGs was sold to India. When India was again at war in 1965 (this time with Pakistan), the Soviet Union took no sides - despite Pakistan's membership in the American CENTO Pact. The USSR was arranging a ceasefire between the contestants and emerged, in January 1966, as peacemaker between them with the Tashkent Declaration (28).

In the decade under consideration, the Soviet Union came closest to actual extrabloc intervention in the case of Egypt. During the Suez crisis of 1956 (a result of the nationalization of the Canal) the Soviets resorted to nuclear and intervention threats. On November 5, 1956, N. Khrushchev issued a vague nuclear threat to Britain, France and Israel. His colleague, Marshall N. Bulganin proposed a joint Soviet-American military intervention if the three nations attacking Egypt would not cease operations within twelve hours. The next day Khrushchev threatened for the second time (the first threat dated August 23, before the outbreak of the armed conflict) to send Soviet "volunteers" (29). Given the simultaneous Soviet military involvement in Poland and Hungary, the intervention threat was an empty one. So was the nuclear missile threat. There were no non-experimental rockets in the Soviet military arsenal capable of hitting Israel, France or Great Britain before the SS-4 with a radius of 2,000 km. was introduced (30).

The Soviet Union's close relationship with President Gamal Abdel Nasser of Egypt introduced the Soviet Union to North Yemen. The Imam of Yemen was in conflict with the British in Aden and since the British managed to seal off Western weapon supplies to him, he turned to the Soviet Union. On November 1, 1955, he signed a friendship treaty with the USSR in Cairo and Soviet weapons and Soviet and Egyptian instructors arrived in 1956 to re-equip and train the army of Imam Ahmad. When this feudal ruler died on September 19, 1962, Nasser decided that the monarchy had to make room for a republic. On September 25, 1962, he supported a coup d'etat against Muhammad al Badr, the Imam designate. The new regime of Colonel

Abdullah al Sallal, formerly the head of the royal army, was recognized by the United Arab Republic (Egypt) and the USSR. The shaky new regime was soon waging war with the more traditional elements of Yemen and had to ensure its survival with a defence pact signed with Nasser on November 10, 1962. In the subsequent civil war, the royalists were backed by Jordan, Morocco, Iran, Pakistan and Saudi Arabia, while Egypt, Iraq and Syria backed the republicans.
The Egyptians sent troops - adding up to 40,000 in 1964 and 70,000 men in 1966 - and the first of them were airlifted to North Yemen by the USSR (31). By the summer of 1963 the Soviet Union was engaged in a massive support operation for the Egyptian war effort against the royalists. A complete airport capable of handling the Soviet-built Egyptian TU-16 was built near Sanaa and a port was constructed under the supervision of about 1,000 Soviet technicians and instructors at Hodeida. When the war against the Saudi-supported royalists became ever more expensive and Sallal felt rebuffed by Khrushchev in a meeting in May 1964, he went to Peking for help to pay for the war. All he received was a loan of half a million dollars, while the Egyptian debt to the Soviet Union caused by this expedition into Yemen was already approaching half a billion dollars. Despite the fact that the Soviet Union indirectly paid for the Egyptian war effort in Yemen, the Egyptians appear to have been in control of the situation and, until late 1965, Nasser even banned direct Soviet arms deliveries to Yemen (32). In a meeting between Nasser of Egypt and Feisal of Saudi Arabia in 1965, the withdrawal of Egyptian and Saudian aid was decided. When this peace plan collapsed, Russian, Czech and Chinese military aid was stepped up in early 1966. However, this did not significantly improve the military position of the republican regime.
A dramatic change in the situation was brought about by the Arab defeat in the June War of 1967 against Israel. Nasser was forced to withdraw his troops - by then reduced to 40,000 men - unilaterally. When in the fall of 1967 Sallal was overthrown in a bloodless coup on November 5, 1967, neither Egypt nor the Soviet Union showed regret. With the Egyptians gone, the Soviet advisers in Yemen hoped that the new government would accept some compromise solution with the royalist forces but its military situation was so weak that a compromise would have been more disadvantageous than fighting on. The situation looked so hopeless that all but one foreign embassy - including the Russians but excluding the Chinese - had evacuated their personnel from the capital Sanaa. At this stage Soviet-build aircrafts, piloted by Russians and later by Syrians, took part in the defence of Sanaa (33). Together with other military support measures the Soviet specialists were instrumental in breaking the 70-days siege of the capital in late 1967. Without Soviet military assistance, the Saudi-backed royalists would have won the Yemeni civil war at this stage (34). Yet it would seem that the republican government of al-Amri was more impressed by the Chinese posture. While arms, food, and up to 1,000 technical personnel for the support of the regime came from the Soviet Union, the Yemeni regime at that time leaned more towards China ideologically and only in spring of 1968 the relationship between Yemen and the Soviet Union was normalized.

By that time, the rapprochment with Saudi Arabia had already been initiated and Soviet influence had largely gone when the hostilities ended in March 1970. It was in neighboring South Yemen, which had gained independence from Britain in 1968, that Soviet influence was to play a role in the next decade.

Looking back at the Soviet military involvement in North Yemen one fails to see an aggressive Soviet role in the Egyptian-led military intervention. The Russians were brought into this conflict by Egypt and when Egypt could no longer bear the burden, Moscow assumed Cairo's role. In one way (but not in others) the situation was comparable to the one of the British in Greece in 1947: there too, the burden of supporting the government in a civil war had become too heavy and Washington had to take over from London. The Soviets probably had a special interest in a naval base in Yemen to protect its only all-year sea-transit route to its Far Eastern parts against American submarines. Hence the construction of Hodeida for ships and submarines and the construction of the Sanaa airport for anti-submarine aerial reconnaissance flights. In this sense the USSR supported local regime because it could thereby improve its own position in the world. Doubts about the reliability of the local client must have been a factor in limiting the degree of commitment. In the beginning, however, it is likely that the USSR was simply dragged by Nasser into this adventure as suggested above. Richard E. Bissell, on whose detailed account our summary is mainly based, has concluded, referring to the period before and after the Egyptian withdrawal:

> "The new links with the Yemeni republicans, however, could obviously not be of the same calibre as relations with states professedly 'building socialism' such as Guinea, Syria, Algeria, and the UAR. (...) It had been acceptable to give massive aid to the UAR, being a socialist regime of the Arab version, and, if the UAR in turn wished to aid the Yemenis in their struggle, that was all right. The only justification available for the Soviet aid to the Yemenis directly, however, was the Yemeni role in the anti-imperialist struggle. How much aid does that warrant? (...) The USSR opted for the least possible involvement, a level of aid that barely sustained the regime through early 1968. (...) It clearly took the USSR some time to understand the nature of the problem in the Yemeni civil war. They were dealing with a form of political succession that was rather unfamiliar to them, and for a long time the USSR apparently did not understand that there was no revolution in Yemen, simply a centuries-old method of choosing a new ruler. The true deception came, of course, from the republican side, where Sallal and a few other politicians did consider themselves revolutionaries..." (35)

The eight-year long civil war in North Yemen ended with Saudi Arabia rather than the Soviet Union as the dominant outside power. During the early 1970s Soviet influence steadily declined and in 1976 Soviet advisers were expelled from the republic. In 1980, however, limited Soviet aid and some advisers were again accepted after President Ali-Abdallah Saleh became disenchanted with his Saudi and American friends.

While the developments in North Yemen took us beyond the Khrushchev period, some other Soviet military involvements in the early sixties deserve mentioning: Cuba, Laos and the Belgian Congo. While the Soviet military commitments in Cuba and Laos were successful, its involvement in the formerly Belgian Congo was a failure.

When the mutiny of the Congolese Force Publique and the secession of the Katanga province pushed the newly independent country into a deep crisis in July 1960, the Soviet Union, like the United States, provided some military support in the framework of international aid to the threatened government of Premier Patrice Lumumba. In the case of the Soviet Union this consisted of more than one dozen transport aircrafts, perhaps one hundred trucks and 200 technicians. Lumumba counted on the Soviet Union when he was ousted from power in September 1960 by General Mobutu. Yet Moscow could do nothing for him beyond providing airshuttle services to Lumumba's own troops. The United Nations' command subsequently closed the airport at Leopoldville to prevent a Soviet airlift of troops loyal to the Premier. His appeals for Soviet intervention against the United Nations troops, his internal opponents and the secessionist provinces were not answered by the Kremlin. The Soviet Union could not even save his life when he was taken prisoner in December 1960 as UN forces again prevented the transfer of Soviet supplies to troops still loyal to him in the Stanleyville area (36). However, in 1964 the Soviet Union managed to send small arms to these rebel forces who by then had moved closer to the Sudan border. This support (jointly with Algeria and Egypt) was minimal and was discontinued when it produced no results (37). Soviet air supplies of arms on a larger scale also occurred in the early sixties in the cases of Laos and North Vietnam.

Between late 1960 and early 1961 the USSR carried out about one thousand transport flights from North Vietnam to Laos, bringing military supplies to one side in the civil war. This support for the united front of Prince Souvanna Phouma and the Pathet Lao movement consisted mainly of small arms worth less than $ 10 million. Some of the aircrafts used were flown in from the Congo. Despite its moderate size, this military assistance proved decisive in routing the U.S.-supported forces of General Phoumi Nosavan. American aid was terminated and the neutralization of Laos was declared in the Geneva Accords of July 1962 (38).

Soviet support for the Cuban revolution became substantial after the summer of 1960 and especially once the Castro regime had proven its ability to survive the CIA-organized Bay of Pigs invasion by Cuban exiles in April 1961. In 1962, the Soviet Union had, according to Fidel Castro, more than 40,000 soldiers and technicians in Cuba. U.S. estimates were about half that number for October 1962. The Soviet had 5,000 ground troops equipped with T-54 tanks, anti-tank missiles and tactical rockets on the island. These were overlooked at the time by the United States and would have made an invasion by U.S. marines more costly than envisaged by the U.S. military (39). Cuba was subsequently supplied amply with equipment and training; so much so, that Cuba, in turn, could send military training missions to Africa in the mid-sixties. In the case of the mission to Congo Brazzaville such a mission was numbering close to one thousand men. Cuban military personnel took part in guerrilla fighting during this period in a number of African nations, notably in Portugese Guinea, Tanzania and Zaire (40). In the course of two decades the Cuban armed forces increased fivefold compared to the 1960 level. Today they number 225,000 men and 190,000 reservists. The people's militia has recently been doubled to more than one million men and women, which means that altogether about 15% of the more than 10 million Cubans are part of the military. Cuba can mobilize more armed forces than Brazil with a population ten times as big. In size, as well as fighting experiences, the Cuban military is second to none in Latin America. In the period 1969-1979 the Soviet Union provided Cuba free of charge with at least $ 900 million worth of military equipment (41). In the early 1980s Soviet military supplies to Cuba increased again: while in the 1970s the average tonnage of weapons supplied was 15,000 per year, the averages for the years 1981-1983 were more than four times higher, according to U.S. sources (42). This armament, the presence of 2,500 military and 8,000 civilian Soviet advisers and a Soviet brigade of 3,000 men in Cuba (43), combined with the fact that the Soviet Union supports the Cuban economy to the amount of $ 1.5 million per day have given rise to the charge that the Cubans have become the "Gurkhas of the Russian Empire" (44). (The notion of the Cubans as Soviet "proxies" will be discussed in the 'Conclusion' of this chapter.)

This has brought us beyond the Khrushchev area, which was an area of pretence, when the Soviet Union was strategically inferior and lacked the means to project its military power successfully to other continents. There was no significant naval activity by the Red Fleet in this period except for the sending of a minor naval contingent to Latakia in the initial phase of a Syrian-Turkish crisis in September - October 1957 (45). Weapon supplies unaccompanied by troops (except in the case of Cuba) were the main expression of military policy in the Khrushchev period. Due to Western opposition or countermeasures these arms were often supplied clandestinely and/or through third parties. The intermediary in Eastern Europe was usually Czechoslovakia, which traditionally had a sizeable weapon industry of its own. On the receiving side the intermediaries varied. In the case of the Algerian struggle for independence, small shipments of arms reached the FLN through the United Arab Republic, Tunesia and Morocco since the late 1950s. Upon achieving independence in 1962, Algeria was openly supplied with a few MiG-15s and 300 tanks. Yet these came too late to influence significantly the outcome of the border war between Algeria and Morocco in 1963 (46). The struggle for independence of the Portugese colonies was supported in the early 1960s by the Soviet Union through Ghana, and, after Nkrumah's overthrow in 1966, through Guinea. During Khrushchev's period in office over 1,000 Soviet advisers were active in Ghana giving training to independence movements, but there were also over 400 Chinese, as well as Yugoslavian, Cuban, North Korean and East European advisers involved in the training of the liberation movements (47). The Cuban role in supporting the anti-colonial struggle in Angola and in Guinea-Bissau was already substantial in the mid-sixties and the liberation forces, in fact, showed a preference for them as trainers (48). But they accepted any help which they could get, be it that almost all of this help came from the East as Portugal was a member of NATO.

The emergence of the Third World, epitomized in the Bandung conference of 1955 where 29 Afro-Asian countries congregated, was seen by the Soviet Union under Khrushchev as an opportunity to win allies while at the same time weakening the Western powers. Khrushchev no longer insisted on Communist party rule in these countries but offered the concept of the 'national democratic state' of progressive orientation advancing on a 'noncapitalist path of development'. These anti-Western, non-aligned nations were, in his view, in a transitional stage on the road towards socialism. Third World nations where the Communist parties were playing an active role in the political process (rather than being suppressed) were labelled 'revolutionary democratic states' in the new ideological terminology evolving under Khrushchev (49). Among these figured Indonesia (until 1965) and presumably also India, while Egypt and Iraq who cracked down on local Communists, belonged to the former group. Given the limited economic resources available to the USSR, arms were the main instrument of influence in these countries. A total of more than $ 2.7 billion worth of Soviet weapons were delivered to Third World nations in the decade 1954-1964. In the 1950s the recipients had been Egypt, Syria, Iraq, North Yemen, India, Afghanistan, Indonesia and Guinea. In the early 1960s Laos, Morocco, Algeria, Sudan, Ghana, Mali, Cambodia, Somalia, Tanzania, Zaire and Nepal became recipients of Soviet arms (50). By providing arms the Soviet Union became co-responsible for the arms race in the Third World and the establishment of military dictatorships *).

The Period 1965-1980s

Under Khrushchev, the Soviet Union sent no Soviet troops abroad into a Third World nation for combat, though he had threatened with "volunteers" during the Suez crisis. Only in the case of Cuba a relatively large number of troops was sent for defensive purposes. Intervention requests like those of Nasser in 1956 or Lumumba in 1960 were declined and no troops were sent to Laos and Vietnam when the Kennedy administration threatened military intervention in

----

*) The number of countries in the Third World under military rule rose from less than 15 percent in 1960 to more than 43 percent by 1980 (for nations with more than half a million people). In the 1970s the Third World nations were to spend between 800 billion and one trillion dollars on their armed forces, about one fourth of this sum going to the importation of weapons - a sum exceeding all foreign aid which these 105 Third World countries received. (Miles D. Wolpin. Reaganism and American National Insecurity. Courier & Freeman (Potsdam, N.Y.), 29 November 1983, p. 4.)

Laos in April 1961 or when 5,000 V.S. troops and a naval task force were sent into Thailand in 1962. In response to the American involvement in Indochina, Khrushchev could only offer a piece of prophecy to the Communists in Laos and North Vietnam by saying that "the Americans may fight fifteen years if they want to, but it will not help" (51).

Khrushchev had put much stress on the deterring effect of his Strategic Rocket Forces, established as a separate service in 1959. Relying on them he had cut back naval shipbuilding programs in the mid-1950s and reduced the size of the total armed forces from 5,763,000 in 1955 to 3,623,000 in 1958 (52). After the Cuban missile crisis, under pressure from the military, this trend was reversed and his successors were preparing for a broader range of possibilities then a "rocket nuclear war" (53).

The first ten years of the Brezhnev period saw an extended continuation of the pattern established under his predecessors. There were two differences, however. First, arms supplies were no longer linked to ideological affinities. The new recipients of Soviet weapons in the Brezhnev period included nations as diverse as Pakistan, Iran, South Yemen, Ethiopia, Nigeria, Cyprus, Uganda, Mauretania and Congo-Brazzaville. Second, since the mid-1970s Soviet military initiatives became markedly bolder - notably in Africa. In the following pages we will survey Soviet military efforts on a regional basis for the period since 1965.

Latin America

In no other region has the Soviet Union shown more military restraint than in Latin America. The Kremlin's refusal to engage in armed adventures in the United States' "backyard" had been a major source of friction with Cuba in the 1960s when Castro and Guevara favoured a strategy of triggering off revolution by armed groups acting as a "foco" for popular resistance. Instead, the Soviet Union generally favoured a "peaceful road to power" strategy for the Communist and other left parties in South America (54). Strange enough, in the one instance where this strategy worked - in Chile in 1970 - the Soviet Union did not come to aid the Allende regime in any major way, when the latter was subjected to North-American economic pressures. When economic support was finally promised on a substantial scale to socialist Chile, it was too late. No Soviet military assistance was given to S. Allende during his reign from April 1970 to September 1973 (55). After Allende was overthrown, Soviet condemnation of the Pinochet regime was vociferous (while the Chinese, in an anti-Soviet vein, established links with the right-wing junta). On the other hand, the Soviet Union has offered military equipment to a number of countries in Latin America (Columbia, Ecuador, Argentina). Yet only the military junta of Peru under Juan Velasco Alvarado and his successors accepted Soviet tanks and fighter bombers between 1972 and 1977 (56). In 1979, Peru ceased buying Soviet weapons. It has been reported that the Soviet Union also provided military support, especially radar equipment, to Argentina during its 1982 war with Great Britain over the Falklands. In addition, the USSR has been reported to offer Argentina weapons in exchange for a naval base in the Cape Horn region (57).

Most of the Soviet military support to Latin America went to Cuba which received military aid to the value of $ 5.1 billion in the last three years alone (58). Part of this equipment was probably transferred to Central America, notably Nicaragua and possibly to insurgents in El Salvador, Honduras, and Guatemala (59). The Soviet Union has remained cautious to show a direct military presence in the region, even on Cuba. In 1970 the Soviets were trying to make the Cienfuegos naval base suitable for missile-firing nuclear-powered submarines. When the Nixon administration termed this a "hostile act" in violation of the 1962 Kennedy-Khrushchev understanding, construction activities at the port of Cienfuegos were halted. However, when the Carter administration in 1979 demanded the withdrawal of a Soviet military brigade of 2,600 men which had been allegedly detected by satellite surveillance, the Soviets refused, pointing out that these troops had been in Cuba for years. They also resumed construction activities at Cienfuegos in 1979, perhaps testing U.S. response again (60).

The political revolution of March 13, 1979, which brought the New Jewel Movement under Maurice Bishop to power in Grenada, was not of Soviet or Cuban making. However, once in power, the new government relied heavily on Cuban advice and Soviet arms which were provided as a gift. The victory of the Sandinista National Liberation Front (FSLN) over the pro-American dictator A. Somoza in July 1979 was also basically "homemade". However, Soviet weapons and Cuban advisers played an important role in the final offensive. With the organization of the counterrevolution by the United States, Cuban military advisers increased to several thousands by the mid-eighties. Cuban and East German specialists are also in charge of Nicaragua's internal security matters. In the case of El Salvador, the Cuban role in the coordination of the insurrection appears to be far more important than in Nicaragua in the last phase of Somoza's reign. However, the degree of Soviet backing of Cuban support to the anti-regime forces of El Salvador remains a matter of conjecture, which in itself, might be an expression of a successful camouflage effort (61).

Asia

On its far Eastern Front the Soviet Union has faced a fairly stable situation once the Korean war was settled. Japanese claims to sovereignty over the Kuril Islands (which together with South Sakhalin had been promised to Stalin at Yalta) were not backed up by force and were ignored by the Soviet Union. The border dispute with China did not produce a renewed major flare-up after a nuclear warning. (Pravda announced on August 28, 1969, that China's territorial claims against the Soviet Union courted nuclear war.) However, substantial numbers of troops were tied down along the border ever since then. In the 1970s the conflict with China was acted out in South East Asia where the Chinese supported rebel groups in Afghanistan and the Khmer Rouge guerrillas in Kampuchea who were fighting the Vietnamese occupation force.

North Vietnam had sided with the Soviet Union after a long balancing act between the rival socialist states enabled it to achieve its military goal after three decades of fighting. While both China and the Soviet Union had not cut their weapon supply to North Vietnam prior to the Paris Peace Agreement of January 1973, they were significantly decreasing the supply of arms in 1973 and were not resupplying North Vietnam in 1974. This would suggest that the Soviet Union was not from the outset treating the Peace Agreement between Hanoi and Saigon as a scrap of paper. However, by 1975, when Hanoi's first tentative spring offensive proved amazingly successful, it is likely that Soviet material support had again increased (62). With Vietnam, the Soviet Union not only shared its enemy with China but also the desire to see the influence of Japan and the United States reduced in the area. Despite this goal consonance, the Soviet-Vietnamese relationship has been a less than harmonious. For one thing, Vietnam, with its more than 50 million people, sees itself as a regional power in its own right, despite its economic and military dependency on the Soviet Union. (Due to the war devastations, between 20-30 percent of the rice consumed in Vietnam in 1980 was of Soviet origin (63).) While there are about 5,000 men of Russian personnel in Vietnam (and 300 in Kampuchea with the 170,000 Vietnamese troops and 500 in Laos alongside 45,000 Vietnamese soldiers), the military relationship is a strained one and the Russians are generally not liked. For all their military support, the Soviets have apparently not received formal base rights at the American-build Cam Ranh Bay naval base in Vietnam, despite repeated Chinese claims to the contrary (64).

When the victorious Northvietnamese regime extended its control to Laos and Kampuchea after 1975, overthrowing the Peking-backed Pol Pot regime in the latter country in early 1979, it was backed by the Soviet Union (65). Prior to the invasion of Kampuchea in January 1979 the Soviet Union had signed a treaty alliance with Vietnam on November 3, 1978, and stepped up military aid to Vietnam (China had withdrawn its advisers in the summer of 1978), financing Vietnam's military policy to a reported amount of 2 to 3 million dollars a day. The new Hanoi-imposed regime of Heng-Samrin in Phnom Penh was immediately recognized by Moscow. This prompted Zbigniew Brzezinski, the U.S. national security adviser, to characterize the Vietnamese invasion as "the first case of a proxy war between the Soviet Union and China" (66). When the People's Republic of China decided to "teach the Vietnamese a lesson" one and a half month later with a punitive incursion into Vietnam, the Soviet reaction was, however, initially rather unsupportive. After the Vietnamese government "urgently called on the Soviet Union" and other fraternal socialist countries for support, the Soviet government flew in some military supplies and sent some war ships up the Vietnamese coast, which were reported as bringing troops from South to North Vietnam. The reason given by Moscow for not providing more substantial aid was rather amazing. Moscow suggested that China's "self-defensive counterattack" had been undertaken in collusion with the United States, adding, that it was in reality a Chinese plot to provoke a war between the two superpowers, so that they would annihilate each other in the confrontation, thereby allowing China a rise to "world hegemony". The Soviet Union, it was stated, would not fall for such a trick. However, after the retreat of the Chinese punitive expedition, the Soviet Union greatly increased its military supplies to Hanoi and continued to do so in the following year when Vietnam received more than $ 1 billion worth of Soviet military equipment. The USSR had in the early 1980s about 5,000 military and civilian advisers in Vietnam and Soviet Aeroflot planes were providing regular airshuttle services for Vietnamese troops destined for the battle zones in Kampuchea. This support of the occupation forces has been judged to be of great help for the Vietnamese ability to cope with the Kampuchean resistance movement (67).

The Chinese incursion into Vietnam and, for that matter, the Sino-Soviet conflict as well, were, of course, also an ideological embarrassment of sorts for those who professed to believe that war was linked to capitalism and would be unthinkable between socialist states. Due to the short duration of the Chinese incursion - they proved inferior to the war-hardened Vietnamese with their more modern equipment - the Soviet Union was not forced to step up its military aid substantially as it was by the turn of events taken in Afghanistan in the same year.

The Soviet involvement in Afghanistan shows some parallels with the U.S. involvement in South Vietnam. The year when both countries started aid programs and begun to provide military training to the client government was the same: 1954 *). When the local regimes proved ineffective in coping with the insurgency, both the United States and the Soviet Union were instrumental in staging coups for their replacement. In the case of South Vietnam the Diem regime was overthrown in 1963; in the case of Afghanistan the coup-cum-intervention against Hafizullah Amin in late 1979 served this purpose. In both cases the intervening superpower had to take over the main defence burden. Whether the Soviet military presence in Afghanistan - now in its fourth year - will be as prolonged as the American one in Vietnam remains to be seen.

While the details of the Soviet invasion of Afghanistan are presented in the last of our case studies, a few more general remarks about this first direct massive extra-bloc military involvement of the Soviet Union since the Second World War will be made here. The Soviet intervention did not come out of the blue but was a result of a century-old interest and cumulative commitments. Russia had intervened militarily in Afghanistan in 1885, 1928, 1930, and almost - it was cancelled at the last moment - in 1934. For many years it had

----

*) Although it should be kept in mind that the bulk of the costs of the earlier French war effort (amounting to 600 million francs per year) was paid by the United States, from 1950 onwards. The American commitment went so far that, in April 1954, John Foster Dulles and Admiral A. Radford made plans ('Operation Vulture') to save Dien Bien Phu by utilizing atomic bombs against the Vietminh. However, President Eisenhower was not prepared to intervene without allies, especially the British, and the latter favoured a peaceful solution at the conference table in Geneva.

given substantial economic credits to the country, as much, in fact as it spent on all African nations over the same period (68). A Communist party, the People's Democratic Party, had been in existence for 15 years, although it split the following year (1965) into two quarreling factions, the Khalq ('Masses') led by Nur Muhammad Taraki and Hafizullah Amin and the Parcham ('Banners'), led by Babrak Karmal. The initial coup against Prime Minster Daud which brought them to power in April 1978 is unlikely to have been encouraged by the Soviet Union (69). The Soviet Union was certainly worried by the close links which the repressive Daud regime appeared to develop with Pakistan and Iran. An anti-Soviet Islamic coalition on the southern borders of Soviet Turkmenistan and Tadjikiistan, linked to the United States (who had some 24,000 military advisers in Iran alone before the fall of the Shah) was conceivably a cause of concern for the Soviet leaders. The coup of April 1978 against the Daud regime (which had came to power five years before, also by a coup) was provoked by Daud himself.

When he attempted to arrest the leadership of the People's Democratic Party of Afghanistan (united again in 1977) the Communist party, with the support of elements from the Soviet-trained military, retaliated and managed to seize state power on April 27, 1978 (70). Once in power, the government under President Taraki and Prime Minister Amin received active Soviet backing. However, the pace at which the new regime introduced and enforced land and educational reforms in the tribal and religious country produced growing popular opposition (71). During 1979 the Soviet Union had already sent more personnel to Afghanistan, altogether some 7,000 military and civilian advisers. Amin called for more Soviet aid to cope with the rebellion. At the same time he apparently also sought to come to terms with Pakistan. This might have raised Soviet fears that Amin was about to become a "second Sadat". Apparently the Soviets also felt that Amin was too ruthless

----

*) According to an American document seized by Iranian students during the occupation of the American embassy in Tehran in 1979, the Soviet Union actively encouraged a coup d'etat for the removal of Amin. They had sent Vasily S. Safronchuk, a diplomat, to Kabul, to prepare the installation of a less hated regime. The American embassy in Tehran was informed about the planned Soviet coup, apparently by Safronchuk himself, as well as by the East German ambassador in Tehran, Hermann Schwiesau. On July 18, 1979, Schwiesau had told the American chargé d'affaires in Tehran, Bruce Amstutz, about the planned changes: "Schwiesau confirmed that Safronchuk is charged with bringing about a radical change in the government ...", Amstutz wrote, continuing "Schwiesau clearly aimed at a coup within the party by which the Soviets would remove Amin and perhaps others as well". The Americans were amazed and puzzled about these confidentialities from Safronchuk and Schwiesau. They concluded that these were meant to forestall in advance American protests against a greater Soviet presence in Aghanistan. (72)

and too fast in his policy of bringing about socialist changes. They urged President Taraki to remove the much-hated Prime Minister and form a more moderate and broadly-based government *). Amin, however, moved faster when these plans came to his knowledge. In a shoot-out on September 16, 1979, Taraki was killed and Amin assumed power himself. Had this power struggle ended differently the Soviet intervention of December 1979, which brought Babrak Karmal to the Afghan presidency, might not have been "necessary".

The internal opposition, in turn, was given military support by Pakistan, and from early 1979 onwards, by China, while Arabic states also provided weapons. The United States encouraged Egypt and Pakistan to provide such support already prior to the Soviet invasion of December 1979 (73). After the Soviet invasion, the same states and Saudi Arabia and other Persian Gulf states were reported to provide arms and aid to the anti-regime forces (74).

This sequence of events has been recalled here in order to indicate how much internal factors in Afghanistan affected Soviet moves. These should be carefully assessed before one rushes to the wide-spread notions that some geostrategic design - a Soviet advance to the warm water ports of the Indian Ocean or to the Western oil supplies - was the prime reason for the invasion of Afghanistan. Strategic considerations did play a role. They were probably more defensive than offensive. Brezhnev's assertion in August 1981 that the situation in Afghanistan posed "a direct threat to the security of our southern frontier" (75), exaggerated as it was, can be interpreted as an indication in this direction. While this does not excuse the Soviet intervention, it places it in a different framework for interpretation, one formulated in the Brezhnev Doctrine at the time of the Czechoslovakian invasion in 1968. At that time Brezhnev asserted that historic progress could not be turned back: once that a country had become socialist, it could not be allowed to fall back into capitalism and rejoin the imperialist camp.

Afghanistan and Vietnam represent the primary examples of Soviet military commitment in the Asian region under Brezhnev. Throughout the period, from 1965 onwards, India has acquired most of its military equipment from the Soviet Union with which it shares its apprehension of China and Pakistan. During the war between India and Pakistan over the secession of East Pakistan (December 4-17, 1971), the Soviet Union strongly backed India, while the United States sided with Pakistan. In 1971 India received Soviet arms to the value of $ 1.1 billion and about 15 Soviet aircrafts were transferred from Egypt to India in response to a similar transfer of American aircrafts from Jordan and Libya to Pakistan (76). At the same time, the USSR sent units from its Pacific Fleet to the Bay of Bengal in order to check the American naval task force. The Indian government was, according to the CIA, assured by the Soviet ambassador that the USSR "will not allow the [U.S.] Seventh Fleet to intervene" and "would open a diversionary action" in Sinkiang if China intervened on behalf of Pakistan. Soviet troop movements towards the Sino-Soviet border were at that time signalled, presumably as a warning to China. The outcome of the Indian invasion of East Pakistan was the dismemberment of an ally of both the People's Republic of China and the United States. The U.S. Secretary of State, Henry Kissinger, characterized this Indo-Pakistani war as "the naked recourse to force by a partner of the Soviet Union backed by Soviet arms and buttressed by Soviet assurances". With his characteristic preoccupation to place local issues into a geopolitical straight jacket, he forgot to mention that America's close ally Pakistan was engaged in little less than genocide (between 500,000 and three million people were slaughtered) and that the Indian intervention was above all a humanitarian one (77).

In May 1980 another major armament programme to the value of $ 1.6 billion (over five years) was signed between the Soviet Union and India (78). This continued military relationship has not made India politically dependent on the Soviet Union in any significant way. As A.Z. Rubinstein has noted:

> "... Moscow did not receive what it really wanted: naval facilities for its Indian Ocean flotilla; support for Brezhnev's plan, floated in June 1969, for an Asian collective security system, and a special relationship that would keep India at a distance from China." (79)

While the USSR remained the main source of weapons for India in the 1980s, India has diversified its buyings, acquiring French, British and German (but not American) weapon systems.

Another recipient of Soviet military support in the region has been Sri Lanka. When pro-Chinese "guevarrists" in a period of economic crisis, attempted to seize state power in April 1971, the Soviet Union offered the left-of-center coalition government of S. Bandaranaike two helicopters and 4-5 MiG 17 aircrafts together with pilots. Such military help was, however, also provided by Great Britain, the United States, India, Pakistan and Yugoslavia - a rather mixed collection of friendly powers (80).

The Middle East

Soviet Naval Interest, Arms Transfers and Bases

Russian interest in the region has been of long standing as the only short, year-round open, searoute linking the Western parts of the Union of Soviet Socialist Republics with its Far Eastern parts is passing from the Black Sea and Bosporus to the Mediterranean Sea, Suez Canal and Red Sea. As such the significance of this route is comparable to the one of the Panama Canal for the United States. Attempts to make the Red Sea passage an "Arab Lake" have therefore met strong resistance from the USSR. It is likely that Soviet attempts to obtain a U.N. mandate over colonial territories in Libya and Eritrea (with its port of Massawa) were influenced by naval considerations although the Soviet Union at that time had no sizeable deepwater navy. Soviet demands on Turkey for control of the Bosporus and to Greece for Rhodos in the same period can also be explained in this light (81).

In the Brezhnev period, Soviet relations with Turkey became very good, partly because the United States were backing Greece on the question of Cyprus. Despite its NATO membership, Turkey has also become one of the major Soviet aid recipients. This can be seen as a way of guaranteeing a flexible Turkish interpretation of the 1936 Montreux Convention with regard to the passage of warships (82).

The securing of the Suez passage, on the other hand, has cost the Soviet Union more efforts than the one at the Bosporus. The conclusion of the Baghdad Pact in February 1955 between Turkey and Iraq (and later Great Britain, Iran and Pakistan), conceived by the United States as a "northern tier" defence of the Middle East against the Soviet Union, alienated India and Egypt. When the latter sought arms from the Soviet Union in 1955 and nationalized the Suez Canal Company in July 1956, a more secure Canal passage for Soviet ships than under English control seemed to be in the offing. However, the contrary was true: following Arab defeats, the Canal was closed between November 1956 and March 1957 and between June 1967 and June 1975. Soviet interest to keep this sea lane out of the hands of hostile powers has contributed to Soviet entanglement in the Arab-Israeli conflict, and, on the shores of the Gulf of Aden, the Yemeni conflict, and the Ogaden conflict.

Partly as a consequence of this, no Third World region has imported more weapons in general, and also more Soviet weapons, than the Middle East. For the 1970s Table IV gives an indication of the Soviet share.

Table IV: Exports of Major Weapons to Third World, according to SIPRI (1980) (83)

Region	Total Value of Weapon Imports (in millions of dollars)		Share of Soviet Exports (in percentages)	
	1970-74	1975-79	1970-74	1975-79
Middle East	9,344	20,141	51	15
Far East	3,738	6,679	28	21
North Africa	783	4,848	17	62
Black Africa	1,276	4,021	17	31
South America	1,479	3,936	not known	not known
South and Southeast Asia	1,869	2,031	54	42
Central America and Caribbean Region	231	624	66	45

Soviet arms transfers were confined to Egypt, Syria, North Yemen and Iraq and Algeria in the Khrushchev period. Thereafter South Yemen, Sudan, Libya, Iran, Morocco, Lebanon and Kuwait were recipients of Soviet military equipment. Due to the shifting alliances all of these countries (except South Yemen since 1968) were also recipients of American weapons, and many of them received arms from British, French, West German, Italian and Chinese sources. These countries also provided weapons to a number of Middle Eastern countries where Soviet military assistance was not welcomed: Quatar, Israel (after 1948), Tunesia, Saudi Arabia, Oman and Bahrain (84).

Since these weapon deliveries usually involved military training, they were generally accompanied by military advisory missions, which in the case of the Soviet Union have generally been sizeable. Where weapons could not be fully paid for (which is not uncommon, except for the oil-exporting nations) base rights have sometimes been offered in return by recipient nations. The Soviet Union has not been very fortunate to obtain permanent air or naval bases in the region. In the Mediterranean, its only naval support facility in the 1950s was Vlonë in Albania, which was lost in 1961 when Enver Hoxha switched to the Chinese side. Only after the June War of 1967 were air and naval bases obtained in Egypt. However, these were partly lost again in 1972 and completely lost four years later. In the period 1962-1968, North Yemenese facilities were accessible to the Soviet airforce and navy but this was far away from the Mediterranean. From 1969 onwards South Yemen became an ally of the Soviet Union but it shared the distant position disadvantage with North Yemen. After the October War of 1973, Syria granted naval access to Soviet ships, but it curtailed access somewhat in 1976, the year the Soviet Union disagreed with Syria's intervention in the Lebanon. However, in that year Iraq was beginning to grant quite extensive access to the Soviet Union to its naval and air facilities. Compared to the numerous bases of the Western powers (Cyprus, Turkey, Egypt, Iran, Libya, Bahrain, Oman, Morocco, Abu Dhabi, Aden in the 1960s and 1970s) the Soviet position has been smaller and less stable *).

Soviet Military Interventions

In the 1950s the Soviet Union did not intervene directly in Middle Eastern conflicts. However, on a number of occasions Khrushchev had used nuclear language, for the first time towards the end of the Suez War in 1956. In 1957 during the Syrian-Turkish crisis, 'rocket-rattling' was accompanied by a visit of a Soviet cruiser to the Syrian port of Latakia. In both the Syrian-Turkish crisis of 1957 and the Lebanese-Iraqi crisis of 1958, large-scale troop manoeuvres under a prominent Soviet general in the southern parts of Russia were staged for a show of Soviet determination to support the Arab cause (86).

Only the June war of 1967 brought a major change. This war, which closed the Suez Canal for eight full years, was inadvertedly triggered off by the Soviet Union. The Palestine Liberation Organization, backed by Syria, had been engaged in small-scale cross-border attacks on Israel, which created expectations of an Israeli counterstrike on Syria. When the Syrian government, which maintained friendly relations with the Soviet Union, was in internal difficulties, Moscow

----

*) The imbalance between Western and Soviet bases in the Mediterranean is even more pointed on a global scale: While the United States had, in 1980, about 1,600 foreign bases in approximately 100 countries, the USSR had perhaps as many as 3,000 in about 20 countries, most of them Warsaw Pact allies (85).

tried to rally support for it in May 1967 by spreading unsubstantiated
rumours of an impending attack by Israel against Syria. President
Nasser, who had linked Egypt in a defense pact to Syria, mobilized
his army in the Sinai and asked for the removal of the United
Nations' buffer force which had been stationed between his troops
and Israel for the last ten years. To defuse the situation, Israel had
invited the Soviet ambassador to visit its border area with Syria, so
that he could see for himself that Israel had not significantly built up
its forces there. (There had been a small build up which the Soviets
might have overestimated.) The Soviet ambassador declined this offer.
Nasser's next step was the announcement of the closure of the Strait
of Tiran, which was a casus belli for Israel: a pre-emptive Israeli
strike (launched in part from an Ethiopian airfield) marked the
beginning of the Six Days War and turned the false intelligence
spread by the Soviets into a self-fulfilling prophecy (87). As in 1956,
when it announced that "volunteers" were enrolling in the Soviet
Union for the fight on Egypt's side, the Kremlin declared to be on
the side of the Arabs and made some threats of intervention but
ultimately did not answer Arab appeals for military help. Neither
were substantial military supplies sent nor did the Soviet naval forces
play an active role. The Soviet fleet in the Mediterranean, however,
was substantially increased during the May-June period, ultimately
counting more than fifty ships, many of them shadowing the U.S.
Sixth Fleet (88). Only at the very end of this 'Blitz Krieg', when the
Israelis appeared to be pushing towards Damascus, did the Soviet
Union issue an "ultimatum" to Israel via the United States, warning
"that unless Israel unconditionally halted operations within the next
few hours, the Soviet Union would take necessary actions, including
military" (89). This threat of direct intervention with combat forces
in an ongoing armed conflict was more credible then the 1956
rhetoric. However, Soviet rapid power-projecting capabilities were
still very modest in 1967.
Soviet support came only after the Arab defeat in the form of a
re-equipment of the defeated Egyptian and Syrian armies. Egypt alone
received Soviet military support worth more than $ 4.5 billion from
1967 to 1973. This enabled President Nasser to start, in March 1969,
against the wishes of Moscow, a "war of attrition" in the form of
raids and bombardments across the Suez Canal (90). Israeli retaliation
in the "Canal War" consisted of aerial bombardments against
infrastructural targets in the Egyptian hinterland and at the Suez
front. To this Egypt had no reply of its own. On January 22, 1970,
President Nasser secretly went to Moscow asking the Soviet leaders
for a complete air defence system to be manned by Soviet personnel
until Egyptian officers had acquired the necessary skills in the USSR.
To the consternation of the Kremlin top he reportedly threatened to
resign if the Soviet Union would not grant his request, adding that in
this case he would hand over power to a pro-American successor.
After some hesitation, the Soviet leaders honoured Nasser's desperate
plea for military assistance. As a consequence the aerial defence of
Egypt was delegated to the Soviet Union. The USSR provided Egypt
with a complete air defence system with radar, ground-to-air missiles
and fighter aircrafts, and the personnel to man and defend this

system. In March and April 1970 Soviet MiG-21 pilots and SAM-3 crews and support units arrived, altogether ultimately some 20,000 men by 1972. When in May 1970 the Israeli deep-penetration bombings had been halted, the Soviets were not pushing Egypt's advantage. In June the Soviet leaders made it clear to Nasser that the Soviet military contribution would not be substantially augmented. Returning from Moscow, Gamal Abdel Nasser announced that he was prepared to accept the cease-fire proposed by the United States in the Rogers Initiative. By mid-July the Israelis, under American pressure and after increased losses of aircrafts, also accepted in principle. The next day, however, on July 24, 1970, and again on July 30, when the Israeli government officially announced its adherence to a cease-fire, Soviet and Israeli pilots clashed in airbattles in which the Soviets lost four MiG-21 aircrafts. Until the cease-fire took effect on August 7, Soviet planes avoided the Canal zone (91).

The summer of 1970 marked the zenith of Soviet military presence in Egypt. Six airfields in Egypt were under the almost complete control of the Soviet military. Its 150 fighter aircrafts and 75-85 surface-to-air missile sites were manned by more than 200 pilots and between 12,000 and 15,000 missile crew men. Soviet ships received facilities at the ports of Alexandria, Port Said and at Mersa Martuh. Then, in the fall of 1970 Nasser suddenly died and the Soviet Union, apparently eager to institutionalize its commitment in the face of an internal struggle for power, concluded a Treaty of Friendship and Cooperation with Egypt on May 27, 1971 (92). However, Nasser's successor Anwar Sadat announced the expulsion of all Soviet military personnel (between 15,000 and 21,000 men) on July 18, 1972, leaving the Soviets with little more than some access to port facilities. This break with the Soviet Union was, however, healed to some extent before the outbreak of the October war in 1973.

The Soviet air presence in Egypt after the Six Day War had given the USSR an opportunity to interfere, indirectly and directly, in Nigeria and the Sudan in the period 1967-1971. In the case of Nigeria, which was engaged in a civil war over the secession of its oil-province Biafra, the USSR sided with the central government rather than with the more "progressive" secessionist government of Biafra. They sent more than 50 fighter and bomber aircrafts to Lagos and were instrumental in arranging the transfer of Egyptian pilots and planes to Nigeria to fly missions for the government side (93). During the spring of 1969 the Egyptian pilots were reportedly replaced by East German ones as well as by others from Eastern Europe (94). In the Sudan, the central government was faced by an insurgency by the Christian negro movement Anya Nya (which was supported by Uganda, Zaire and Ethiopia). The Soviet Union sent and manned aircrafts for the suppression of the rebellion. Soviet aircrafts were reported to be involved in rocket, strafing and bombing missions in southern Sudan. Apart from the tactical air support and the provision of helicopter pilots, Soviet ground advisers were also reported in the Sudan in 1970-1971. Relations with President Jaafar el-Nimeiry deteriorated sharply after it was discovered that the Soviet Union was indirectly involved in a coup attempt in 1971. They came to an end in May 1977

when Nimeiry expelled 90 Soviet military advisers and when he entered into defence alliances with Egypt and Saudi Arabia (95).
While none of these military involvements brought the USSR in conflict with the United States, there was a crisis in mid-September 1970 between Syria and Jordan where the United States reacted much stronger than to the Soviet military presence at the Suez Canal. Following a Palestinian triple hijacking of Western airliners ending on 'Revolution Airstrip' in Jordania, King Hussein became involved in a civil war with Palestinian fedayeen. Syria sent, according to Israeli intelligence, more than one hundred tanks to northwestern Jordan to the aid of the Palestinians and Soviet advisers (who had been rebuilding the Syrian army after the defeat of 1967) were suspected by the Americans to be accompanying the Syrian units crossing into Jordan. (It turned out the Soviet advisers had stayed behind the border.) The Nixon administration felt that this intervention would not have taken place without Soviet approval. When both Israel and the United States made preparations to save Hussein's regime by a military intervention, the Soviet Union called upon Syria to recall its troops, to which the Syrians acceded (96).

The October War of 1973 (Yom Kippur War for the Jews, Ramadan War for the Arabs), made possible by renewed Soviet arms supplies to Egypt after a reconciliation of sorts had taken place in early 1973, again led to a heavy Soviet postwar commitment, but this time mainly on the Syrian side. The Soviet Union had provided Anwar el-Sadat with a missile screen guarding the troop crossing at the Suez Canal on October 6, 1973, and its ample supply of anti-tank rockets inflicted heavy losses on the Israeli side. This novel strategy brought about a situation which, for the first time since 1948, was not a downright Arab defeat. Soviet military technicians and advisers fulfilled several non combat functions like assembling aircrafts, operating air-defence electronics equipment, and air-traffic control. They also drove tanks from the ports to the Syrian capital. It has been suggested that they probably assisted in the firing of two Scud short-range missiles towards the end of the war. Yet the major contribution was material. Material losses on both sides were so heavy that both superpowers had to resupply their clients during the war. Soviet resupplies to Syria and Egypt began to arrive on October 9 or 10, as did U.S. resupplies for Israel. The Soviet Union airlifted some 14,000 tons of weaponry to Egypt and Syria. An additional 63,000 tons was transported by some 30 cargo vessels. However, this was still too little in the opinion of President Sadat who was furthermore upset by Soviet unwillingness to provide Egypt with information gained from satellite reconnaissance. Prior to the Egyptian surprise attack on Yom Kippur day, Soviet vessels had also shipped a Moroccan expeditionary force of 2,000 tank troops to the Syrian front (97). The Soviet Navy in the Mediterranean was increased to around 90 ships by the end of the conflict.
Despite this Soviet backing of the Arab war effort, the Kremlin was less than enthousiastic about the war. In June 1973 R.M. Nixon and L. Brezhnev had held a summit meeting. Détente was going well, so well indeed that the Egyptian leader was afraid that the superpowers

would make a new Arab-Israeli war impossible, leaving Israel with the
gains of 1967. Sadat had informed the USSR only at the last moment,
on October 3 and more precisely the next day, about the actual date
of attack. The Soviet leaders, in the words of one analyst "... were
resigned to its outbreak, or at least did nothing effective to stop it."
Once war had been started, the USSR supported the Arab war effort,
but privately the Soviets recommended an early cease-fire to Egypt.
Sadat rejected, and when the fortunes of war turned in favour of
Israel, the Soviet leaders were negotiating the terms of the
cease-fire with the American Secretary of State. Henry A. Kissinger
arrived in Moscow on October 20, 1973, following a hot-line
invitation from the Kremlin leaders. Agreement between the
superpowers was quickly reached. This led to the United Nations
Security Council Resolution 338 in the early hours of October 22. To
bring Sadat to the point of accepting the cease-fire, Brezhnev gave
assurances that the Soviet Union would, if necessary, enforce its
observation unilaterally. When Israel did not observe it, violating two
cease-fires, the Soviet Union put all seven Soviet airborne divisions
on increased alert. On October 23 Brezhnev warned that if the
United States should "find it impossible to act with us in this matter,
we should be faced with the necessity urgently to consider the
question of taking appropriate steps unilaterally" (98).

The Soviet threat - to which the United States reacted with a
worldwide nuclear alert on October 25 and pressure on Israel - was
not implemented, as a cease-fire that held could finally be
established in time. Soviet troops did not intervene unilaterally either
though they had come close to send airborne troops in order to halt
an Israeli advance on Damascus. The only direct Soviet material
losses were a Soviet merchant vessel and a transport aircraft which
the Israeli had intentionally bombed in Syria at the beginning of the
October War (99).

By its credible intervention threat, the Soviet Union saved Egypt and
Syria from another disaster. Had it gone less far, its prestige within
the Arab world and its image as a world power would have suffered.
For Anwar Sadat the Soviet Union had, however, not done enough. He
resumed diplomatic relations with the United States within one month.
In due time he broke completely with the Soviet Union, abrogating in
March 1976 the Treaty of Friendship and Cooperation and
withdrawing all privileges granted to the Soviet navy. As an
unintended consequence of the October War, oil prices rose steeply
and permanently. The oil embargo accompanying the war brought
great wealth to the Arab oil-exporting nations, thereby lessening the
Arabs' dependence on the Soviet Union.

The Soviet military presence in the Middle East was, however,
assured by the role the USSR could play in the affairs of South
Yemen, Syria and Iraq.

In Iraq the rebellion of the Kurdish minority had suddenly gained
force in the early 1970s after the United States decided to finance
this rebellion as a way of taking pressure from the Israeli front. Iran
was used as a conduit to distribute from the CIA $ 16 million to the
Iraqi Kurds. The Soviet Union, which had a Kurdish minority within
its own borders, supported the central government in Baghdad in 1974

with tactical airstrikes by Soviet-piloted MiG-23 aircrafts against the secessionist insurgents. In March 1975 Iran decided to reach a settlement with Iraq and ceased support of the Kurds. The Soviet involvement is held to have been of crucial importance in Iran's decision to terminate its assistance for the rebellion (100). Despite repeated Iraqi government repression of the Communist Party and the execution of leading Communists, the Soviet Union has supported the Ba'thist regime and, after some wavering, also sided unequivocally with Iraq in 1983 with regard to the border war with Iran. Iraq has apparently also offered some naval facilities to the Soviet navy (at Umm Qasr, Basrah and Al Fan) but its foreign policy has not become consonant with the one of the Soviet Union (e.g. the Iraqi regime supports the Eritrean secessionist against the Soviet-backed central Ethiopian government). In the 1980s France became the most prominent supplier of Iraq, delegating Soviet influence to a secondary level (101).

To South Yemen (Aden), which became independent after the British withdrew in 1967, the Soviet Union became a weapon supplier in August 1968. Renamed the People's Democratic Republic of Yemen (PDRY), the country became a Soviet ally in the early 1970s after the goverment had declared itself to be Marxist-Leninist. In 1973 Soviet ships transferred PDRY troops from Aden to the border of the province of Dhofar (Oman) where these troops apparently took part in the insurgency against the troops of Sultan Qabus bin Said (102). Soviet support for the Popular Front for the Liberation of Oman (PFLO) had been increased but could not match the Shah's assistance to the sultan of Oman. One author has termed this support for the guerrilla war in Oman a precedent: "the first time that the Soviet Union openly encouraged a client to upset the existing territorial status quo..." (103) After a period of PDRY-Saudi rapprochement in the mid-1970s, when the Soviet influence appeared to be waning, an internal power struggle again brought pro-Soviet leaders to the foreground in 1978 - possibly with some Cuban and Soviet involvement in the coup. The Soviet Union concluded a Treaty of Friendship and Cooperation with the PDRY and in 1983 there were 1500 Soviet, 500 East German and 800 Cuban military advisers in the country (plus 500 more Soviet advisers in North Yemen). The USSR also received naval facilities in Aden, Al-Mukalla, Turba, and on the islands of Socotra and Perim. In addition, it obtained access to the airfields of Aden, Lahej and Mukalla. South Yemen, with its control of the access to the Red Sea from the Indian Ocean, is politically probably the firmest Third World base the USSR has apart from Cuba. The United States is therefore expecially apprehensive about developments in Yemen. When in late February 1979 some 3,000 men from the People's Democratic Republic of Yemen violated the borders of North Yemen, the American government saw the hands of the Soviet Union and Cuba behind it. Massive military assistance was consequently promised to North Yemen and a U.S. naval task force headed for the Gulf of Aden. As it was, the border clash ended in mid-March, mainly through Saudi mediation (104).

The most extensive Soviet military involvement in de Mediterranean region since the Canal "war of attrition" in 1970 has been the support of Syria, after its near-disaster on the Golan Heights in 1973. On October 24, 1973, President Assad of Syria had apparently requested Soviet troops to intervene on the Syrian front (105). Major Soviet support came after the cease-fire when the Syrian army was re-equiped by the USSR and an air defence system was set up which was reportedly manned by North Vietnamese soldiers and pilots. It was also reported that two Cuban armoured brigades were brought in with Cuban airliners to train Syrian tank corpsmen. Between February and May 1974 a "war of attrition" was fought on the Golan front in which Cubans fought in mixed tank crews, supported by artillery units commanded by Soviet and East German officers. Cuban pilots also fought on the Syrian side, alongside Saudis, Jordanians and Moroccans, the so-called 'solidarity front' *). The degree of coordination with the Soviet Union is a matter of conjecture.

The Soviet rebuilding of the Syrian army allowed President Assad to intervene in the civil war in Lebanon in 1975, against the protests of the USSR. To signal its displeasure, the Soviet Union thereafter cut arms supplies to Syria. However, after the Egyptian-Israeli peace treaty was signed on March 29, 1979, Soviet military supplies to Syria began to flow more profusely again. In 1980 Syria concluded a Treaty of Friendship and Cooperation with the Soviet Union (107). The Lebanese intervention brought the Syrian forces in Lebanon - some 50,000 men - into renewed conflict with Israel after the Israeli intervention in Lebanon in June 1982. In the ensueing air war over the Bekaa Valley Soviet SAM-7 missiles have been used. The Syrian air space was at the same time protected by Soviet missile crews and other support troops, some 7,000 men in total. In 1983 the Soviet Union introduced new surface-to-surface missiles into Syria. These SS-21 rockets have a range of more than 120 kilometres and can be equipped with nuclear warheads. The Syrian Minister of Defence, Mustafa Tlas, claimed in 1984 that the Soviet Union had given Syria a guarantee against a nuclear attack by Israel in the form of providing Syria with the means for nuclear retaliation (108).

The Soviet Union is also militarily present in Libya where, in 1981, some 60 Soviet (and 60 Cuban) pilots were reported to fly Libyan aircrafts in addition to North Korean, Pakistani and Palestinian pilots (109). Despite the fact that it has received arms worth several billion dollars from the Soviet Union since 1974, Lybia has not made any concessions to Soviet interests with regard to naval or refuelling bases (110). In his Islamic fervour, Colonel Qaddafi has been firmly anti-communist. Like in the case of President Assad of Syria who occasionally cracks down on local Communists, Qaddafi's military dependence has not led to a parallel political subservience to Soviet interests.

----

*) The presence of Cuban combat troops in the Mediterranean was not altogether new: already in 1963 Fidel Castro had sent about 400 tank troops to Algeria when it was at war with Morocco. A Cuban mission, 700 men strong, was also in Yemen in 1973, when Iran intervened in Oman (106).

While weapons have been an entry ticket to the Middle East for the Soviet Union, these have not "finlandized" any of these countries. Even such a heavily dependent country as Ethiopia could afford to expel Soviet diplomats on charges of espionage in 1984. In an assessment of Soviet successes and failures in the Third World, Joseph L. Nogee has concluded:

"The Kremlin's greatest success to date has been in the Arab world, and this was a consequence of the Arab-Israeli conflict, a situation it did not create. Moscow cannot determine the domestic or foreign policy of any of its clients, and... many of the largest recipients of Soviet arms have in recent years opposed Moscow on very important issues." (111)

The Soviet Union in Africa

In recent years the Soviet Union has repeatedly been accused for its military role in Africa. Frank Carlucci, Deputy Director of the CIA, for instance, told the American Congress that the Russian involvement constituted "the most determined campaign to expand foreign influence in this troubled region since it was carved up by the European powers in the late Nineteenth Century" (112). The arrival of the Second Cold War has been linked to the Soviet record in Africa by U.S. foreign policy officials. Henry Kissinger is quoted as saying that SALT II began to die in Angola and President Carter's National Security Adviser Zbigniew Brzezinski said that the SALT treaty died in the Ogaden desert of Ethiopia (113). It has been noted by Arthur Jay Klinghoffer that 'Angola' and 'Ethiopia' have joined 'Yalta' and 'Vietnam' as "pulsating schizoid facets of the Western political psyche" (114). Given this wider significance, we will mainly concentrate on these two episodes of Soviet (and Cuban) military involvement in the following pages.

In the 1970s the Soviet arms sales to sub-Saharan Africa increased significantly, amounting to four times as much for the whole decade as American arms sales. From a level of $ 90 million in 1974 military deliveries rose to a value of $ 1.2 billion in 1978. Eighteen countries in black Africa were recipients of Soviet arms, among them Angola, Benin, Burundi, Ethiopia, Ghana, Guinea, Mali, Mozambique, Nigeria, Somalia, Upper Volta, and Uganda. Sometimes these arms were traded rather than sold: in the case of Mali and Congo-Brazzaville the arms served as payment for aircraft landing rights and in the case of Somalia and Guinea-Bissau they were given in exchange for naval facilities (115). This quid pro quo approach has become more marked since the late 1960s. Due to the absence of a Communist or working class party in most African countries, alliances had to be made in the first instance with anti-Western civilian or army rulers. However, due to the political instability and the frequency of military coups, "progressive" and other friendly heads of state have had short political lives or were sometimes apt to change sides in the Cold War. In this way the Soviet Union lost over the years influence in a number of African countries such as the formerly Belgian-Congo (1960), Ghana (1966), Mali (1968), Guinea (1975), and Somalia (1977). The backing which the Soviet Union gave at various times to a regime through military aid was often a matter of "Realpolitik". In the case of Idi Amin of Uganda, who came to power with British and Israeli support (116), the Soviet decision to back the bloodthirsty dictator with arms in 1971 might have been influenced strongly by the fact that the neighbouring country Tanzania was receiving substantial aid from the People's Republic of China. Rivalry with China has also led to Soviet support for different liberation movements in countries like Angola, Mozambique or Rhodesia. In the latter case, for instance, the USSR and Zambia supported in the period 1976-80 the Zimbabwe's People's Revolutionary Army (ZIPRA), while China, Tanzania and Mozambique supported the Zimbabwe African National Liberation Army (ZANLA) (117).

In the case of the Nigerian Civil War (May 30, 1967 - January 15, 1970), the Soviet Union backed the conservative Federal government in Lagos, while China, France, Israel, Portugal, Spain and South Africa supported the Biafran secessionist regime of Lieutenant Colonel Emeka Ojukwu to varying degrees. Although Great Britain was the principal arms supplier to the military regime of Colonel Yakubu Gowon, the Soviet support was important in that it involved offensive weapons (about 50 MiG-17 and MiG-19 fighters, 4 Il-28 bombers and heavy artillery, among other equipment), denied by the United Kingdom and the United States. It was the desired access to these types of weapons which led the Nigerian government to approach the Soviet Union. As it turned out these weapons had no decisive influence for the course of the Civil War. The marked ineffectiveness of the airstrikes also throws some doubts on the alleged role of East European pilots (118). At any rate, the side backed by the USSR won in the Nigerian Civil War, giving the Soviet Union access to Africa's most popular nation for the rest of the decade.

The influence which the Soviet Union has been able to build up in Africa has, on the whole been modest. With the possible exception of the Ethiopian Dahlak Islands, the Soviet Union has not been granted the use of territory to establish a permanent air or naval military base *). Even Guinea, which after a Portuguese invasion of its capital Conakry in November 1970 had obtained Soviet support in the form of a permanent naval task force patrolling its coastline (the United States had not answered to a similar request as this would have offended its NATO ally Portugal) was not very generous with granting base rights. In 1977 Ahmed Sékou Touré withdrew the privilege granted earlier to the USSR to use Conakry airfield for reconnaissance flights over the Atlantic. No country has turned into a centrally directed non-market economy and only one, Ethiopia, has sought association with the Comecon. In no case has the Soviet Union instigated a government in Africa to change the political map of

----

*) However, Soviet ships have been allowed the use of the ports of Arrab and Massawa in Ethiopia and they are allowed to harbour in Antaranana (Madagaskar), Maké (Seychelles), Port Louis (Mauritius), Nacala-Beira and Maputo (Mozambique), Luanda (Angola) and, until 1979, Luba (Equatorial Guinea).

Africa through redrawing border lines. It has followed the policy of the Organization of African States which regards the borders drawn by the colonial powers as permanent. In accordance, it has generally supported the central governments where secessionist movements have been active, such as in Biafra or in Eritrea (119).

In addition, the Soviet Union has given support liberation movements who were opposing established Western powers and their African clients. Until the collapse of the Portuguese colonial empire in 1974 and the overthrow of the pro-Western emperor Haile Selassie in Ethiopia - events wherein the Soviet Union had no part - Soviet support for African liberation movements has been modest. Support went to the movements aiming at the elimination of white supremacy in Namibia (SWAPO) and Rhodesia (ZANU, ZAPU), to the rebels in Angola (MPLA), Mozambique (Frelimo) and Guinea-Bissau (PAIGC) and to a few others (ANC in South Africa, Frolinat in Chad, Polisario in the former Spanish Sahara). Support also went to governments in power opposing Western influence. These governments were also recipients of East German and Cuban military advisers and training personnel.

In the early 1980s the Soviet Union had 7,830 military personnel in Africa. This total represents slightly more than one third of the total Soviet military personnel abroad (21,800 according to one source) - excluding the 95,000 Soviet troops in Afghanistan and the 584,000 stationed in Eastern Europe (120).

In terms of size of military personnel, the Soviet presence is about half the French presence, which, however, counts fewer advisers and more combat troops in the countries of francophone Africa. In 1980, for instance, the French had advisers in nine African countries and advisers and troops in five more countries (121). In all cases - the French, the Russian and the Cuban - these military advisers and troops are there mainly because the local government has asked for them. Even when it comes to the support of insurgents the Russians have not been alone. The French, at one time, supported the Biafran insurgents and, the FNLA in Angola, while the Soviet Union supported, in 1976, the Polisario in the formerly Spanish Sahara, together with Algeria, which, in turn, was fought by Morocco with American and French support (122). As one looks closer at the African scene, it becomes difficult to find the Soviet Union doing in Africa things which other powers are not also doing and have been doing for a much longer time, with much greater frequency. France, notably, has sent troops to African states at least eighteen times in the twenty-five years preceeding 1982 (123). Indirect intervention by third parties have also not been restricted to the Cubans as a closer look at the events in Angola in 1974-1975 and in the Ogaden in 1977-1978 makes clear.

The Cuban-Soviet Intervention in Angola

Various liberation movements in Southern Africa fighting white supremacy in South-West Africa, Rhodesia and the Portuguese colonies Mozambique and Angola have received Soviet and East European weapons and training ever since the early 1960s. This was effectuated either through intermediaries, such as Algeria, Egypt and the Liberation Committee of the Organization of African Unity, or bilaterally. In the 1960s, China was a serious rival in that many of these movements had more confidence in the Chinese model of revolution and development. An exception was the Popular Movement for the Liberation of Angola (MPLA - Movimento Popular de Libertaçao de Angola) whose links with the Soviet Union date back to 1955 (124).

Cuban support for the MPLA dates back to 1965 when Che Guevara, on a four-months tour to African countries, met with leaders of liberation movements from Angola, Mozambique and Portuguese Guinea in Congo-Brazzaville. Subsequently Cuban ships delivered arms to the MPLA's training base in Congo-Brazzaville. By the fall of 1966 the Cuban military mission to Congo-Brazzaville had grown to 1,000 advisers though not all of them were assigned to the MPLA. When the MPLA moved its training base to Zambia in 1970, Cuban instructors apparently moved with them (125). During this period, especially around 1966-1967, Cuban-Soviet relations were at a breaking point due, mainly, to differences over guerrilla support in Latin America (which Moscow disapproved of). Cuban involvement in Africa was initiated independently from the Soviet Union in an attempt to create "many Vietnams". The Soviet non-reaction to the American intervention in the Dominican Republic in 1965 and the insufficient support given to North Vietnam, were viewed as betrayal by Castro as was the establishment of diplomatic relations between the Soviet Union and anti-Castro governments in Latin America (126). In short, Cuba was an unlikely proxy for the Soviet Union in its initial support for the MPLA.

The events in Southern Africa entered a new phase with the overthrow of the Portuguese dictatorship of Marcello Caetano on April 25, 1974. At that time the Soviet Union had suspended its support for the MPLA after a leadership split in the movement in 1973. The Chinese were, in 1973, sending arms to the National Front for the Liberation of Angola (FNLA - Frente Nacional de Libertaçao de Angola). In July 1974, the United States also began small-scale financial support of the FNLA. One month after the Central Intelligence Agency initiated U.S. assistance of the FNLA through Zaire, the Soviet Union resumed aid to the MPLA, and in March 1975 Soviet aircrafts were airlifting armaments for the MPLA to Congo-Brazzaville (127).

While the motives for the Soviet Union's re-entry in Angola can only be guessed (presumably at the very least to prevent that the Chinese and the Americans were alone in the field), more is known about the background of the American involvement. A report of the U.S. Congress' House Select Committee on Intelligence from January 1976 has this to say:

"Dr. Kissinger has indicated that U.S. military intervention in Angola is based on three factors: Soviet support of the MPLA and the USSR's increased presence in Africa, U.S. policy to encourage moderate independence groups in southern Africa, and the U.S. interest in promoting the stability of Mobutu and other leadership figures in the area. Past support to Mobutu... make[s] it equally likely that the paramount factor in the U.S. involvement is Dr. Kissinger's desire to reward and protect African leaders in the area. The U.S.'s expressed opposition to the MPLA is puzzling in view of [CIA] Director's Colby's statement to the Committee that there are scant ideological differences among the three factions, all of whom are nationalists above all else. (...) Until recently, the U.S.-backed National Front was supported by the People's Republic of China, which had provided about 100 military advisers. Mobutu has provided a staging area for U.S. arms shipments and has periodically sent Zairois troops, trained by the Republic of North Korea, into Angola to support Roberto's operations [Roberto Holden, a longtime associate and kinsman of President Mobutu was the leader of the FNLA - AS]. Small numbers of South African forces have been in the country and are known to have been in contact with Savimbi's UNITA troops." [UNITA - the National Union for the Total Independence of Angola (Uniao Nacional para a Independência Total de Angola), under J. Savimbi, was the third rival independence movement - AS] (128)

While the Zairian and South African armies were already actively intervening on behalf of their clients, the FNLA and UNITA, in 1974, the first Cuban combat units - 700 men - arrived in Angola only in October 1975, fifteen months after the American C.I.A. operation in Angola had begun (129). This was at a time when the Alvor Accords, signed between the representatives of MPLA, UNITA and FNLA on January 15, 1975, had broken down. The Alvor agreement contained provisions for a transfer of power to Angolese representatives to be elected in October 1975 prior to the proclamation of independence on November 11, 1975. Portugal, in early 1975 itself in the grip of revolution, was not in a good position to arrange an orderly transfer of power in Angola (as was the case in Mozambique, Guinea Bissau and the Cape Verde Islands). Some members of the Portuguese government saw the 230 Cuban civilian and military advisers entering Angola on behalf of the MPLA in June 1975 apparently as less problematic than the invasion of the oil-rich Cabinda enclave in March 1975 by regular Zairian troops who were joined by the FNLA. It was the Cabinda invasion which led to fighting between the MPLA on the one side and the FNLA and Zairian troops on the other in April and May 1975. This clash led to the request of MPLA leader Agostinho Neto for Cuban shipments of arms. The rival liberation movements also appealed for more foreign support. UNITA and FLNA were at that time supported by China (until October 1975 when it withdrew all advisers and support), India, North Korea, Romania and Zaire. On June 18, 1975, the American government appropriated covert military aid amounting to $ 30 million to the FNLA and UNITA, to be distributed via Zambia and Zaire. This was a considerable increase over the $ 300,000 which the U.S. National Security Council had appropriated for the FNLA on January 22, 1975 (130). By late July 1975 U.S. arms began to arrive in greater quantities and outside involvement generally increased. A Swedish analyst of interventions in civil wars summarized the general pattern:

"No less than eight states intervened. The MPLA was assisted by the Congo, Cuba and the Soviet Union. (...) The anti-MPLA side was backed by France, the People's Republic of China, the USA, South Africa and Zaire. The most notable military connections were with the South Africa-USA-Zaire triad. Troops from both South Africa and Zaire invaded Angola and headed for Luanda. There are strong indications that these invasions were co-ordinated to some extent (and South African instructors were reported to have joined the Zairians). (...) The South African invasion, for instance, seems to have been discussed with the USA. Moreover, South Africa has intimated that the invasion was supported by the USA and it was reported that South Africa wished for US involvement and had even hoped for more decisive North American efforts. There is evidence about the co-ordination of some actions in the field. There were even unsubstantiated reports about an understanding that the USA would rush sufficient weaponry to counter the Soviet-supported movement. (...) Between the USA and Zaire there were close contacts. For one thing, Zaire served as a conduit for US funds and American weapons were supplied partly in the form of swap operations with Zaire. (...) China had contacts primarily with Zaire. Chinese instructors were training FNLA soldiers there. (...) French funds were funnelled via Zaire..." (131)

In this intervention escalation Mobutu played a crucial role as a pull factor for attracting American involvement and, in reaction, Soviet involvement (132).
South African regular troops intervened in Angola on August 9, 1975, (after one prior incursion in July) justifying their move with the protection of hydroelectric plants at Calueque and at Ruacana Falls which supplied electricity to Namibia, the UN territory illegally held under occupation by South Africa. The South African armed forces set up two military bases inside Angola at Cunene and extended their help to UNITA which, in turn, aided them in destroying the South West African People's Organization (SWAPO). In response, the Portuguese Revolutionary Council dissolved the provisional government of Angola and assumed all administrative powers, as far as it still exercised control over events in Angola. It also held discussions with the Cuban government. Given the obvious foreign links of UNITA with South Africa and FNLA with Zaire, the Portuguese Revolutionary Council viewed the MPLA with its Cuban connection as the least neo-colonialist threat and the expectation rose that power would be handed over to the MPLA on the preset independence date on November 11, 1975.
The South African intervention of August apparently led to a Cuban decision to send fighting units to Angola, just as the Zairian intervention in March had led to the decision to send 230 advisers from Cuba. In the United Nations the Cuban representative stated on October 10 that

"... in view of the scandalous interference on the part of the imperialists, colonialists, and racists, it is our elementary duty to offer the people of Angola whatever aid is necessary to guarantee the true independence and the full sovereignty of their country."

The week before, on October 4 and 7, the first Cuban troops, which had left Cuba on September 5, arrived at the Congolese port of Pointe Noire and at Porto Amboin near Luanda (133). As the date of independence approached, the race for the capital Luanda was on. South African troops with heavy artillery and armoured vehicles, estimated at a strength of 10,000 men, staged an invasion on October 23, 1975, advancing 40 miles per day. On November 5, 1975, they attacked a training camp at Benguela, run by Cuban instructors. The Cuban government, according to its own saying, took the decision to send its first regular military units on that day "at the request of a sovereign government". The MPLA, while the de facto government in an encircled Luanda, was not the de jure government until the 11th of November, as Nelson P. Valdes has pointed out (134). The Cubans were no longer the only ones to intervene on behalf of the MPLA. The chronology and participants in this period have been recorded by Valdes (who, however, fails to mention the mercenary units recruited by the CIA which entered the fight in October 1975):

"At no point during the whole war did the MPLA confront such an overwhelming situation as on November 7, when the FNLA had forces just nine miles from Luanda. The next day, Guinea-Bissau, Mozambique, Cape Verde, the People's Republic of the Congo, and Guinea formed a coordinating committee to provide whatever the MPLA needed from abroad. On the night of November 10, Portugal granted independence to the Angolan people. Immediately three different governments were officially formed - by the MPLA in Luanda, the FNLA at Carmona, and UNITA at Huambo. The MPLA held effective control over just 20 percent of Angolan territory. By November 11, 1975, there were close to twelve hundred Cuban military men who had come from Cuba and other parts of Africa. (...) From November 7 to December 9, Cuban planes made seventy trips to Angola from Havana by way of Barbados, Guinea-Bissau, and the Congo Republic. (...) The number of Cuban troops increased rapidly, as published estimates of American and Swedish intelligence show: November 15, 1975: 2,000; November 20, 1975: 3,000; November 30, 1975: 5,000; January 6, 1976: 9,500; February 3, 1976: 14,000. (...) The Cuban forces reaching Angola in the second week of November were joined by elite forces from Mozambique, Guinea, Guinea-Bissau, and the Congo Republic. Some Algerian, Yugoslav, and Nigerian advisers may have helped too. (...)
By December 16, 1975, Zairian forces had retreated from the vicinity of Luanda. (...) In mid-December the Cubans concentrated their forces near Quibala to contain the South Africans. The South Africans, who had stopped their offensive on November 23, after taking 1,974 miles in thirty-three days, began pushing north again. In the second week of December they were just seventy miles south of Luanda. Between December 9 and December 18, the Cubans and South Africans clashed in the largest battle of the war, at the Salazar Bridge over the Cuanza River north of Mussende. This was the farthest north the South Africans

advanced. (...) On December 28 the South African forces expressed their willingness to withdraw from Angolan territories. UNITA and FNLA were weakened when they broke their political-military alliance and declared war on one another at the end of the year. (...) By February 22, 1976, the military confrontation, for all practical purposes, was over. Symbolically, that same day, the Portuguese government established diplomatic relations with the People's Republic of Angola. (...) ... on April 5, 1976, Angola and South Africa signed a diplomatic agreement..." (135)

This brief summary leaves out the role of the Soviet Union and the United States. The larger context of international politics in the mid-seventies, especially in Indochina, where North Vietnam was undoing the diplomatic peace achieved in 1973, played a role, as well as the domestic paralysis of the Nixon administration in the days of Watergate and the Congressional hearings disclosing illegal practices by the U.S. intelligence services. The détente between the USA and the USSR, as well as the American rapprochement with China, the revolutionary fervour in the NATO country Portugal and the granting of most-favoured nation status to the Soviet Union as well as the linkage of this to Jewish emigration from the Soviet Union - all these entered the local struggle for power as background factors. Some of these aspects have been touched by René Lemarchand writing about the Portuguese administration of Angola in 1974:

"... a highly competitive - if not openly antagonistic - relationship emerged between Portuguese and U.S. intelligence officials during the brief term of office of Rosa Coutinho as High Commissioner of Angola in 1974. That Coutinho used his authority to facilitate the entry of substantial though unknown quantities of Soviet military hardware for the M.P.L.A. is a well-established fact. The nexus of interests between Coutinho and Agonstinho Neto, backed by strong ideological affinities, was seen by Henry Kissinger as thoroughly incompatible with the spirit of détente... (...) Whether there is any truth to the intriguing thesis that Kissinger's move in Angola was really intended to placate the Chinese Communists, so as to allay their suspicion that the U.S. was too accommodating towards the Soviets, is difficult to say. What is beyond dispute is that the initial involvement of the C.I.A. in Angola stemmed from the radically divergent appraisals made by U.S. and Portuguese officials of the cold-war implications of the struggle between pro-Soviet and pro-western (and pro-Chinese) factions." (136)

The operations of the CIA in Angola in 1975, consisting in the provision of arms and money to UNITA and FNLA, the supervision of logistical operations on the ground in Zaire and Angola and the hiring of mercenaries in Europe and the United States, were officially discontinued when in December 1975 the U.S. Congress voted for the halting of further support for UNITA and FLNA. Inofficially some support continued to go to FNLA despite congressional prohibition, as the chief of the CIA task force in Angola was later to reveal (137). On December 9, 1975, the U.S. government managed to disrupt the airbridge Cuba had established with Angola (138). After that date, no

Cuban reinforcements appear to have reached Angola by air until at least Christmas due to American pressure on countries granting refuelling to Cuba's short-range Bristol Britannia aircraft. In late December 1975 or early January 1976, however, Soviet Aeroflot IL-62 began flying Cuban troops to Angola, carrying them nonstop to Guinea first before heading for Angola. By the end of January 1976 this airlift was discontinued (139).

Much less is known about the Soviet decision to intervene than about the American one. An interesting though dubious piece of information about Soviet decision-making has been brought to the West by a high-level defector, Borris Rabbot. He depicted the decision to intervene in Angola as the result of a power struggle in the Kremlin:

> "Former KGB chief Alexander Shelepin, who was Brezhnev's major opponent in the Politburo in 1974 and 1975, said the Jackson proposal [linking trade preferences for the Soviet Union to Jewish emigration, AS] would "amount to selling human beings, an unacceptable affront". Shelepin recommended aggressive counteraction. The Caetano dictatorship had collapsed in Portugal with prospect for revolution, so Shelepin urged the Politburo to send 'volunteers' on the model of Soviet support for the Republican forces in the Spanish Civil War nearly forty years before. Brezhnev's political position had been deteriorating, along with his health. He retreated to his dacha, where he rested and licked his wounds, trying to counter the moves of Shelepin. He emerged with a different idea - sending Cuban troops to assist the Communist side in the civil war in Angola. The Politburo accepted the new policy, and Brezhnev emerged victorious. On April 16, 1975, PRAVDA announced that Shelepin had retired. So, as Rabbot interpreted it, the real Soviet response to the Jackson amendment was the adventure in Angola. The collapse of the dream that significant trade and aid would be coming from the United States intensified the struggle between 'hawks' and 'doves' in the Soviet leadership. (...) ...on Independence Day, November 11, the MPLA announced in Luanda the creation of the People's Republic of Angola, which was immediately recognized by the Soviet Union. The Soviets began to carry out Brezhnev's plans, developed earlier that year." (140)

There are several questionable elements in this account. The principle one is the depiction of the Cubans as simple pieces in a geostrategic chessboard game, as "surrogate soldiers" of the USSR. This vision has been offered frequently in American interpretations of these events. U.S. Air Force general S. Brown, for instance, wrote that "...through the employment of the surrogate Cuban force in Angola , the Soviet Union recently has been successful in expanding its influence in Africa at a relatively low cost and risk" (141). The official Soviet version has been different. Andrei Gromyko, the Minister of Foreign Affairs, stressed in a conversation with Kissinger in January 1976 that the Cuban intervention was a decision which the Cubans had made themselves (142). Fidel Castro himself reiterated this on April 19, 1976, when he said:

> "Cuba made its decision completely on its own responsibility. The USSR... never requested that a single Cuban soldier be sent to

that country. The USSR is extraordinarily respectful and careful in its relations with Cuba. A decision of that nature could only be made by our own party." 143)

While one can only smile at the 'extraordinary respectfulness' of the Soviet Union vis-à-vis Cuba in the light of earlier evidence (as during the Cuban missile crisis), the possibility that "the tail wagged the dog" cannot be excluded. One Soviet official said: "We did not twist their arms. The Cubans wanted to go for they are more radical than we are." (144) Cuba was asked to intervene by the leaders of the MPLA and requests for support in the hour of need were also addressed to and honoured by, a number of other nations such as Tanzania, Algeria, Mozambique, Guinea, Congo-Brazzaville, Cape Verde, Guinea Bissau, and, from further away, Denmark, Yugoslavia, Sweden, the Soviet Union, the German Democratic Republic and even North Vietnam. By mid-January 1976, twenty-two African states had recognized the MPLA as the legitimate Angolan government (145). They may, however, not all have been willing to aid the MPLA, taking their position perhaps as much from revulsion over the fact that the FNLA and UNITA collaborated with the racist South African regime. In addition, they were probably opposed to the fragmentation of an African state which the other two factions in the struggle appeared to bring about. To exclude all these other actors, which in material and diplomatic ways backed the MPLA, and explain the Angola events only in terms of Soviet machinations and aggressiveness, is a reduction of historical complexity to Cold War ideology. This is not to say that the Soviet role was as noble as was depicted by Leonid Brezhnev on the occasion of the 25th Congress of the Soviet Communist Party, on February 24, 1976, when he said:

"Our party supports and will continue to support peoples fighting for their freedom. In so doing the Soviet Union does not look for advantages, does not hunt for concessions, does not seek political domination or exact military bases. We act as we are bid by our revolutionary conscience, our Communist convictions... (...) We make no secret of the fact that we see détente as the way to create more favorable conditions for peaceful socialist and communist construction." (146)

The Soviet intervention in Angola in 1975-1976 was probably as decisive to turn the tide as was the Cuban one. It took place in two stages. From October 1975 onwards, military material was airlifted and shipped to the MPLA and to the Cuban advisers and combat troops with them. Soviet, Bulgarian and Yugoslavian ships arrived with 370 armoured vehicles, 319 T-54 and T-34 tanks, helicopters and 29 MiG-17 and MiG-21 fighter-bombers, 122-millimeter rockets and other equipment to the value of nearly $ 200 million (147). The second stage of Soviet intervention took the form of airlifting Cuban troops to Angola after, in the words of Fidel Castro, "imperialism had cut off practically all our air routes in Africa" (148). However, the Soviet Union did not step in immediately after the cessation of flights from Cuba on December 9, but waited at least for two weeks, also halting arms transfers for this period. Whether this delay has been due to fear of a reaction from the side of the United States - a fear that must have been considerably reduced after the U.S. Congress prohibited further covert aid to Angola on December 19, 1975 - is an unresolved question.

In the course of 1976 Cuban troop strength increased to between 20,000 (Western estimates at that time) and 36,000 (according to a later statement by Fidel Castro). Between November 1975 and January 1976, Soviet military advisers, an estimated 500 men, are also likely to have entered Angola. Once the war was practically over their numbers increased. Ultimately there were about 1,000 Soviet military advisers and about 1,400 Soviet and East European "economic technicians" in Angola, plus about 8,500 such Cuban civilian technicians. They were presumably filling the vacancies created by the exodus of more than 100,000 Portuguese (149). The basis for this postwar intervention was the Treaty of Friendship and Cooperation signed by Agostinho Neto in Moscow in October 1976. Eight years later this involvement still continued, surviving the death of Neto in September 1979. However, Angola has not turned into a Soviet satellite and has rejected (as did Mozambique) Soviet requests for naval base rights. (However, limited use of naval and air facilities has been granted to the USSR.) Rather it had to submit to a humiliating security treaty with South Africa in 1984, after the country had been brought on the brink of collapse by military attacks of UNITA (with its 25,000 fighters numerically as strong as the Cuban force) and the South African troops on Angolan soil. Unable to obtain sufficient economic support from the East Bloc, Angola has made openings to the West.

In the light of these subsequent developments it appears difficult to see a 'grand design' in the Soviet involvement. Rather, the process by which the Soviet Union became involved has been a familiar one in which rival domestic parties seek external allies to help them to consolidate or improve their positions. It was the same process which had first let to Western intervention. Furthermore, one should not forget that it was not the Soviet Union which sought to exclude other parties than the MPLA from power. Rather, as Kenneth Grundy has written:

> "Both (the USSR more than Cuba) sought compliance with the Alvor agreements calling for a coalition government in Angola until the West and its clients jeopardized such a trilateral transition to independence." (150)

By the mid-eighties, the United States and South Africa were still working hard to restore their blunders of 1975. Discussions were held in 1984 between the United States and President Jose Eduardo dos Santos of Angola over the withdrawal of Cuban troops and South African troops from Angola and Namibia.

The Soviet Union and the Ogaden War in the Horn of Africa

The Soviet interest in the Horn of Africa, in conjunction with the Soviet presence in South Yemen, has sometimes been depicted as a pincers movement intended to cut the West off from the Persian Gulf

(151) *). A less offensive version of geopolitics traces the Soviet interest back to the architect of the modern Russian Navy, Admiral Sergei G. Gorshkov, whose strategy is said to call for naval facilities all around the coast of Africa. Colin Legum, who interprets Soviet actions in these terms, has written:

> "The emergence of the Soviet Union as a world naval power for the first time in its history has created new strategic interests for Moscow in obtaining naval facilities in all the major oceans. Moscow has three objectives: first, to be capable of effective defensive reaction to any new threat of strategic superiority by the Western alliance; second, to develop its ocean and air supply routes around, and across, the African continent from the Indian to the Atlantic oceans as well as to develop its communication lines through the Red Sea to the Indian subcontinent in order to contain what Moscow sees as a deadly threat from China; third, to enlarge the Soviet sphere of political and economic influence. (...) It would require nothing short of a major reversal of Gorshkov's strategy for the Soviets to loose interest in any of these areas - but it is by no means clear just how heavy a political and economic commitment Moscow is ready to make to secure military facilities around the coasts of Africa. However, the importance Moscow gives to this aspect of its policy is verified by the bold and imaginative gamble it took in the Horn of Africa in the 1960s and 1970s. In pursuit of Gorshkov's strategy, the Russians agreed in the early 1960s to train and equip the Somali Army in exchange for obtaining naval facilities at Berbera on the Red Sea." (152)

Such a line of explanation not only "explains" Soviet interest in the Horn but also in Angola. The only trouble with it is that in "explaining" everything it explains nothing in the end. If we look at the historic evolution of Soviet involvement in the Horn, it is difficult to see a grand design. This is not to deny that the Soviet Union was interested in having one or more friendly states at the entrance of the Red Sea and the northwestern littoral of the Indian Ocean.

When Somalia, which gained independence from Italy and Great Britain in 1960, showed an interest in strengthening its position in the sixties via-à-vis its great neighbour and rival, Ethiopia, it was a natural thing to turn to the Soviet Union for economic and military aid since Ethiopia was an American client since the early 1950s. Somalia had territorial claims on the Northern Frontier District of Kenya, on Djibouti, which was under French control (until 1977), and on the Ogaden which belonged to Ethiopia. In all these regions there were Somalis living, and to bring them together into one nation was

----

*) The charge is reminiscent of another one from the same geopolitical school of thought which interpreted the victory of Salvador Allende, in Chile in 1970, as part of a Soviet design to 'sandwich Latin America', with Chile on the bottom and Cuba on the top side of the South-American continent.

an understandable dream but also one which clashed with the Charter of the Organization of African States, according to which the existing boundaries of Africa were not to be redrawn. A first arms deal with the Soviet Union was concluded in 1963 after Western powers had refused to sell arms to Somalia. It allowed for an expansion of the armed forces from 4,000 to 10,000 troops. In 1969, the armed forces seized power for themselves. The Soviets were probably not fully aware of the Somalian plans to create a greater nation. They were providing training and equipment and, in return, were allowed to develop a port, a communications station, an airfield and naval missile storage and handling facilities at Berbera, Mogadiscio and Uanle Uen. The United States had a communications station ('Kagnew') at Asmara in Ethiopia, manned in peaktime by 3,000 Americans. It maintained other facilities there as well and it is likely that the 5,000-6,000 Soviets in Somalia were more concerned with these, and the activities of the U.S. Seventh Fleet in the Indian Ocean, than with Somalia's own concerns (153).

In 1974, Somalia and the Soviet Union concluded a Treaty of Friendship and Cooperation. More important, on September 12, 1974, Emperor Haile Selassie was ousted from power after a reign of 44 years. A period of internal power struggles among the military powerholders followed. Half a year after the deposition of the autocratic ruler, the new regime sent a secret mission to Moscow in order to explore the possibilities of Soviet assistance for consolidating the Ethiopian revolution. However, at that time - spring 1975 - there were still a number of pro-Western leaders in the Provisional Military Administrative Council (PMAC or Dergue) and the Kremlin was not anxious to step in quickly. This changed when in February 1977 Colonel Mengistu Haile Mariam managed to seize power in Addis Ababa. The following month Fidel Castro arrived for a two-day visit and shortly thereafter a Cuban military delegation arrived for a week-long visit at which arrangements were discussed for training the Ethiopian People's Militia. Castro was no stranger to this region; a Cuban mission was also active in Somalia since 1974, and in the 1960s Cuba had apparently given support to the Eritreans in their secession struggle from Ethiopia (154). Ethiopia was in a precarious position as secessionist movements were active not only in the Ogaden (where the Western Somali Liberation Front - WSLF - was operating) but also in Eritrea and Tigray, and amongs the Afars and the Gallas.

Castro apparently tried his hand as a peacemaker in the region in March 1977 as he arranged a meeting between the new Ethiopean leader Mengistu and President Mohammed Siad Barre of Somalia. The Cuban Prime Minister apparently proposed at this meeting in Aden that the local conflicts should be solved on the basis of socialist brotherhood, within a Marxist federation of Ethiopia and Eritrea and a confederation of North and South Yemen, Djibouti, Somalia and Ethiopia. However, Siad Barre rejected the proposal, pursuing his own ambition of a greater Somalia. Castro's attempt at conflict resolution was backed up by the Soviet President Nikolai Podgorny who was touring Africa at that time. In the Somali capital Mogadiscio he urged "patience" (155). However, from the point of view of Somalia, this was not a moment for "patience" but of "opportunity" as the neighbouring country was in a process of disintegration. Ethiopia, armed by the United States, had been cut off all American aid in February 1977 (156). An attack by Somalia's 22,000 men army on Ethiopia for the liberation of the Ogaden became a distinct possibility despite the fact that Ethiopia's population was ten times as big as Somalia's.

The Soviet role in the prewar phase, as far as it is known, has been delineated by Richard Remnek, a researcher for the U.S. Center for Naval Analysis:

> "While we do not know that the Soviets threatened to apply the stick to Somalia to avoid a war, we do know that they were offering a carrot to promote what would have become a pax Sovietica on the Horn. In what appears to have been a counter initiative to Saudi/Sudanese efforts to forge an Arab bloc of Red Sea States, the Soviets, following close on the heels of the Cubans, proposed in April that Ethiopia and Somalia join South Yemen and independent Djibouti in a federation of Marxist states, in which Eritrea and the Ogaden would receive substantial autonomy. Regardless of whether the Soviets thought that the Somalis would readily accept the plan, they seem nevertheless to have hoped that Mogadiscio would realize that its ambitions could be accommodated best through Moscow's mediation. The Soviets might have been prepared to offer Somalia anything short of hoisting a Somali flag over the Ogaden (e.g. uninhibited rights of passage for Somali herdsmen, restrictions upon the Ethiopian military presence in the region, etc.). However, the Soviets appear to have consistently abided by the principle of the inviolability of sovereign borders even during the critical period after the Somali assault when the battlefield situation was in doubt. As matters turned out, of course, the Somalis rejected the Soviet/Cuban federation scheme and opted for a military solution to Somalia's national problem. (...) They [the Soviets, AS] had little choice but to support Ethiopia, particularly against an act of aggression committed with Soviet-made weapons. The Somali attack also represented an open challenge to Soviet policy on the Horn, which, if unanswered, would tarnish the USSR's image as a bona fide superpower. (...) However, the Soviets came to Ethiopia's aid slowly, in a manner indicative of their increasing difficulty in straddling both camels on the Horn." (157)

The Western role in Somalia's decision to send its army across the Ethiopian border in July 1977, was ambiguous. The Saudi Arabian government, with its own plans to turn the Red Sea into an "Arab lake" had reportedly promised up to $ 300 million for the eviction of the Soviets from Somalia in 1977 (158). With their base in Ethiopia gone, the Americans were also watching developments in Somalia with an eye of weakening Soviet influence in the region. When the Somali government expressed an interest in Western weapons, the United States, Great Britain and France agreed to supply Somalia with "defensive arms" (159). In June 1977 guerrilla activity in the Ogaden desert had increased sharply. In the same month high-level officials of the State Department reportedly told the personal physician of

Siad Barre, the American citizen Dr. Kevin Cahill, that the American government was not averse to further guerrilla pressure in the Ogaden. Cahill was told that the United States would provide arms if wealthy Arab states were paying the bill. Washington was said not to be opposed to Somali extension over the Ogaden; it would teach Ethiopia a lesson for having deserted the Western camp. On July 23, 1977, the Somali regular army invaded the Ogaden and Washington declared, on July 26, that it agreed "in principle" to meet Somalia's legitimate defence requirements (160).

An American arms sales announcement to Somali had already been made on July 15, 1977 (161). The Somali offensive, begun one week later, met little resistance at first and led to the capture of Jigjiga after two months. However, the other two major towns of the Ogaden, Harar and Dire Dawa did not fall and by November the front began to stabilize (162). The Carter administration was increasingly embarrassed by the association of the United States with an offensive in Africa which stood in flagrant contradiction to the principles of the Organization of African Unity (OAU). In late August, it withdrew its earlier promise to supply arms to Somalia and the French and the British also dissociated themselves publicly from the Somali invasion. The CIA, however, reportedly did send covert supplies to Somalia and late in 1977 Iran was reportedly providing military aid to Siad Barre at the request of the American government (163). But this aid was probably far from sufficient and Somalia's leader must have felt betrayed by the United States (as South Africa did in the case of Angola in 1975). Somalia later claimed that the United States had encouraged the offensive. The U.S. Assistant Secretary for African Affairs, Richard Moose, however said that "... our assurances were not of such a nature that a prudent man would have mounted an offensive on the basis of them." (164).

Let down by the United States and with a difficult situation at the front in the Ogaden, Siad Barre took a gamble in November 1977 which was meant to bring in the Western powers more decisively on his side. In the words of Kenneth Weiss:

> "By November, the Somali offensive had bogged down. (...) In the hopes of securing arms from the West, the Somalis built a case for such support by claiming that a Soviet-inspired Cuban-Ethiopian invasion was imminent. (...) In a desperate gamble that Western aid would be forthcoming in reward, Siad Barre on November 13 abrogated the 1974 Soviet-Somali Treaty of Friendship and Cooperation, expelled Soviet advisers, revoked Soviet use of military facilities, reduced Soviet diplomatic representation in Mogadiscio, and severed relations with Cuba. On November 13, there were still 1,678 Soviet advisers in Somalia, representing implicitly the Kremlin's interest in the country. (...) The Soviet airlift to Ethiopia, signalling a more active role for Moscow in the struggle, did not begin until the end of November. (...) Since both the Soviet airlift and the arrival of Cuban troops began after Somalia's November 13 offensive against Harar had failed, Moscows's intervention was probably geared more to the expulsion than the offensive." (165)

Siad Barre's gamble had backfired and the Soviet Union rather than the United States was thereby drawn into the Ogaden war. The intervention came in response to a request for help from Ethiopia's leader Mengistu in October 1977. He secretly went to Moscow and to Havana, where his foreign minister asked for Cuban troops (166). By mid-October 1977, Soviet weapon deliveries to Somalia, already greatly reduced, were halted (167). The Soviet airlift brought large amounts of military material to Ethiopia, beginning on November 26, three days after Siad Barre publicly complained that the United States had rejected his appeal to counter Soviet support for Ethiopia. Cuban troops began to arrive in December (168).

The Soviet airlift of arms and men in December 1977, involving some 50 transport planes and 100 flights over more than 2,000 kilometres, was the culmination of a military commitment. The year before, on December 14, 1976, the Soviet Union had first agreed to provide small arms, anti-tanks and anti-aircraft weapons, to the amount of $ 100 million to Ethiopia. In April 1977, the USSR had supplied Ethiopia with heavier weapons such as tanks and aircrafts, possibly in an attempt to deter a Somali attack. In September 1977, Moscow agreed to provide Ethiopia with 400 tanks, 48 MiG-21 fighter planes, SAM-3 and SAM-4 missiles and other equipment to the value of $ 385 million (169). In the year before December 1977, the Soviet Union had, in fact, already committed around $ 1 billion in military supplies to Ethiopia (170). Not all of this was linked to the Somali threat alone.

Arab states like Saudi Arabia, Egypt and Sudan, but also the Soviet military clients Iraq and Syria, were supporting the Eritrean moslim secessionist movement as well as other Ethiopian opposition forces. In fact, the Soviet Union had in the past also armed and supported the Eritrean Liberation Front (ELF) and the Eritrean People's Liberation Forces (EPLF). After some mediation attempts to reach a political solution failed, the USSR backed the new central government. After the overthrow of Haile Selassie, the Soviets viewed Arab support for the Eritreans as part of a conspiracy to turn the Red Sea into an Arab lake, to create a new conservative military block aimed at keeping the Soviet Union out of the Red Sea and the Middle East in general (171). By strengthening Ethiopia's non-Arab Marxist-orientated central government, the Soviet Union could hope to maintain a presence in the area which would safeguard Soviet shipping through the Red Sea.

The airlift of December 1977 was preceeded by the arrival of V.I. Petrov, First Deputy Commander-in-Chief of the Soviet Ground Forces, in November. He apparently assessed Ethiopia's defence strategy. When in mid-January the Cuban-Ethiopian counter-offensive began, combat operations in the Ogaden (as well as in Eritrea) were reportedly under his control, with three other Soviet generals assisting him in coordinating eight Ethiopian divisions, the Cubans and 100,000 peasant militia men. A special satellite, Cosmos 964, was launched on November 26, 1977, to coordinate the logistics of the intervention. In total, between 1,000 and 1,500 Soviet military advisers and between 11,000 and 18,000 Cuban troops arrived (172). For Cuba, the Ethiopian commitment came on top of other commitments in eleven other African nations, which already absorbed

40,000 Cuban men and women in 1978 (173). This was more than one tenth of the American commitment to Vietnam in the peak period, while Cuba's population was less than one twentieth the size of the U.S. population. To lessen the strain on Cuba's defence at home, the Soviet Union sent about 30 Russian pilots to Cuba in 1978 to replace the Cuban ones fighting in Ethiopia - a practice already initiated during the Angolan conflict in 1976 (174). Apart from the Cubans, units from South Yemen were also flying combat missions in the Ogaden and Soviet military men were involved close enough in the combat operations to be wounded and killed (175). They appear to have manned helicopters in the Ogaden and later also in Eritrea (176). More than twenty Soviet ships were protecting these operations from the sea although there was little risk of Western involvement once the Carter administration had dissociated itself openly from the Somali attack. The covert support from Iran also remained limited, perhaps due to the rising internal problems facing the Shah. By March 15, 1978, the Cuban-Ethiopian counter-offensive on the ground had been successful and the Somali government had withdrawn its troops behind the Somali border after having obtained a pledge that the Soviet Union would prevent an Ethiopian pursuit into Somali territory. However, WSLF guerrilla activity continued in the years to come and some 13,000 Cuban troops stayed on to "keep peace" in the Ogaden, harassed by some 20,000 Somali backed liberation fighters. By early 1984 there were still 10,500 Cuban troops in Ethiopia but it was announced that their strength would be reduced to 3,000 by mid-year.

An assessment of the Soviet role in the Ogaden war has been made by the analyst Richard Remnek, which, coming from the American side, is not likely to be overly biased in favour of the Soviet Union. Nevertheless he had this to say:

"If the ultimate objective of Soviet policy in the Horn was to establish a pax Sovietica, in which all states in the region would be linked in a federation that would resolve age-old hostilities, and with each country making sure progress under Soviet tutelage towards socialism, then obviously Moscow has not succeeded. What the Soviets have clearly accomplished has been to bring an appreciable degree of stability to Ethiopia and in so doing they may have cut short any remote plans to establish a conservative military bloc of Arab states in the region. With Somali armed forces (but not guerrillas) expelled from the Ogaden and insurgency in Eritrea and in other regions in a state of remission, the radical leftist military leaders of Ethiopia are far more secure today than ever before. But the Dergue's [the Provisional Military Administrative Committee of Colonel Mengistu, AS] dependence upon Soviet support does not appear to have given Moscow great influence in shaping the subsequent course of the Ethiopian revolution. (...)

By performing their 'proletarian internationalist' duty towards a revolutionary regime in extremis, by defending the inviolability of sovereign borders, by assuming responsibility for past decisions (e.g. to arm first Somalia and later Ethiopia), and finally, by acting boldly but not rashly, when openly challenged, the Soviets 'walked on the side of the angels' in the Horn. (...) From the Soviet perspective, therefore, it seems that Moscow gained more than it lost on the Horn. The Soviets also can claim that in supporting Ethiopia, they were doing the right thing. Through the course of their involvement, they did indeed pursue (more than less) a 'principled policy'." (177)

If one has to pass a judgement on the Western policy in the Ogaden war and in Angola, the notion of a 'principled policy' is not the first one which comes to mind. Indeed, if it is true, as Henry Kissinger said, that the SALT II treaty began to die in Angola, and if it is true, as Zbigniew Brzezinski said, that SALT II died in the Ogaden desert, any one-sided guilt attribution for the end of détente is doing less than full justice to the historical record.

Conclusion

There have been more than a dozen revolutions in the Third World in the last decade which have reduced Western influence. In the Middle East the Shah of Iran (1979) and the Emperor of Ethiopia (1974) were overthrown; in Africa white supremacy in Rhodesia disappeared (1980) and the Portuguese colonial empire crumbled, leading to changes in Angola, Mozambique, Cape Verde, San Tomé and Guinea-Bissau (1975); in Indochina Cambodia, Laos and Vietnam have been removed from American influence (1975) and in Central America the Somoza dynasty has gone (1979) and in Afghanistan a pro-Soviet regime came to power (1978). For those who see the game of nations as a zero-sum game between only two actors (or blocs of actors), these are all Western "losses", following the "loss of China" in 1949 and the "loss of Cuba" ten years later. From this perspective, the Soviet Union, especially in the Brezhnev period, has "gained".

However, by the same type of calculation, one can also say that the Soviet Union "lost" China in 1960, Indonesia in 1965, Ghana in 1966, Mali in 1968, North Yemen after 1968, Chile in 1973, Somalia and the Sudan in 1977, Equatorial Guinea in 1979, Guinea in 1984. The degree of Soviet influence has declined in a number of other countries such as Algeria and India. Even in the Middle East the record is not one of successes. Galia Golan has made this overall assessment:

"A stock-taking of the Soviet position in the Middle East after twenty-five years of activity reveals a sharply ascending and then a descending curve which tends in the direction of relative failure. On the success side of the ledger there is the Soviet treaty with Iraq; the legalization of the Syrian Communist Party and its inclusion in a front with the ruling Ba'ath Party; the Marxist orientation of South Yemen; improved relations with Libya, Kuwait, Jordan and, within limits, pre-Khomeini Iran, as well as with Turkey; and Soviet identification with the PLO as it has gained world recognition. (...)

On the negative side of the ledger, Soviet relations with Egypt... have been entirely eroded. Syria has guarded her independence jealously, even defying Moscow over such issues as the Lebanese war, while she periodically represses or restricts the local

> Communists. Iraq has proved problematic, and Libya is a highly erratic political partner. Moreover, Soviet support for Ethiopian action against Eritrea has raised problems for Soviet relations with the radical Arab states. (...)
> Even in the realm of strategic interests, Soviet policy has met with certain failures: the port and air facilities lost in Egypt and Somalia have not been fully compensated for by moves elsewhere; and neither Libya nor Syria has been as co-operative as Egypt, nor has Iraq (or, to date, Ethiopia) been as forthcoming as Somalia once was. Only in South Yemen (formerly Aden) does there appear to have been whole-hearted co-operation." (178)

In the book-keeping system of the Soviet Union there are two categories of Third World countries, those which are ruled by Communist parties and those which are 'socialist-orientated'. The first group consists of Mongolia, North Korea, Laos, Cambodia, Vietnam, Cuba, Afghanistan, and China. The second group presently includes 16 members (the 17th, Grenada, has been "lost" in 1983 and the 18th, Guinea, in 1984): Algeria, Angola, Benin, Birma, Guinea-Bissau, Cape Verde, San Tomé, Syria, South Yemen, Lybia, Nicaragua, Mozambique, Congo-Brazzaville, Tanzania, Madagascar and Ethiopia. In addition, Ghana and Surinam were apparently considered candidates to this group (179).

The degree of control which the Soviet Union can exercise on these countries varies but the relative ease with which a country can change sides, exemplified most dramatically in the case of Egypt, indicates that Soviet military power does not automatically translate into political influence. In the case of Syria, the Soviet ambassador in Damascus has, for instance, complained that the Syrians take everything from the Soviet Union except its advice (180). In the case of Iraq the government opposes the Soviet Union over the question of Eritrea and Afghanistan (181). The links created by military dependency of a Third World client from a superpower appear to be weaker than economic links which tie a Third World country to the world market, the International Monetary Fund and Western aid. The fact that the Soviet Union can deliver weapons, both old and new, about twice as fast as the United States due to its production structure (182) has, on the other hand, been an advantage. The inability of the Soviet Union to accompany military aid by substantial economic support (except in a few cases) has been a disadvantage. The ideological product which the Soviet Union has to offer to Third World nations ("scientific socialism" with its inherent atheism, collectivization of agriculture, and emphasis on heavy industry) has a declining attractiveness. The Soviet Union is no longer considered the developmental model par excellence.

"Proletarian internationalism", or, in the words of Brezhnev at the 25th Party Congress in 1976, the "support to peoples who are fighting for their freedom" (183), has become an instrument of Soviet foreign policy which selects some liberation movements but not others by a process based on Soviet interest (support, though not unqualified, for the Palestinians; no support for "progressive" Eritreans; suppression of the Kurds in Iraq). The backing provided to rulers like Idi Amin of Uganda and Jean Bedel Bokassa of the Central African Republic at one time or another (184) can be explained only in terms of 'my enemy's enemy is my friend'. This kind of foreign policy is understandable in the case of a small and threatened nation like Israel (which also, at one time supported Idi Amin of Uganda and which also trained Ethiopian troops in counter-insurgency in Eritrea until April 1978). To a great power it is certainly no tribute.

Nevertheless, on a number of occasions, notably in the Ogaden War and in Angola, the Soviet Union has backed the "right" party in the view of at least the majority of African states. It has come to the help of two countries under aggression (although the MPLA and the Ethiopian revolutionary leaders were only bona fide representatives of "their" countries). However, in the case of Cambodia, the Soviet backing for the intervening nation Vietnam meant a siding with the aggressor. Had the Vietnamese intervention been humanitarian in nature or at least provoked (as was the case in the Tanzanian counter-invasion of Uganda) by the overthrown regime, mitigating circumstances could be pleaded. But that was not the case. Another question is whether the Soviet Union could have stopped Vietnam from intervening. The answer is, that given the pro-Chinese orientation of the Pol Pot regime, it had no interest in doing so.

More in general, the question of control of client behaviour is a difficult one. It would seem that this control is rather weak. In the case of Syria, the Soviet Union could not prevent Syria to intervene in Lebanon in 1976, nor could it stop the Syrian attack on PLO leader Yassir Arafat in northern Lebanon in 1983. The most intriguing question of control is of course the one of Cuba. Are the Cubans "all purpose mercenaries" intervening as proxies wherever and whenever the Soviet Union asks for it, sacrificing some 4,000 men in Africa in support of Soviet policies? The economic dependence of Cuba on the Soviet Union (financially as well as in terms of oil) and the military dependence (in terms of arms and protection) is beyond doubt. But that alone is not sufficient reason to assume that Cuba has not, at times more, at other times less, been acting on its own initiative when sending military personnel to more than 30 countries in the 1960s and 1970s *).

To view the Soviet-Cuban relationship as one of paymaster and mercenary by referring to the fact that for many years the Soviet Union has subsidized the Cuban economy, is a caricature of the complexity of the circumstances surrounding the Cuban intervention. If one accepts this type of reasoning based on a cash nexus as sufficient, the American support for Israel (amounting to more than $ 1,000 for every Israeli citizen per year) could also be interpreted in such terms. In the case of the Vietnam war, the United States has directly

----

*) There are more Third World exporters of troops in the world. Pakistan is an example of a Western "Cuba". It has troops in Saudi Arabia, Jordan, Abu Dhabi and Libya and has military missions in 22 different countries. Other examples are North Korea with military training advisers in about a dozen countries, and India, which in 1980, had provided 26 countries with military assistance (185).

paid the Philippines, South Korea and Thailand for sending troops to South Vietnam (186). Given the unequal pattern of interdependence it is of course true that Cuba or Israel can only intervene in Angola or Lebanon with the assurance of the patron superpower that it will come to its aid if the other superpower intervenes directly. Yet one should not underestimate the extent to which small client nations in strategic places can pull their patrons along in pursuit of their local ambitions. In the case of Angola, the pull factors of small movements and states (the MPLA and Cuba on the one hand, the FNLA and Zaire on the other) were probably decisive in bringing in the superpowers and their auxiliaries.

Mitchell has formulated two hypotheses with regard to the involvement of external parties in civil strive. These appear to offer a more fruitful explanatory model than a "war by proxy" theory. Mitchell wrote, in 1970:

> (1) "That external parties tend to become highly involved in violent civil strife through a process by which rival domestic parties seek external allies to help them maintain their position in the conflict.
>
> Linked with this is the proposition:
>
> (2) That the allies chosen are already to some extent involved in domestic affairs, and that the extent of this prior involvement helps in deciding to whom the appeal for help is directed, and whether it is answered by positive action." (187)

In the case of Angola, various liberation movements appealed to several external parties (e.g. the MPLA to Cuba and to the Soviet Union) and they responded primarily because of "prior involvement" and because they had an interest of their own in the situation (the Soviet Union presumably did not want to leave the field to China and to the United States; Cuba saw its ten year-old alliance with the MPLA threatened and possibly also saw the oil-rich Cabina province as an alternative source for covering its energy requirements if the Soviet Union should again coercively cut back oil supplies as happened in early 1968; in addition there was a genuine feeling of 'revolutionary solidarity' among many Cubans). In other words, both Cuba and the Soviet Union had reasons of their own to intervene. Given their uneven resource bases, the one intervened with men and the other with weapons mainly. In a military alliance these complemented each other. To term the Cubans "the Surrogate Forces of the Soviet Union" (188) is simplistic. Rather, it was a case of "military co-operation", to use a term introduced by Bertil Dunér after dismissing the proxy concept as an unsatisfactory explicatory theory. Dunér has written:

> "The starting-point for any idea of a proxy-relationship must be that the relationship is asymmetrical. The proxy is, in one sense or another, subordinate to his principal. (...) It can be shown that the only logically tenable and theoretically appropriate attitude is to regard a proxy relationship as a question of power – the principle is a state which gets another state to intervene by using positive or negative sanctions. However, with a definition like this, it seems to be impossible to demonstrate a single case

of proxy intervention. For example, no one has been able to show that Cuba yielded to Soviet persuasion or coercion in Angola, no more than it has been proved that South Africa yielded to American persuasion or coercion. (...) In the end, one is confronted by a problem that is general in all power research - that of trying to determine the aims and intentions." (189)

Cuba and the Soviet Union had parallel interests in Angola, as had the United States and South Africa. The difference was that the Soviet Union made the Cuban intervention effective, while the United States government, in the wake of Vietnam and Watergate, was not allowed by Congress to back up South Africa sufficiently to check or beat the Cuban troops. In Ethiopia, Cuba and the Soviet Union presumably also had parallel interests although the distance of Ethiopia from Cuba somewhat weakens the power of "revolutionary solidarity" as an explanation of Cuban interests. Cuba's interest, however, was parallel only with regard to the situation in the Ogaden. With regard to Eritrea, the Soviet Union and Cuba disagreed and the suppression of the Eritrean secessionists was, according to most sources, apparently done without substantial Cuban help (190).

The notion of "parallel interests" combined with the one of a "division of labour" between intervening powers seems to be able to explain military cooperation between big and small intervening powers better than a simple proxy concept. The term "cooperative intervention", introduced by Stephen T. Hosmer and Thomas W. Wolfe, is more adequate than "intervention by proxy" (191). Another example will illustrate the point. In this case the smaller power was a medium power, France. During the invasion of northern Chad by Lybian-supported troops in 1983, the United States pressed France to intervene strongly. The French socialist government, however, after much hesitation, sent only limited reinforcement to Chad, just enough to create a stalemate with Libya (which had between 6,000 and 7,000 troops south of the Aouzou strip) while the United States' government would have liked to see an all-out French effort against Qadaffi. The parallel interests of the United States and France, in other words, diverged after a certain point. France has sometimes been termed the NATO's policeman in Africa but it has played this role only insofar as France's own interests were at stake. It is quite unthinkable that France would act as a simple proxy. France, of course, is less dependent on the United States than Cuba on the Soviet Union but degree of dependence does not automatically translate into degree of obedience.

Military cooperation is not confined to dyadic relationships. The French-American military cooperation in Africa and the use of Moroccan troops in Zaire in March 1977 and of Belgian troops in May 1978 during the Shaba invasions from Angola by Katangan exile forces introduced a third tier to military cooperation. Such a third tier has also been observed in the case of the East bloc. An U.S. State Department official noticed a 'division of labour' in Black Africa:

"The bulk of the manpower has been supplied by Cuba. The Soviet Union has supplied the equipment and, undoubtedly, much of the

financing. The East Germans supplement these contributions with
technical skills and sophisticated equipment." (192)

In a certain sense the world military order can be conceived as a
multitier system. For the West, the first tier would be filled by the
United States, the second by France and Great Britain, among others,
the third by countries like Iran (before 1979), Egypt (after 1976) and
Pakistan. The fourth tier would consist of local actors in the
contested Third World countries where most military interventions
take place: Oman, Nicaragua, Chad, etc. Such a model has been
suggested by Richard Bissell who exemplified it by a reference to the
position of North Yemen before 1967:

"The Soviet relationship with Yemen before the June war can be
conceptualized as a four-tiered system. This model, which
conveys a sense of much of Soviet foreign relations during its
present growth period into a superpower, includes the Soviet
Union as the top (first) tier, Eastern Europe as the second tier,
and various other countries divided into the third and fourth tiers
according to their importance to the USSR. Khrushchev created
that division as he bestowed honours on countries that were
presumably on the road to socialism: The UAR, Syria, Burma,
Ghana, Guinea, and Mali. Other countries were grouped into the
fourth tier, including Yemen and those countries' relations with
the Soviet Union were governed, by and large, with the advice
and understanding of a third-tier country. The situation in the
lower Red Sea was compatible with the interests of both the
USSR and the UAR, since the former did not wish to invest too
much prestige in a civil war, and the latter wished to limit the
direct influence of the USSR in the UAR sphere of influence.
Nearly all political and military aid, therefore, arrived in Yemen
with an Egyptian label." (193)

Such a model can serve as a heuristic tool which is more
illuminating than a simple proxy theory. The Soviet Union 'used'
Egypt in Yemen, but Nasser also 'used' the Soviet Union to enlarge
Egypt's role in the Middle East. Both, in turn, were used by the
post-1962 Yemeni leadership and, after 1969, the latter could do
without them, having aligned with Saudi Arabia, which was backed by
the United States.

Alliances in the Third World are apparently easily made and easily
broken, often without too much cost. Nigeria is a case in point: in its
civil war with Biafra the central government was aided by Great
Britain and the Soviet Union and, after victory, maintained a close
military relationship with the USSR. In 1979, however, the Soviet
advisers were expelled from the country. The same pattern of
military aid and rejection characterized the Soviet relationship with
Indonesia, Egypt, Sudan, Somalia, Ghana and Guinea and other
nations. In the case of the United States a similar row would include
the names Cuba, Iran, Ethiopia, Nicaragua. There are, of course, also
permanent Third World allies, but in the case of the Soviet Union the
list is short: Cuba, Vietnam, South Yemen, perhaps Ethiopia and
Afghanistan, and, less likely Mozambique and Angola.

The military relationships between a patron and a client nation are
rarely simple command-obey relationships. The possibility to exchange

one patron for another (China for the Soviet Union, or the United States for either of them) provides a client with bargaining strength. The forms of military relationships vary greatly and bring with themselves varying opportunities and risks for both client and patron. 'Peace-time' military assistance can lead to 'war-time' military intervention. In reality, the borderline between assistance and intervention, between war and peace, has become fuzzy. Table VI, derived from Milton Leitenberg, is an attempt to categorize the types of military ties which can exist between patron and client nation.

Table V: Types of Military Assistance and Military Intervention (194)

Military Assistance	Military Intervention
1. Arms donations; 2. Arms sales; 3. Cash donations for arms sales; 4. Supplying mercenaries; 5. Training local forces locally; 6. Training local forces in donor country; 7. Training local forces in friendly countries; 8. Supplying specialist forces for peacetime operations of defence equipment (radar, pilots, anti-aircraft systems, etc.); 9. Building defence(-related) infrastructural facilities (harbours, airfields, etc.); 10. Providing satellite and other intelligence to local military; 11. Maintenance of military equipment.	1. Peacetime stationing of troops as deterrent against third parties; 2. Providing body guards and palace guards to local government; 3. Military mission at headquarters for planning local operations without direct combat participation; 4. Combat participation of foreign special forces (tank operators, pilots, radar, etc.); 5. "Volunteers" serving in combat; 6. "Regular troops" engaged in combat; 7. Providing naval or air protection in or near combat zone; 8. Mobilization, troop movements in border areas, deployment of special weapons into forward positions; 9. Special weapons supplies during combat phase; 10. Armed blockades to prevent weapons reaching opponent of supported party; 11. Providing logistics (air and naval transport) for combattants.

If we link the category "military assistance" with the second hypothesis of Mitchell (see above, p. 120), an indexation of the various subcategories might provide us with useful predictors for forecasting "military intervention" in times of crisis.

However, in an important sense "military assistance" is already a form of intervention of the distributing country in the recipient country. With regard to the Soviet military assistance as a means of creating ties with the nations of the Third World, J.L. Nogee has noticed:

"The objectives of Soviet military aid are to undermine and supplant Western influence, to contain Chinese influence, to establish military bases to project Soviet power, and to gain economically. (...) On the negative side, however, it needs to be noted that a substantial portion of Soviet military aid is simply never repaid. Military assistance... has proven to be one of Moscow's most effective, flexible, and enduring instruments for establishing a position of influence in the nonaligned countries." (195)

This "military assistance" business has entangled many Third World nations into more or less close relationships with the four nations which dominate the world's arms trade. In the late 1970s these were the United States (with a global market share of 49 percent), the USSR (28 percent), France (5 percent) and the United Kingdom (4 percent) *). Between 1979 and 1983 - as for most of the time in the previous two decades - the Soviet Union was the largest Third World supplier of major weapons (the USA was the largest supplier to the industrial countries of the West). Almost 70 percent of Soviet major weapon exports go to the Third World (the figure for the USA is 50 percent; these exports are spread over twice as many recipients than the Soviet exports). Third World nations have increased their arms imports from $ 2.5 billion in 1965 to $ 9.8 billion in 1976. This quadrupling of imports parallelled a quadrupling of Third World military spending, which in the late 1970s already exceeded $ 100 billion per year (197).
The Third World nations have become the testing ground of the weapons for the northern medium and great powers. The local instability and the fluid character of regional power constellations has invited great power interference and rivalry in the new nations. The East-West confrontation is, in a way, fought out in the Third World and a major goal of the superpowers appears to be to deny access to each others' client states. The location of military conflicts

----

*) The concentration of 86 percent of arms sales in the hands of four major powers suggests an almost equally limited number of distributing relationships for military assistance. However, since this percentage figure excludes some types of arms transfers and the provision of military services, it is misleading. Leitenberg has pointed out that
"There are more than twenty nations now known to be on the distributing end of these relationships, some during open hostilities and others as a part of peace-time military operations (USA, USSR, France, UK, Saudi Arabia, Israel, Egypt, Cuba, Pakistan, India, Taiwan, North Korea, Libya, Morocco, etc.). There may be others for which documentation is lacking. The number of recipients probably runs to well over 50 nations. The assistance may be in the form of money, weapons, specialized military personnel (pilots, submarines crews, radar operators, aircraft repair technicians, tank crews, etc.) or information (satellite reconnaissance photographs or intelligence obtained by other means, either ground-based or satellite systems)." (196)

in the contemporary world - over 90 percent of all armed conflicts since 1945 have taken place outside Europe, the Soviet Union and the United States - combined with the fact that the West took part in half of them, according to one count (198), is probably linked to the patron-client relationships between northern and southern nations.

Clients do not have to be governments in power but can be exile groups or internal liberation movements. In the case of the Soviet Union, clients have been governments in power engaged in the suppression of internal insurgents (as in North Yemen, Iraq, Nigeria, Sudan, Sri Lanka, Ethiopia/Eritrea) or governments of nations at war with another nation (as in Indonesia, Egypt, Syria, Ethiopia/Ogaden) as well as insurgents seeking state power (as the MPLA in Angola, PAIGC in Guinea-Bissau, SWAPO in Namibia, Frelimo in Mozambique). From the client's point of view, superpower backing can enhance its power with regard to local rivals and opponents. From the patron nation's point of view, the arming of clients can be seen as an investment, as the opening of a channel of influence into a region which is economically and/or strategically interesting.

According to Barry Blechman, author of a study on the use of American armed forces as a political instrument, the utility of superpower activity in the Third World can be seen on two levels:

> "first, such activity can serve to protect the specific interests of client states and, presumably, whatever values cause the superpower to seek or to accept such a patron/client relationship to begin with;
> second, use of armed forces serves to demonstrate to a global audience the strength and resolve of each super-power and thus the value of their patronage, thereby contributing to their continuing quest for political influence throughout the world."
> (199)

In their competition to influence the outcome of Third World confrontations, the superpowers appear to have reached some basic understanding as to what is tolerable behaviour. James McConnell and his associates have described the pattern of behaviour emerging from US-USSR competition in the Third World as one wherein it is

> "permissible for one superpower to support a friend against the client of another superpower as long as the friend is on the defensive strategically; the object must be to avert decisive defeat and restore the balance, not assist the client to victory. The issue of who began the war is not central; it is the strategic situation of the client at the time of the contemplated intervention that counts. (...)
> The realistic aim of both sides, then, is not to maximize gains but to reduce losses. The patron threatening intervention is limiting the losses of his own client against the other client; the countering patron is limiting the scope of the threat to his client by the other patron." (200)

Applied to a concrete situation like the Ogaden War this "rule" of superpower gaming in the Third World would postulate a greater toleration of Soviet than American intervention since its client Ethiopia was strategically on the defensive. Once the tide had turned it was the United States that was "limiting the scope of the threat to his client" - Somalia - by asking (and obtaining) a guarantee from the Soviet Union that the Cuban-Ethiopian counter-offensive would stop at the Ethiopian-Somali border line in the Ogaden desert. In Angola, on the other hand, the Soviet Union had apparently broken the rule by "assisting the client to victory". But this was an internal conflict with no clear borderline and the MPLA was about to be crushed by US-supported clients. It is also not clear whether victory has been achieved. UNITA was still very active in 1984 receiving support from South Africa, Saudi Arabia and Morocco among others. The FNLA also survived until 1984 when it apparently decided to demobilize.

McConnell's rule of tolerated latitude of action for an intervening superpower, fits Third World interstate conflicts generally better than internal ones. With regard to a particular case like Afghanistan it is difficult to make it fit. The Soviet Union treated this adjacent country as if it were an intra-bloc rather than an extra-bloc country. The American indifference to Afghanistan's coup of April 1978 - which brought a Communist group into power - might have made Moscow overly confident that it could get away with its intervention without major international political damage being done. Yet in this case the Western reaction was strong, perhaps also because there were no Cubans this time who could confuse the question of responsibility.

Since 1945 there have been more than one hundred wars, most of them in the Third World. According to one count, the Soviet Union has been involved in about twenty of these conflicts as major arms supplier and diplomatic actor (201).

Especially in the last decade there has clearly been an upward trend in Soviet military involvement in the Third World. Yet it should not be forgotten that the Soviet Union, with the probable exception of Afghanistan, has intervened because threatened or adventurous local Third World actors have extended an invitation. And not all invitations have been accepted by the Soviet Union. However, where such invitations for military intervention were honoured, Third World conflicts have also obtained a substitute function for the "impossible" - because nuclearly deterred - central conflict between the superpowers. This view also appears to be implicit in the evaluation of the role of military force in international relations by the Soviet author V.M. Kulish of the Moscow Institute of World Economy and International Relations. He wrote, in 1972:

> "... military power is the decisive instrument of present-day international relations and the foreign policy of states. And although the sphere of its immediate, direct use is to some extent limited at the present time, that has not decreased but, on the contrary, has increased its role... Military power, of course, is not the only foreign policy instrument that the state has at its disposal. Political, economic, ideological, and cultural instruments also exist, but the employment of military power... is the ultimate remedy, dangerous not only to those it is directed against but also to those who use it." (202)

Case Study X

THE SOVIET INTERVENTION INTO AFGHANISTAN (1979-)

Russian interest in Afghanistan, which dates back to the middle of the 19th century, initially took the shape of economic assistance after the Second World War. The Kingdom of Afghanistan received economic aid from the United States as well in the 1950s. American aid was primarily aimed at the improvement of agriculture, public health, education and the like, and it remained smaller than the amount of Soviet aid. By the 1960s American interest in Afghanistan had all but disappeared, while Soviet aid had greatly increased, concentrating on strategic infra-structure projects. Young Afghan army officers received their military training in the Soviet Union.

After a coup d'etat in 1973 the Democratic Republic of Afghanistan was proclaimed, with Mohammad Daud Khan as President. At first the regime enjoyed Soviet approval but Moscow became increasingly discontented, especially after Khan's purge of leading Communists in the People's Democratic Party of Afghanistan (PDPA). A coup d'etat on April 27, 1978, brought a pro-Soviet regime into power, with Nur Mohammad Taraki of the Khalq ("The People") faction of the PDPA as President. As in 1973 the the coup was led by Afghan army officers. The Soviets financially supported the new regime and increased the number of Russian advisors in every field of Afghan life. Nevertheless it seems plausible that the 1978 coup was neither instigated by, nor had the active support of the Soviet Union. Rather, it was a result of internal tensions (1).

The Taraki regime launched a sweeping program of reform aimed at rapid economic development and modernization. However, the mass of the Afghan population, fiercely Islamic, illiterate and committed to a rigid social structure, opposed the atheistic, marxist central government. Resistance to the alien philosophy of life, which from 1973 onwards had developed under the guidance of the religious leaders, became substantial soon after the so-called April Revolution. This was facilitated by the fact that Afghanistan is an ideal country for guerrilla warfare due to its many inaccessible areas and a tribal population of some 15.5 million of which barely two million live in the cities. By early 1979 the government still held the towns, but it had lost control of large parts of the countryside, and one year after the April coup most of the provinces were in a state of rebellion. According to a guerrilla spokesman, 250,000 people were killed between the coup in April 1978 and the Soviet invasion in December 1979 (2).

In the West, these events in Afghanistan evoked little reaction, but the Soviet Union was alarmed. It supplied the Afghan army with more weaponry and it raised the number of its advisors from some 1,500 before April 1978 to 5,000 or more in 1979. The Soviet Union seems to have favoured a slow-down in the pace of reforms, contrary to the wishes of hard liner Hafizullah Amin who became Prime Minister in March 1979. Reportedly, Amin learned about a plot against him by

Taraki and the Soviet Union in September 1979; he quickly reacted and as a result Taraki was killed (3). Amin became President. After Americans in the US embassy in Tehran were taken hostage in the first week of November 1979, the Soviet Union reportedly exerted pressure on Amin to acquire the exclusive use of the military base of Shindand near Afghanistan's border with Iran. Amin refused to comply (4).

The Soviet Union may have started to prepare for an intervention during the spring of 1979, and it continued to do so after Taraki's death. The final decision to invade was probably not taken until December. The visit of Soviet Lieutenant-General V.S. Paputin to Kabul in early December is generally considered to have been a vain effort to force President Amin out of office and to obtain a formal invitation for Soviet intervention (5). The call up of Soviet reserves was begun by mid-December. During December various Soviet units arrived in Afghanistan; if they were noticed at all, they might have been taken for reinforcements of the Afghan army in the struggle against rebels. On Christmas eve the Soviet Union began to fly thousands of troops to a military airfield near Kabul.

On December 27, 1979, Soviet forces were brought by air into Kabul to secure the key points while at the same time more than 50,000 men from ground units crossed the border into Afghanistan. Afghan troops offered incidental resistance, but reportedly many units had been neutralized in advance by Soviet advisors who had made them disarm under various pretexts. During and shortly after the invasion more than 40,000 men are alleged to have deserted from the 80-100,000 strong Afghan army. The invasion caused an estimated 2,000 Afghan deaths (6). On the first day President Amin was also killed, perhaps in a shoot-out with Paputin who apparently committed suicide on December 28, 1979.

In the course of 1980, the Afghan army further shrunk to about 30,000 men. Figures of losses amount to 10,000 desertions and 5,000 fatalities a year (7). The government started a mobilization campaign to replenish its armed forces. Pay was raised, the age for conscription was lowered and the conscription period was extended, and older men were redrafted. There have been many reports of forced recruitment. According to American estimates the Afghan troop strength thereby increased from about 25,000 in 1982 to some 40,000 or 50,000 in 1983 (8).

On the morrow of the Soviet invasion, Babrak Karmal was installed as President of Afghanistan to succeed the widely hated Amin. In addition, Karmal became Prime Minister and Chairman of the Revolutionary Council. Karmal, who was the leader of the Parcham faction, had been fired as Deputy Prime Minister in July 1978. After the invasion he returned from Eastern Europe to Afghanistan. Despite the moderateness of his measures, however, Karmal was looked upon as a Soviet puppet by most Afghans. A general strike broke out in Kabul and other major cities in February 1980, with thousands of demonstrators chanting anti-Soviet slogans. In May and June students and schoolchildren demonstrated. During the night curfew in the cities 'Allah is Great!' was shouted from the rooftops, and by the morning the streets were scattered with so-called night letters, crudely printed lampoons. At the end of February martial law was declared. The strikes were broken up and the demonstrations were violently suppressed, causing many casualties. The Karmal regime introduced identity papers in the big cities, and tried to bribe tribal chiefs.

The religious leaders have since declared resistance against the Soviets to be 'Holy War', and morale is very high among the numerous guerrilla movements. The groups are of different orientation. Co-ordination is generally lacking, and sometimes clashes occur between the groups. Early in 1980, various resistance movements tried to unite to form the so-called Islamic Alliance, but this effort was not successful. Many of the guerrilla movements are based in Peshawar in Pakistan. In Afghanistan the mujaheddin ("fighters") generally stay in the villages, enjoying strong support from the local population, with whom they are ethnically and tribally linked. It is generally estimated that the resistance movements dominate 80 per cent of the country. The Soviet and Afghan troops hold control of the major towns and roads, and other strategic points. The guerrilla strategy consists of sabotage, ambushes, political assassinations, and the encouragement of desertions from the Afghan army on the condition of bringing one's own weapon. Manpower is no problem for the guerrillas but weapons are in short supply, notably heavy weapons and anti-aircraft guns.

In their present counterinsurgency campaign the Soviets make frequent use of helicopters. A great number of villages have been bombed, because they were suspected of harbouring mujaheddin, or to intimidate the population. Crops have been destroyed and irritant gases have been used. Some reports state that lethal gas and other chemical weapons have been used as well. As a result of non-discriminating military actions casualty rates among civilians, especially among males and children, are very high compared with the number of guerrillas killed. Casualties among the children are frequent due to small plastic mines which are dropped in large numbers throughout the rebel areas and on the mountain passes along the border with Pakistan (9). From the urban population many males flee to the countryside to evade military service in the Afghan army. Moreover, about one million Afghans are in refugee camps in Iran, and over 3 million in Pakistan. A high proportion of them are women. Millions of Afghans live separated from their relatives nowadays. Soviet fatalities since December 1979 are estimated by the CIA (1983) to amount to 15,000 (10). To keep fatality rates low, the Soviets tend to place Afghan troops in front line positions when battles are fought. The strength of the Soviet army in Afghanistan was estimated at 130,000 by late 1984. It is generally agreed that it would take twice or thrice this number to crush the Afghan resistance completely. On the other hand, the Soviet presence appears to be big enough to prevent the insurgents from gaining victory. The present situation is therefore one of a stalemate.

Obviously, the Soviet Union did not expect substantial resistance when it decided to intervene. Nearly all identifiable invading divisions originated from the Central Asian and Turkestan military districts, where reserve troops were readily available. It is almost certain that the reservists from Central Asia received only marginal military training (11). Apparently the Soviet Union intended to use its forces for occupation duties rather than for combat operations, hoping for a political advantage due to the ethnic and religious similarities of the majority of the Soviet troops with the peoples in the north of Afghanistan. Afghan resistance to the invasion was, however, considerable and Soviet soldiers fraternized to some extent with the Afghan population, buying religious books, attending places of worship and the like. From about February 1980 onwards these forces were replaced by new troops of Slav or other non-Muslim nationalities, mainly from units in the German Democratic Republic, Poland, Czechoslovakia and Hungary (12). They were better suited to the task in Afghanistan. By mid-1980 several thousand troops had been replaced and a major offensive was started. In such a way the 'win-the-hearts-and-minds' approach was substituted by a 'search-and-destroy' strategy. From early 1981 onwards this was supplemented by a non-discriminative strategy of destruction, including high altitude bombings of villages (13). Ever since the beginning of the occupation the Soviets are reported to have launched two major offensives a year, one of them during the harvest period. Its military involvement in Afghanistan is estimated to cost the Soviet Union many millions of dollars a day (14). Trade between Afghanistan and the Soviet Union has greatly increased. Afghanistan supplies natural gas, fruits, carpets, fur and minerals, while the Soviet Union provides Afghanistan with vehicles, heavy materials, consumer goods and oil products and renders financial aid (15).

There has been a great deal of speculation concerning the motives behind the Soviet intervention. The most likely one seems to be that the Soviet move was determined by the internal situation in Afghanistan and the errors of its local ally, the PDPA. To cite Fred Halliday:

> "the level of Russian presence in Afghanistan only increased dramatically in mid 1979, when substantial rural resistance to the regime's reforms broke out. Later in that year, the Russians tried to help a faction inside the government to remove the most hated man in the regime, Premier Hafizullah Amin, and it was only in December that they managed to do so. Amin had so weakened the structures of party and state and so inflamed the tribal rebellion by his repression that the Russians decided they could only restabilize the situation by sending in thousands of their own troops." (16)

In contrast to this interpretation many other observers consider the Soviet intervention in the first place as part of a "masterplan". They point at a Soviet quest for control of the oil resources around the Persian Gulf in order to dominate western oil supplies and to compensate for future oil shortages within the Soviet Union (17). Many authors also assume a Soviet fear of Islamic resistance spreading into the Soviet Union. Furthermore, the natural resources of Afghanistan are mentioned as a cause, as well as a Soviet fear of an American intervention in Iran in connection with the hostage crisis (a small-scale U.S. rescue operation was indeed attempted on April 25, 1980).

The Soviet ambassador at the UN Security Council cited article 4 of the Soviet-Afghan Treaty of Friendship and Co-operation of December 5th, 1978, as the basis for the intervention. The article provides for military co-operation. It is not entirely clear whether President Amin asked for the intervention. Amin must have approved of the presence of numerous Soviet advisors, and at the very least he must have known of the arrival of Soviet troops weeks before the invasion. In an interview on December 26, one day before he was killed, Amin welcomed the military aid and said that the Soviet Union respected the independence and integrity of Afghanistan (18). Amin's death, whether caused by accident or on purpose, discredited any possibility of a Soviet claim that the Amin government had asked the Soviet Union to intervene. The late Amin was depicted as an agent of the CIA. Immediately after the removal of Amin, a radio broadcast reported that the new President of Afghanistan had asked for military assistance from the Soviet Union (19).

After more than a quarter of a century of Soviet influence, the role of the Soviet Union in Afghanistan was in jeopardy by late 1979. Afghanistan being within the Soviet sphere of influence, the Soviet Union could be certain that no military confrontation with the West would result from its decision to intervene. However, Afghanistan was formally non-aligned and the invasion constituted the first direct use of Soviet ground forces in divisional strength outside the Soviet block since the Second World War. The international reaction to the events must have been much greater than the Soviets had expected. On January 7, 1980, the Soviet Union vetoed a UN Security Council resolution on Afghanistan. A few days later, during an emergency session of the UN General Assembly, 17 Third World countries in a draft resolution called for the "immediate, unconditional and total withdrawal" of foreign troops from Afghanistan (20). In November 1980, 1981 and 1982 the resolution was repeated. The Olympic Games in the Soviet Union in 1980 were boycotted by athletes of various nations. The United States' Congress postponed ratification of the SALT II treaty and restricted grain deliveries and the transfer of high technology to the Soviet Union. Within the Soviet Union, dissatisfaction with the intervention in Afghanistan seems to have been voiced by "the simple people, often from the provinces, who think it is wrong for the government to help foreign countries when there is a shortage of goods at home", rather then by the critical intelligentsia. The latter takes the reactionary regime in Afghanistan before the intervention into consideration, and the alleged threat from China (21). The Soviets claim that during the Amin period both the CIA and China were giving support to the rebellious tribes (22).

Compared with the general indignation against the Soviet invasion, foreign support for the Afghan resistance has remained rather small. Aid programmes concentrate on the refugees. Egypt is the largest supplier of weapons, and Saudi Arabia provides the finances for arms purchases. Minor deliveries by Iran and China are also reported. It is generally thought that direct American involvement is negligible. Pakistan has recognized the six major Afghan resistance movements and has provided them with headquarters in Peshawar. The high

numbers of refugees destabilize Pakistan's life and President Zia Ul Haq has demanded financial assistance and weapons from the West.
As a result of the Soviet intervention in Afghanistan East-West relations have substantially deteriorated and the overall advantages gained by the invasion must be open to question in Soviet eyes as well. However, as Fred Halliday cogently put it,

> "if it is false to argue that the Russians entered Afghanistan because of marginal strategic benefits, it must also be false to expect them to leave in order to improve the international climate. They will only leave when the Kabul government itself is strong enough to cope with the rural opposition that remains". 23)

Both the Afghan and the Soviet governments take the position that the 'Afghan revolution of December 1979' cannot be turned back.

EPILOGUE

PAST AND FUTURE OF SOVIET MILITARY INTERVENTIONS

Introduction

If the "Past is Prologue", our survey of Soviet military interventions should enable us to draw some lessons from history - provided there are no pronounced breaks with the past. There are, however, at least three possible turning points, two internal and one external one in 20th century Russian history. The first internal turning point is the October Revolution of 1917: many will argue that the change from Nicolas II to V.I. Lenin, from Czarism to Communism, was a clear breaking point. The second possible internal breaking point is the death of Stalin in 1953. N. Khrushchev's critique of Stalin's despotic type of rule at the 20th Party Congress in 1956 marked, according to many, an end to the "Cult of Personality" and initiated "Destalinization". The external breaking point is the advent of the nuclear age in 1945 and the fuller realization thereof in the Cuban missile crisis in 1962. With regard to all three of these events one can have doubts whether they may legitimately be dubbed turning or breaking points: some statesmen still conduct international affairs as if we lived in a pre-nuclear epoch; Destalinization has not gone far enough to become irreversible, and Stalin and his successors, some would argue, have more in common with the Czars than they would like to believe.

In our view, a case can be made for the thesis that the Soviet Union is the heir of the expansionist Czarist tradition. Both before and after 1917 a major impetus for expansion was a sense of insecurity, made real by the experience of foreign invasions. From the Mongolian Tartar Khans to Napoleon and to the Russo-Japanese war of 1904/05, Russia stood wide open for military conquest. Since 1917, the Soviet Republic has been the victim of aggression four times (see Table VI).

Table VI: Foreign Interventions in the Soviet Union Since 1917

1. Febr. 17, 1918:	Following the breakdown of an armistice, German, Austrian, Hungarian and Turkish troops intervene in Russia; some of these push toward St. Petersburg. In the resulting Peace of Brest-Litovsk (March 3, 1918), 400,000 skm and 60,000,000 people are detached from Russia.
2. June 23, 1918:	The Western Allies begin to intervene in Russia in support of the anti-Bolshevik forces and their own interests with 40,700 British, 3,900 Canadian, 13,600 French, 13,700 Americans, 3,000 Italian, 80,000 Japanese, 3,000 Serbian, 42,000 Czechoslovakian, 40,000 Greek, 32,000 Polish, 29,000 (?) Estonian, 6,500 (?) Lithuanian, and 33,000 Romanian troops.
3. April 25, 1920:	Poland intervenes in Russia on a 1,000 km wide front with about 150,000 men, conquering the Ukrainian capital Kiew on May 6, 1920.
4. June 22, 1941:	Nazi Germany invades the Soviet Union with more than 3,000,000 men, 2,000 aircrafts, 3,350 tanks and 7,000 guns.

Yet Russia, the victim of aggression, has also been a frequent aggressor, both before and after 1917. Through continuous territorial expansion and annexation Russia sought to resolve the security problem posed by the outside world. According to one count, Russia has, from Czar Ivan III (1462-1505) until the decade Stalin died, fought 74 aggressive wars under the Czars and 12 under the Soviets. While the Czars managed to establish a record of 69 annexations in the period of four centuries, Lenin and Stalin could look upon a record of 20 annexations in less than half a century (1). (See also Table VIII.)

What is remarkable is that Stalin succeeded in reconquering most of territories lost as a consequence of the First World War and the Peace of Brest-Litovsk. With its land- rather than sea-based empire, the Soviet Union could until now successfully resist decolonization in a way the British and the French empires could not (see Table VII).

Table VII: Size of British, French and Russian Empires (in skm)

	1914	1970
British Empire	31,600,000 *	216,000
French Empire	10,418,000	151,000
Russian Empire	22,385,000	22,270,000

* Figure for 1933

Sources: A. Küng. Estland zum Beispiel. Stuttgart, Seewald, 1973, p. 144; David K. Fieldhouse. Die Kolonialreiche seit dem 18. Jahrhundert. Frankfurt a.M., Fischer, 1965, p. 214.

The restoration of the Czarist empire was a goal of Stalin's foreign policy. V.M. Molotov, Stalin's Commissar of Foreign Affairs, told a Finnish armistice negotiation delegation on March 29, 1944:

"The re-establishment of our frontiers is self-evident to us. The entire Russian people want it, and they regard the war from that point of view. (...) People would laugh at us if Finland could actually force us to sanction the new frontiers. The basic purpose of our war is to re-establish our old boundaries. Germany did not understand this, but after the present war she will remember it for many years to come. The Soviet Union's frontiers cannot be made the object of business transaction." (2)

Stalin not only recovered Finnish territory, but also Czechoslovakian and Romanian lands. At the Yalta conference South Sakahlin and the Kurile Islands (which had passed to Japan in 1905 and 1875 respectively) were promised back to the Soviet Union. In the same Allied conference in February 1945, the USSR recovered 179,000 square kilometres of Polish territory. At the Potsdam conference in July, 1945, East Prussian territories were transferred to the Soviet Union. When Stalin broke his Neutrality Pact with Japan on August 8, 1945, and invaded Manchuria, he termed this the revenge "for the criminal Japanese attack" of 1904. When Japan was defeated, follow-

Table VIII: Soviet Military Interventions and Annexations; 1918-1945

Nov. 29, 1918:	Estonian Soviet Republic set up with Russian military assistance.
Febr. 1918-1923:	Campaigns against Turkestan government (set up in Nov. 1917) and occupation of 4,000,000 km^2 of territory, including Khiva and Bukhara (which, though vassal states of the Czar, were not part of the Russian Empire).
April 1920:	Soviet troops, invited by local Bolsheviks, put end to independence of Azerbaijan with the occupation of its capital Baku and announcement of formation of Soviet republic.
1920-1921:	Soviet troops came to aid of a local rebellion in a province of northern Persia where the Soviet Republic of Ghilan was proclaimed.
Nov. 1920:	Soviet troops, invited by local government for the defence against Turkish invaders, entered the Armenian capital Erivan. Subsequently they overthrew the local goverment and established a Soviet regime. On December 20, 1920, Armenia became an 'independent' Soviet republic.
Febr. 1921:	Soviet troops overthrew the Menshevik government of Georgia in Tiflis (after Lenin had recognized the country's independence in May 1920).
1921:	Soviet military force used to create the 'independent Tuvian People's Republic (Tannu Tuva, a region of 160,000 km^2 on the northwestern border of the Mongolian People's Republic, had been a Russian protectorate until 1911).
1921:	Soviet troops liberated Outer Mongolia from White occupation by Baron R.F. von Ungern-Sternberg and recognized Mongolian 'sovereignty' in November 1921.
1933-1934:	Soviet troops and aircrafts intervened in China on behalf of the General Sheng Shih-ts'ai, governor of the semi-independent province of Sinkiang, and repressed Muslim rebels.
1936-1939	Soviet Union organized through Comintern International Brigade of 40,000 men for participation in Spanish civil war. No Soviet communists were officially allowed to join them. However, some of the more than 3,000 Soviet military advisors under General J.K. Berzin also took part in tank and air combats.
July 1938 - Sept. 1939:	Serious military clashes between Japan and the USSR at Changkufeng (Khasan) and in Nomonhan (Khalkin-Gol), with as many as 30,000 Soviet casualties in these border conflicts with the Japanese puppet state of Manchukuo.
Sept. 17, 1939:	700,000 Soviet troops invaded East Poland (following the Molotov-Ribbentrop Pact of Aug. 23, 1939), bringing 11 million people under Soviet rule.
Nov. 30, 1939:	30 Soviet divisions invaded Finland (the independence of which the USSR had recognized on December 31, 1917) and annexed part of it in peace treaty of March 12, 1940.
June 14, 1940:	300,000 Soviet troops marched into Lithuania, annexing it on Aug. 3, 1940.
June 14, 1940:	Soviet troops invaded the Romanian provinces Bessarabia and northern Bukovina, annexing these on Aug. 7, 1940.
June 17, 1940:	Soviet troops marched into Estonia, annexing it on Aug. 5, 1940.
June 17, 1940:	Soviet troops marched into Latvia, annexing it on Aug. 6, 1940.
1937-1941:	Soviet military aid, including 200 'volunteer' pilots and 885 aircrafts furnished to Chinese nationalists against Japanese (earlier Soviet support to Chinese nationalists and provincial warlords was given in the period 1923-1927).
1942-1946:	Soviet troops occupied northern Iran an helped to establish allegedly autonomous Azerbaijan and Kurdish republics.
Nov. 1944:	Soviet troops entered and incorporated the Czechoslovakian province of Ruthenia (Carpatho-Ukraine) into Soviet Ukraine.

Sources: Ladislaus Singer. Sowjet-Imperialismus. Stuttgart, Seewald, 1970; The Russian Empire, 1533-1963. London, Today Publ., n.d.: Ken Booth. The Military Instrument in Soviet Foreign Policy, 1917-1972. London, RUSI, 1973; Stephen T. Hosmer and Thomas W. Wolfe. Soviet Policy and Practice toward Third World Conflicts. Lexington, D.C. Heath, 1983; and various others.

ing the second atomic bomb, Stalin declared on September 2, 1945, (referring to the Czar's defeat against Japan in 1905): "For fourty years, we, the men of the older generation, have waited for this generation, for this day. And now this day has come..." (3)
There is, in our view, continuity between the essential foreign policy goals of the Czars and Stalin. The recovery of former Czarist territories and the restoration of the Russian Empire were close to Stalin's heart.
The basis of the Czarist Empire and the Stalinist one have been essentially the same. In the words of the Russian Chairman of the Council of Ministers in 1905-1906, Count S. Witte:

> "In reality, what was the Russian Empire based on? Not just primarily, but exclusively, on its army. Who created the Russian Empire...? It was accomplished strictly by the army's bayonets." (4)

The same applies to "the commonwealth of socialist states" (A. Gromyko). It was not some Marxist law of capitalist development which brought the first Communist regime into power but a coup d'etat in a situation of military collapse. It was not the rising of the working classes which led to the successful revolutions in Eastern Europe but the export of "the revolution on the points of the bayonets", a concept first propagated by General M.N. Tukhachevsky in 1920, when the counteroffensive against the Polish invasion opened the prospects of carrying the revolution into the capitalist countries with the help of the Red Army. Lenin liked the idea to "probe Europe with the bayonets of the Red Army" though he later regretted, in the light of his army's defeat, to have done so (5).
This brings us to the second possible breaking point: Stalin's death. Under Khrushchev there was an attempt to reduce the role of the armed forces in Soviet society, to place more stress on civilian than military products. Between 1955 and 1960, Soviet troop strength was reduced by 2,740,000 men and N. Khrushchev put his hope on the newly formed Strategic Rocket Forces, which, while small in size, could pose a bigger threat to the United States than huge land armies (6). Yet Khrushchev was also dependent on the military, as can, for instance, be gathered from his decision-making during the Hungarian crisis in 1956. Veljko Mićunović, the Yugoslavian ambassador in Moscow at the time, noted:

> "Khrushchev turned again to the question of intervention by the Soviet Army. He said that there were also internal reasons in the Soviet Union why they could not permit the restoration of capitalism in Hungary. There were people in the Soviet Union who would say that as long as Stalin was in command everybody obeyed and there were no big shocks, but that now, ever since they had come to power (and here Khrushchev used a coarse word to describe the present Soviet leaders), Russia had suffered the defeat and loss of Hungary. (...) Khrushchev said this might be said primarily by the Soviet Army, which was one of the reasons why they were intervening in Hungary." (7)

The Yugoslavian ambassador noted dryly: "And this was happening at a time when the present Soviet leaders were condemning Stalin." (8)
As can be gathered from the role the Soviet military played in 1964

in Khrushchev's fall, he had not done enough to please them (9). This lesson was not lost on L. Brezhnev. The external and internal security forces, which had been the mainstay of Stalin's regime, lost none of their influence. At the end of his reign, Brezhnev left his successors with "a militarized KGB Party state" (10). This was, as Gerner argues, the price of empire:

> "The Soviet security zone in Central Europe, established by Stalin, has reemerged in almost original shape as part of an empire that is based upon military power. Militarization of the Soviet Union itself is the outcome of the attempts to create military security at the cost of the nations of Central Europe." (11)

In this, the death of Stalin marked no radical break with the past.

The third possible breaking point which might interfere with the extrapolation of past trends into the future are the constraints imposed by the existence of nuclear weapons of mass destruction. When the American atomic bomb came into existence, Stalin's armies had, except in Manchuria, already reached the points from which they would not return. Not until 1979 did his successors send ground combat troops into action to secure an enlargement of the "socialist commonwealth". It is difficult to pinpoint the influence of nuclear weapons on superpower military behaviour. It is reasonable to assume that the "absolute weapon" has made them more cautious most of the time, especially since 1962. Yet caution was also characteristic of Stalin's moves on the geographical map, as can be witnessed from his comment on Communist guerrilla warfare in postwar Greece to Tito's envoy in Moscow:

> "What do you think? That Great Britain and the United States - the United States, the most powerful state in the world - will permit you to break their line of communications in the Mediterranean Sea? Nonsense. And we have no navy." (12)

Peaceful Co-existence, propagated by N. Khrushchev, was a realization of how dangerous the world had become and how important it was to avoid World War III - without, however, refraining from the support of wars of national liberation.
In conclusion, one can say that there is continuity in Soviet military behaviour and that, whatever lessons the past contains, these are not without significance for the future. In the following pages, we shall summarize our findings in the form of three tables, referring to intra-, inter- and extrabloc interventions respectively. On the basis thereof some more general observations on past and future of Soviet military interventions will be attempted.

Intrabloc Interventions

Table IX summarizes Soviet intrabloc interventions since 1945.
A number of Soviet intrabloc interventions are closely linked to the outcome of the Second World War. In these cases the term intrabloc is premature in the sense that a bloc had not yet been formed. Table IX covers a broader area than the Warsaw Pact bloc alone since Yugoslavia and China, members of the socialist bloc, are included.

Table IX: A Survey of Soviet Intrabloc Military Interventions Since 1945 (including China)

Event, Place, Year: / Type of intervention:	Bulgaria	Romania	Hungary	Czecho-slovakia	East Germany	Poland	Yugo-slavia	Lithuania	Latvia	Estonia	China
1. Peacetime stationing of troops as deterrent against 3rd parties		+ (1944-1958)	+ (1945-)	+ (1945) + (1968-)	+ (1945-)	+ (1945-)		+ (1944-)	+ (1944-)	+ (1944-)	
2. Providing body guards and palace guards to local government											
3. Military mission at headquarters for planning local operations	?? (1944-)	+? (1944-)	+? (1945-)		+? (1953)	+ (1945-1948) + (1956)		+ (1944-)	+ (1944-)	+ (1944)	
4. Combat participation of foreign special forces (tank operators, pilots, radar, etc.)								+ (1944-1953)	+ (1944-1953)	+ (1944-1953)	+ (1950)
5. "Volunteers" serving in combat											
6. "Regular" troops engaged in combat			+ (1956)	(+) (1968) ! (1969)	+ (1953)		+? (1948-1951)	(+)	(+)	(+)	+ (1946/47) + (1960s)
7. Providing naval or air protection in or near combat zone											+ (1950-1953)
8. Mobilization, troops movements in border areas, deployment of special weapons into forward positions		+ (1968) + (1971)		+? (1948) + (1968)		+ (1956) + (1980-1981)	+ (1948-1951)				+ (1950-1953) + (1960s) + (1971)
9. Special weapons' supplies during combat phase											
10. Armed blockades to prevent weapons reaching opponent of supported party					+ (1953)			+	+	+	
11. Providing logistics (air and naval transport) for combattants											+? (1950-1953)

Legend: + = verified; +? = probable but not verified; ? = possible; ?? = doubtful; ! = threat of intervention; (+) = not fully in accordance with definition.

From the point of view of the Soviet Union the three Baltic States formed an organic part of the Union of Socialist Republics since 1940 and should therefore not be considered as separate bloc units. However, this interpretation is not unchallenged: the United States, for instance, has never recognized the annexation of Lithuania, Latvia and Estonia.

If we take pro- and anti-regime interventions together, we find that the Soviet Union has intervened militarily in all intrabloc countries except Albania which was protected by the Yugoslavian buffer and the presence of the American fleet in the Adriatic. Bulgaria, a country which had been pro-Russian ever since it received its independence from the Ottoman Empire after the Russo-Turkish War of 1877-1878, was invaded after a Soviet declaration of war in September 1944, despite the fact that it was not formally at war with the Soviet Union. After the war Bulgaria became the most faithful ally of the Soviet Union even without the presence of sizeable Soviet forces on its soil. In the whole postwar period Bulgaria was unique in that there has been no anti-communist or anti-Soviet uprising. Postwar intervention, in other words, was not required. Romania, which in 1944 changed alliances, was a faithful ally of the Soviet Union until at least the late 1950s it took part in the suppression of the Hungarian revolution though it left the fighting to Soviet troops entering from Romanian territory. In 1958 Romania managed to get rid of Soviet troops, probably by successfully playing the China card and by making economic concessions to the USSR. Since the mid-1960s Romania's leadership calls for the liquidation of military blocs and the abolition of military bases and of troops on the territory of other states. Consequently, it refused to participate in the Warsaw Pact intervention in Czechoslovakia in 1968. Later it also condemned the Moscow-backed Vietnamese invasion of Kampuchea in 1979. In late 1980 Romania called upon the Kremlin leaders to withdraw the Soviet troops from Afghanistan. Despite all this, Romania was never facing a direct intervention, although there were two instances, in 1968 and 1971, where Soviet naval forces were used for the intimidation of Romania (13). Yugoslavia, on the other hand, was subjected to Soviet military pressures soon after the end of January 1948, when <u>Pravda</u> attacked Tito's independent role and his plans for a (con-)federation of Balkan states consisting of Romania, Bulgaria, Greece, Albania and Yugoslavia (14). In the late 1940s and early 1950s Soviet troops on Yugoslavia's border created countless border incidents but ultimately did not invade the country. On the other hand, interventions did take place in East Germany (1953), Hungary (1956) and Czechoslovakia (1968).

Why has the Soviet Union intervened in these cases but not directly in the others? Geography appears to be one variable in explaining Soviet intrabloc interventions. Albania, Romania and Yugoslavia, which managed to shake off Soviet control were all situated on the southern rim, not on the central front with the Western powers. Another factor which is important is that the rule of Communist regimes was not in question in any of these countries, only their loyalty to the Soviet Union. On the other hand, in Hungary, and to a lesser extent in East Germany and in Czechoslovakia, the leading role of the Communist party was at stake in the crises of 1956, 1953 and 1968. Perhaps the crucial factor, however, was the degree of control on their armed forces which local Communist leaders could still exercise within the Soviet military bloc. Christopher Jones has argued rather convincingly that there where local military resistance could be expected on a major scale, such as in Poland in 1956 and in Yugoslavia earlier and in Albania and Romania later, Soviet intervention was effectively deterred. He writes:

> "Tito, Gomulka, Hoxha, Gheorghiu-Dej, and Ceausescu had been able to deter Soviet military interventions by mobilizing regular and paramilitary forces for prolonged resistance to the installation of a pro-Soviet faction of the Communist party. The Yugoslavs and Romanians have institutionalized such mobilizations by adopting strategies of territorial defense. (...) Yugoslav and Romanian military planners seek the following:
> 1. to deny an agressor any collaborators, military or civilian, by branding potential collaborators as traitors, even before the outbreak of war, and by eliminating opportunities for the Soviets to recruit collaborators in the national armed forces;
> 2. to use patriotic appeals to mobilize the entire national population for waging a prolonged war of national liberation; these strategies also expect that military actions of the invading army will actually intensify the popular determination to resist;
> 3. to generate international sympathy and eventually international logistical support for a struggle of national liberation against the Soviet army;
> 4. to provoke a crisis of morale among Soviet soldiers over the course of a long war in which Soviet personnel will conclude that they have been sent to suppress a nation intent on defending its sovereignty. The territorial defense strategies of Yugoslavia and Romania seek to intensify the moral-political strains on Soviet soldiers by forcing them to fight in small units in which the Soviets will lose the psychological and military advantages of their superior numbers and directly experience the hostility of the local population." (15)

Deterrence in this sense was also achieved by the People's Republic of China. Military intervention beyond the border incidents in the 1960s and the nuclear threat to "take out" China's nuclear test sites in Lop Nor (Sinkiang) on August 28, 1969, was apparently never considered by the Soviet Union. Before Sino-Soviet relations became hostile in the early 1960s, the Soviet Union had intervened three times in China: first in Sinkiang on behalf of a secessionist East Turkestan Republic, then in 1950 to "clean up" the last pockets of Nationalists' resistance and then during the Korean War when China was provided with a deterrent air cover by the Soviet airforce. This military intervention can be regarded as a quid pro quo for the willingness of the Chinese Communists to save Stalin's Korean protegé Kim il Sung from defeat in the war with the United States. In addition to air cover and material aid, the Chinese profited little during the Korean War nor were they reimbursed in 1958 during the Taiwan Straits crisis over the islands Quemoy and Matsu when a

Soviet nuclear umbrella was promised too late to make an impact on the outcome of the crisis.

A different category of military intervention by the Soviet Union took place in the Baltic States. There local armed resistance survived an incredibly long period of eight years (much longer than in the Ukraine and Poland in 1946-1947). However, since these small states could not, in the terms of Christopher Jones above, "deny an aggressor collaborators", "generate international sympathy and eventually international logistical support for the struggle of national liberation" or "provoke a crisis of morale among Soviet soldiers" they were doomed to failure.

This leaves us with the recent case of Poland where in December 1980 a Soviet intervention was apparently seriously considered and then cancelled though threatening military manoeuvres in and outside Poland were a recurring theme. Still too little is known to reconstruct the decision-making in the Kremlin in the Polish crisis in the early 1980s. According to Richard D. Anderson, a former CIA analyst, there was a power struggle between "hawks" and "doves" in the Soviet top, who respectively favoured or discouraged direct military intervention. In this interpretation L.I. Brezhnev managed to prevent the victory of the hardliners in the Kremlin after these proved incapable to get the Soviet military intervention machinery into readiness. Anderson writes:

> "The reason for Brezhnev's resurgence probably lies in a factor that was not known in the West until February 1981. A correspondent in Moscow received a report of extraordinary disorders accompanying the mobilization in the Carpathian Military District, one of the three along the Polish frontier. Reservists called up for the crisis had supposedly deserted in numbers too large to punish, and units had moved back and forth in a disorganized fashion. If true, this report explains much. The troubles would strengthen the hand of political leaders opposed to the invasion, since the Soviet army's ability to defeat Polish resistance would be lowered if its troops were unreliable. The troubles would also discredit some advocates of invasion. (...) Brezhnev's countermove was to turn to an alternative group of military experts. (...) By promoting such generals - Petrov, Zaytsev, Govorov, Popkov - Brezhnev converted the Ground Forces headquarters from a center of champions of intervention to a center of opposition to it. (...) In Brezhnev's case, personal interests in the Polish crisis would consistently have favored delaying intervention as long as alternative methods showed any sign of working. Brezhnev's interest in delay can be deduced from reports that Brezhnev had given Kania until the summer of 1981 to restore order - reports which were lent credibility by the Soviet-sponsored coup attempt against Kania in mid-summer and the eventual transition to Jaruzelski." (16)

Brezhnev's decision not to intervene directly might also have had to do with the prospect of a bloody fight with parts of the third largest army in Europe, an army of 317,500 regular troops of which many probably sympathized with Solidarity, the newly-founded independent trade union organization. Yet even if part of the Polish troops would not have fought (or could not have fought due to Soviet control of their munition supplies), the price of direct intervention would have been high. Détente with the West would have become impossible for many years to come. The Siberian pipeline project would have been dead and American grain exports to the USSR unlikely while the Soviet Union would have had to feed the Poles. Most important perhaps, Western banks would no longer have loaned money to the East European countries which would have increased the burden of the Soviet Union to support the failing economies of these countries.

The solution short of actual intervention which finally emerged was elegant for the Soviet Union (though less so for the communist parties in Eastern Europe): the Polish military leadership carried out a self-occupation of Poland with the introduction of Martial Law on December 13, 1981. At the same time the military leadership under W. Jaruzelski unofficially dropped hints that thanks to the introduction of martial law an imminent Soviet military intervention was avoided (17). In the case of Poland, the Brezhnev Doctrine had not to be enforced by the Warsaw Pact. Whether the Soviet Union could have counted on its allies in an occupation of Poland has been questioned by A. Ross Johnson et al.:

> "Multilateral participation in the invasion of Czechoslovakia notwithstanding, the Northern Tier military establishments [Poland, East Germany, Czechoslovakia, AS] may be of dubious utility to the USSR in intra-bloc "policing" actions. The unopposed operations of the Polish and GDR armed forces in the Czechoslovakian invasion created severe morale problems. The Soviets would probably be reluctant to attempt a multilateral suppression of a national uprising in Eastern Europe such as the Hungarian Revolution..." (18)

Such a multilateral intervention was apparently not considered in December 1980. The Hungarians would have been unlikely participants and the East Germans would also have thought twice knowing that while there was a chance that some of the Polish troops would not shoot on the Soviet army, they would certainly have used their limited munition supplies on any German intruders.

What lessons are there in this for the future of Soviet intrabloc interventions? The Soviet military preponderance over its Warsaw Pact members is much more pronounced than in the case of the United States and NATO. (In terms of military expenditures the respective ratios are 10:1 versus 3:2 (19).) From the point of view of military capabilities, the superiority of the USSR is overwhelming, the more so as the Soviet Union enjoys an intrabloc nuclear monopoly. Even if the East European military establishments were stronger in terms of hardware they could probably not challenge the Soviet Union since they have, with the exception of Romania and Yugoslavia, been largely integrated into the Soviet Armed Forces (SAF). T. Rakowska-Harmstone et al. have argued that

> "the Soviet Union has attempted to solve the problem of East European reliability by fragmentating national military forces along service lines, detaching elite and specialized units from

> national control and incorporating these units into a "Greater
> Socialist Army" build around the SAF and under the operational
> control of the Soviet General Staff." (20)

How successful this Soviet attempt has been in undermining potential
East European challenges at achieving greater political autonomy
remains a debatable point. Given the asymmetry in military strength
it is likely that any challenges to Soviet hegemony will take the form
of "peaceful counterrevolution" rather than of armed confrontation.
To such a challenge, there are no perfect military solutions, as the
continuing conflict in Poland in the 1980s indicates.
In terms of frequency, the majority of postwar intrabloc interventions
took place in the periode 1945-1956, with another major eruption in
1968. The 1970s were a period of relative stability until the advent
of the Polish crisis of the early 1980s. This stability was linked to
the increased consumer-orientation of the East European economies
and collapsed when the recession of the capitalist world economy hit
the communist bloc as well (21). Whether the Polish crisis will be
repeated in other East European society will depend to a large extent
on the length of the capitalist recession and the Comecon's ability to
cushion the impact of it on its members' economies. If the East
European economies continue to deteriorate, local Communist elites
will be hard-pressed to find local solutions to their problems. These
might, however, not be tolerated by the Soviet Union. While the goals
of the various communist elites are the same - system reproduction *)
- the interdependence of their economies creates bigger strains for
the smaller national units than for the one of the hegemonic power.
If this is true, only a change of the Soviet system can lead to a
situation where future military interventions within the bloc -
'fraternal solidarity and support' in current Soviet terminology -
become unlikely.

----

*) Zdeněk Mlynář has written:
   "The vicious circle of the development of systems of the soviet
   type until now is caused by the fact that the reproduction of the
   existing (totalitarian) power structure has become practically the
   main goal of the whole process of reproduction of social life, in
   the realm of the economy, social relations and culture in the
   broadest sense of the word. At the moment where the autonomous
   requirements of the reproduction of economic, social or cultural
   relations in the society of a Soviet type endanger the given power
   structure, the political power represses these autonomous
   requirements of society in the name of the preservation of itself.
   If one would like to create an abstract model of the process of
   reproduction in the Soviet systems following the classical method
   of Marx, then the self-reproduction of the totalitarian political
   power as a goal in itself and supreme aim would take the place of
   the goal in itself of capital reproduction." (22)

Interbloc Interventions

Table X summarizes Soviet "interbloc" interventions since 1945.
There has been no direct interbloc armed conflict in the postwar
period. However, there are four episodes of potential or near
interbloc interventions in Europe. The first is the Greek Civil War. In
our case study we could not find evidence of direct Soviet
involvement in terms of the eleven categories of our classification.
Even Stephen T. Hosmer and Thomas W. Wolfe, two keen observers of
Soviet "trespassing", do not go further than saying that "Some
indirect Soviet support was rendered to communist-dominated
guerrillas in Greece" (23). The second episode never became a reality,
if it was ever seriously considered: the sending of Soviet volunteers
to revolutionary Portugal in 1974-1975, for which we only have the
testimony of a high-level Soviet defector, Boris Rabbot. The third
episode is the enormous intensification of Soviet "submarine
diplomacy" against Sweden in the early 1980s, where 59 out of a
total of 143 possible and probable incidents took place in the last
three years of the two decades preceeding 1982 (24). The inclusion of
these provocative intrusions of Soviet submarines into Swedish
territorial waters under the caption "military intervention", depends,
however, on the interpretation of "deployment of special weapons
into forward positions" (category 8, see p. 123). Sweden, of course, is
not part of the NATO bloc and in this sense the inclusion of these
episodes is not correct. If we take bloc not in a broader sense as
meaning Western and pro-Western nations (and include only post-1949
incidents (when NATO was created)), then indeed only two episodes
would fall under it: the Berlin crisis of 1958-1961 and the
non-effectuated threat of a Soviet invasion of Western Europe after
1951. The Berlin crisis was accompanied by nuclear threats. These,
however, fall outside our definition of military intervention unless
they are accompanied by a forward deployment of nuclear weapons.
For the remaining episode, we have only two witnesses (K. Kaplan
and M. Rejman) for the allegation that Stalin actually planned, at one
point, to invade Western Europe. Nevertheless, the fear that the
Soviet Union was and still is eager to overrun Western Europe, looms
large in Western perceptions (25).
This apprehension is fed by the fact that present Soviet military
planning for warfare together with the Warsaw Pact allies is still
based on an advance into Western Europe. A. Ross Johnson et al.
state:

"Doctrinally and organizationally, all Northern Tier countries [of
the WTO, AS] are prepared for one kind of military role:
participation in a rapid, massive, offensive strike into NATO
territory, as postulated in Soviet doctrine. The respective
national military and political leaderships appear committed to
this mission. (...) Soviet "lightning war" strategy may constitute
one of the strongest Soviet levers for ensuring substantial
Northern Tier military participation in a European war. In this
contingency, given Soviet concerns about the reliability of the
East Europeans, it would be to Soviet advantage to minimize
consultation and preparation time and achieve quick multinational

men and women, capable of putting up a fight far surpassing the one of the Afghan resistance.

Those who conjure up the spectre of Soviet military threats to Western Europe therefore usually put it in terms of "Finlandization" rather than outright military attack. One such scenario has been given by Leopold Labedz:

> "The assumption that the Soviet Union is now a status quo power is questionable. In any case it would seem a prudent policy to avoid leading it into temptation. Virtue, in morals and politics, may consist of a chronic lack of opportunity. But such opportunity may arise. If détente leads to American withdrawal from Western Europe, if Western Europe is unable to fill the gap resulting from contraction of American power, thus leaving each West European country to deal with the Soviet Union on a bilateral basis, the road will be open to 'Finlandization' of the whole area." (33)

However, the assumption that Western Europe would, after an American withdrawal into fortress America, be reduced to a series of independent non-aligned states is highly questionable. Nor would France (or even Great Britain) easily give up their nuclear weapon systems in case of American withdrawal. Given the manpower reserves of Western Europe, the replacement of some 360,000 American troops would pose no insurmountable problem either. The defence budgets of Western Europe, taken together, are formidable by any standards. Even the nuclear arsenal of Western Europe, though only a fraction of the one of the superpowers, is sufficient for nuclear retaliation. The French nuclear potential of 120 megatons alone equates the destructive power of about 6,000 'Hiroshimas' and the submarine-based part of the French 'force de frappe' is quite invulnerable to a Soviet first strike (34).

Ideologically, the attraction of a Soviet-style Communism has practically disappeared among West European workers and intellectuals. Communist parties as fifth columns of Soviet Communism in Western Europe have become relatively insignificant, their support having been eroded with each new Soviet military intervention in Eastern Europe. After World War II Stalin (together with G.C. Marshall) was, in a sense, the father of Western Europe in that the perceived Soviet threat contributed to European integration. It is, in our view, unduly pessimistic to assume that in a second Cold War European political will would crumble rather than stiffen in the face of Soviet military threats. That, at least, has been the message of the changed mood in Sweden, after its experience of Soviet aerial and submarine provocations in the early 1980s. The subordination of European security interests to Soviet pressures is not something which the majority of the West European public feels inclined to according to opinion surveys (see Table XI).

Table XI :Soviet Domination Versus War (35)

Question: "Some people say that war is so horrible that it is better
to accept Russian domination than to risk war. Others say
it would be better to fight in defence of your country than
to accept Russian domination. Which opinion is closer to
your own?"

Percent in Favor in Each Country

Option	UK	GFR	FR	IT	USA
Better to accept domination	12	19	13	17	6
Better to fight	75	74	57	48	83
Don't know	13	7	30	35	11

'Finlandization', of course, is not so much meant to signify a
conscious choice than a state of affairs.
It has been said that 'Finlandization' has the following
characteristics:

"1. Responsiveness in foreign policy to Soviet preferences;
2. avoidance of alliance with countries deemed by the Soviet
Union to be competitors or rivals;
3. acceptance of neutrality in peace or war;
4. abstention from membership in regional and international
groupings considered unfriendly by Moscow;
5. restraint over the media in one's country to muffle or
minimize criticism of the USSR, so as to avoid possible
provocation;
6. compensatory gestures in commercial and cultural contacts
with the USSR, extending to treaties and diplomatic
consultations, to offset disparities in the relationship with
the USSR, on the one hand, and West European countries, on
the other;
7. openness to penetration by Soviet ideas and media." (36)

It is hard to see that Western Europe is presently showing major signs
of any of these seven deadly sins of 'Finlandization'. The Soviet
Union and Western Europe have some parallel interests - such as the
avoidance of war in Europe - and these should not be misunderstood
as responsiveness to Soviet preference. If some Europeans are no
longer ardent Atlanticists but plead for a European defence effort of
their own, this can make sense in its own right and ought not to be
interpreted automatically as a Soviet success in detaching Europe
from America. As to some other points: there is no sign that Western
European media observe the kind of self-censorship with regard to
anti-Soviet information which is supposedly characteristic for Finland.
The openness of Western Europe to Soviet ideas and media is
practically nil when compared to the United States influence and if
there is a penetration of ideas across the Iron Curtain subverting the
dominant ideology it is going the other way. The 'Finlandization'
metaphor is, in our view, not an accurate description of the present

climate in Western Europe, a political climate which is neither "neutralist" nor "pacifist" (37). Hannes Adomeit has also concluded that no country of the European Community can be said to have fulfilled any of the seven characteristics of "remote control" captured under the label 'Finlandization' (38). It can even be doubted whether the Soviet Union, after abandoning the hope of seeing Western Europe turning communist because of growing Communist parties' strength, is pursuing a strategy of 'Finlandization'. Klaus von Beyme has, in his analysis of the role of the Soviet Union in world politics, pointed out that "it has not been possible to prove the existence of a unitary strategy of Finlandization with regard to Western Europe" (39).

Despite increased tensions, the likelihood of a Soviet interbloc intervention on the central European front seems remote. In the 1950s and early 1960s, Soviet-American confrontations in the Third World, notably over Cuba, made a Soviet military reaction in Europe more likely than today. At that time the USSR did not yet possess the means to project its military power to more distant shores. Today, a Soviet-American duel in the Persian Gulf or in the Pakistan-Afghanistan region might be fought out between the superpowers locally while all remains quiet on the central Western front.

Extrabloc Interventions

Table XII summarizes Soviet extrabloc interventions since 1945.

After Soviet pressure against Iran and Turkey and a claim to ex-Italian colonies in the immediate postwar period came to nothing, it was not until the mid-1950s that the USSR started to make inroads again in the Third World. If we look at the geographic distribution of Soviet military interventions, the prominence of the Middle East is obvious. Asia is second, followed by Africa and tailed by Latin America. If we look at the depth of Soviet military involvement over the past thirty years, there is a clear progression from covert arms sales through third parties (Czechoslovakia) in the cases of Israel (1948) and Guatemala (1954), to overt arms sales in the case of Egypt (1955) to threat of intervention by "volunteers" (Suez, 1956), to demonstrative exercises in areas adjacent to Middle East countries (Syria 1957, Lebanon-Iraq 1958). In the 1960s we see a progression from troop transports for belligerents in the Congo (1960/61) and in North Yemen (1962), to the provision of arms in ongoing conflicts (Algeria-Moroccan war 1963, Biafran war 1967-70). We also see combat participation of Soviet pilots in North Yemen, Egypt, and probably also in the Sudan. In the 1970s the Soviet navy enters the picture, providing protection to Guinea and India in their conflicts with American allies. The transport of troops of third parties by sea and air (Moroccan, South Yemeni, Cuban, Vietnamese) becomes more frequent and in the case of Ethiopia the Soviet Union even takes charge of the battlefield command of such troops. While direct Soviet combat troop intervention was threatened in the Arab-Israeli wars of 1967 and 1973, it finally became a reality in 1979 when Soviet airborne troops and special assault teams took control of Kabul while

Table XII : A Survey of Soviet Extrabloc Military Interventions Since 1945

Type of Intervention	Suez '56	Congo '60	Laos '60-'61	Indonesia '61	Cuba '62	North Yemen '62-'70	Algerian-Moroccan War '63	June War '67	Nigeria '67-'70	Canal War '70	Sudan '70-'71	Jordan '70	Guinea '70	Sri Lanka '71	Bangladesh '71	Dhofar '73	October War '73	Syria '73-	Iraq '74-'75	Angola '74-	Ethiopia '77-	Kampuchea '79	Yemen '79	Afghanistan '79	China-Vietnam '79
1. Peacetime stationing of troops as deterrent against 3rd parties					+																				
2. Providing body guards and palace guards to local government																									
3. Military mission at headquarters for planning local operations					+?						??							??		??	+	?	??	+	
4. Combat participation of foreign special forces (tank operators, pilots, radar, etc.)			(+)		+			+	+?				+?				+?	??		+	?			+	
5. "Volunteers" serving in combat	!																								
6. "Regular troops" engaged in combat							!										!							+	
7. Providing naval or air protection in or near combat zone					?				+				(+)							?	?				
8. Mobilization, troops movements in border areas, deployment of special weapons into forward positions				+				+							+			+	+						
9. Special weapons' supplies during combat phase							(+)		(+)						+			+	+	+	+				+
10. Armed blockades to prevent weapons reaching opponent of supported parties																									
11. Providing logistics (air and naval transport) for combatants		+	+		+?										+	+		+		+	+	+		+	+

Legend: + = verified; +? = probable but not verified; ? = possible; ?? = doubtful; ! = threat of intervention; (+) = not fully in accordance with definition one tank division and four mechanized divisions crossed the borders into Afghanistan.

This gradual but steady increase of Soviet military extrabloc activism has caused apprehension. Trotsky's dictum (often wrongly attributed to Lenin) that "the international situation is evidently shaping in such a way that the road to Paris and London lies via the towns of Afghanistan, the Punjab and Bengal" (40) is sometimes recalled with the implication that there is some grand design behind Soviet military interventions in the Third World. Some voices speak of "an ominous new pattern of Soviet aggressiveness", of a "total offensive against imperialism and world capitalism as a whole in order to do away with them" (41). Other observers cannot detect a Communist master plan underlying Soviet military activity abroad. They see these moves more as products of "low risks, and opportunities provided by previous Western mistakes, defeats, or (as in Afghanistan) indifference" (42).

Two schools of thought thus have emerged: one which attributed a 'grand design' to Soviet policy and one which sees the Soviet Union as moving into the Third World only when there are "targets of opportunity".

Any assessment of the Soviet military role in the Third World has to take into account that some of Russia's activities are no different from that of other great powers and would be no different if the Soviet Union were a "capitalist" state. The special interest which the Soviet Union takes in the Middle East is comparable to the one of the United States in Central America and to grant legitimate involvement to one of the superpowers but not the other is somewhat hypocritical. An explanation of and apology for Western involvement in terms of defence against communist subversion is often unwarranted if the local events are studied in their sequence. A case in point is Guatemala where in 1952 a land reform programme touched the interests of the North-American United Fruit Company. The conflict between the government of Guatemala and the United Fruit Company was translated into one between "Communism against the right of property, the life and security of the western hemisphere", as the president of United Fruit put it (43). When Guatemala bought arms from Czechoslovakia in 1954 (after the United States had refused to sell) this was taken as pretext to overthrow the Guatemalan government by a CIA-organized intervention in June 1954.

An evaluation of Soviet military policy in the Third World varies in accordance with the legitimate role one is prepared to grant the Soviet Union in the Third World and the one one is assigning to the major Western powers. The French government, for instance, intervened twelve times militarily in Africa with its own troops within four years (in the period 1960-1964) and today still maintains troops and/or advisors in more than a dozen African republics (44). This is often viewed differently than when a non-Western nation intervenes. If French troops overthrow the ruler of the Central African Republic, Emperor Jean Bedel Bokassa, and replace him with his cousin, David Dacka, and continue to station troops in the country, this is generally judged differently than when the Soviet Union replaces one communist ruler in Afghanistan with another. When the French and the United States airlift troops from Morocco,

Senegal, Togo and the Ivory Coast to save their client Mobutu in
Zaire (45) this is seen differently from similar undertakings by the
Soviet Union and Cuba.

If one is prepared to grant legitimacy to interventions on the basis of
geographic and historical factors, American interventions in Central
America and French ones in Africa are more 'legitimate' than Soviet
interventions. However, by the same token, one can also "legitimize"
Soviet intervention in Afghanistan by pointing out that both under
the Czar and under Stalin Russian troops had intervened there. Soviet
apprehension about an imminent regime change in Kabul in 1979 was
perhaps not more neurotic than American apprehension with
developments in Nicaragua, following the overthrow of the Somoza
dynasty in the same year. Soviet interest in the Mediterranean can be
compared to American interest in the Caribbean. The desire to break
out of the Black Sea, to have control over the Bosporus has
preoccupied Russia since Catherine the Great and there was nothing
new when Stalin demanded bases in Turkey after the Second World
War. The Soviet desire to stay in Iran after the Second World War II
and to exploit the oil resources of the country was to some extent
comparable to the Anglo-American interest. After the Soviet Union
withdrew its troops from Northern Iran, the Soviet oil concessions
were distributed between the British and the Americans and the
country became, for more than three decades, a Western satellite
(46). In the case of Romania, where the Western powers also had
significant oil investments Stalin, on the other hand, prevailed,
despite a coup attempt supported by Americans in the Allied Control
Mission in August 1945 (47). What made Soviet control different from
Western control was that it signified total control, not just market
control. It was much more visible and also less reversible.

However, if we move away from the immediate southern rim of the
Soviet Union from Romania over Iran to Afghanistan and turn to the
role of the Soviet Union in the Third World in general, it is difficult
to find a similar Soviet ability for control. A look at the genesis of
Soviet involvement in more distant Third World regions and countries
shows that local actors, generally in conflict with major Western
powers or regional rival powers, appealed to the Soviet Union for
military assistance, usually after first having tried in vain to obtain
Western assistance. In some instances, but by no means in all, the
Soviet Union provided such assistance and in a few instances the
resulting military relationship led to request for military
interventions. In the Middle East, the main arena of Soviet extrabloc
military interventions, the arming of opponents and rivals of Egypt by
the Western powers made President Nasser turn to the Soviet Union.
The dynamics of the Arab-Israeli conflict and Nasser's own "Vietnam"
in North Yemen brought the Soviet Union to military interventions.
When Egypt decided to switch alliances in 1972 and 1976, the Soviet
Union was unceremoniously told to go home and excluded from the
settlement in the Middle East between Egypt and Israel. Stefan
Kaplan has once said with regard to the Soviet role in the Third
World that "the status of the Soviet Union typically is not that of
imperial overlord but that of guest worker" (48).

As Table XIV indicates, the Soviet Union has a considerable number of military "guest workers" abroad, but so have other nations. Since its first arms deals in the late 1940s and early 1950s, the Soviet Union has built up a Third World military market second to none (see Table XIII).

Table XIII: Soviet Weapon Deliveries to Non-Socialist Countries, 1976-1980 (in millions of dollars, rounded figures)

Africa:		Latin America:	
Algeria	1,800	Peru	900
Angola	550		
Benin	20	Asia:	
Burundi	10	Afghanistan	450
Cape Verde	50	Bangladesh	20
Chad	5	India	2,300
Congo	60	Pakistan	20
Equatorial Guinea	10	Sri Lanka	10
Ethiopia	1,900		
Guinea	50	Middle East:	
Guinea-Bissau	30	Egypt	20
Libya	5,500	Iran	625
Madagascar	60	Iraq	5,000
Mali	110	North Yemen	625
Morocco	5	South Yemen	775
Mozambique	180	Syria	5,400
Nigeria	90	Other	50
Somalia	150		
Sudan	10		
Tanzania	320		
Uganda	40		
Zambia	220		

Source: U.S. Arms Control and Disarmament Agency. Publication 115, World Military Expenditures and Arms Transfers 1971-1980, March 1983, Table III, pp. 117-120; as quoted in Erik Dirksen. Economische en militaire hulp van de Sovjetunie aan de Derde Wereld. Internationale Spectator, Vol. 37 (1983) no. 7 (July), p. 445.

While the provision of arms has given the Soviet Union access to the Third World, these arms did in most instances not mean lasting influence. What is remarkable is how many Third World nations have switched from one supplier to another. Influence gained through the provision of arms has often been only temporary. Patron-client relationships between the Soviet Union and extra-bloc nations have turned sour and for reasons of state or as a result of regime changes, Third World nations have not infrequently switched sides in the bipolar world of the Cold War. In a few cases nations have switched from one alignment to non-alignment or vice versa. Michael Kidron

Table XIV: Foreign Military (Technicians, Advisers, Troops) Stationed Outside Europe, 1982-83 (33)

Country	USA	FRANCE	UK	USSR	CUBA	GDR	Others
Middle East:							
Saudi Arabia	520						
Egypt	180						
Oman	some						
Iraq				450+	2,200		
Syria				7,000	210		
North Yemen				750			
South Yemen				750	800	325	
Libya				2,300	300	1,600	
Cyprus			some				
Lebanon							50,000 (Syria), 90,000 (Israel)
Iran				100-200			
Africa:							
Somalia	some						
Ethiopia				1,700	5,900		
Angola				700	25,000	450	
Algeria				8,500	170	250	
Mozambique				500	1,000	100	
Namibia							50,000 (South Africa)
Benin				1,200			
Congo-Brazzaville				850	950		
Guinea				350	280	125	
Guinea-Bissau				600			
Mali				630			
Madagascar				370			
Tanzania				300			
Ghana			150				
Zimbabwe			380				200 (North Korea), 100 (China)
Centr. African Rep.			950				
Chad		some					some (Libya)
Djibouti		3,500					
Gabun		500					
Ivory Coast		450					
Mauretania		110					
Senegal		600					
Zaire		100					100 (Belgium)
Uganda							1,000 (Tanzania)
Western Sahara							21,000 (Morocco)
Malawi							100 (South Africa)
Latin America:							
Cuba	2,250			7,400			
Puerto Rico	2,940						
Belize			some				
Panama	9,150						
Peru	175						
Falklands			5,000				
Nicaragua				100	2,000		
Antigua	120						
Asia:							
Diego Garcia	1,840						
Guam	8,680						
South Korea	37,560						
Philippines	15,050						
Japan	50,450						
Thailand	100						
Australia	700						
Afghanistan				120,000	100		
India				200			
Kambodia				300			150,000 (Vietnam)
Vietnam				2,500			
Brunei			some				
Hongkong			7,000				
Laos				500			40,000 (Vietnam)
Various Territories:							
Ascencion	2,200		some				
Mayotte		some					
Réunion		some					
Bermuda	some						

and Dan Smith have identified no less than 28 switchers in this sense
(see Table X V).

Table X V: War Proneness of Countries, according to Cold War
            Orientation (49)

Cold War Orientation (mid-1982)	Involved in Foreign Wars, Average Number of Wars, 1945-1982	Average Years at War (Civil and Others), 1945-1982
Core East (11 nations)	Involved in 1.73 foreign wars (8 out of 11 involved)	9 years (10 out of 11 involved)
Core West (20 nations)	Involved in 4.05 foreign wars (13 out of 20 involved)	9.6 years (15 out of 20 involved)
Non-Aligned (18 nations)	Involved in 0.77 foreign wars (8 out of 18 involved)	11 years (14 out of 18 involved)
Pro-East (10 nations)	Involved in 0.9 foreign wars (5 out of 10 involved)	16.7 years (10 out of 10 involved)
Pro-West (88 nations)	Involved in 0.4 foreign wars (18 out of 88 involved)	6.5 years (69 out of 88 involved)
"Switchers" (East to West or vice versa, also from Non-aligned to East or West or vice versa; 28 nations)	Involved in 1.14 foreign wars (17 out of 28 involved)	14 years (27 out of 28 involved)

While arms have not been the only bond linking Third World nations
to the great industrial powers, they have been the main ones for the
Soviet Union. The Center for Defense Information in Washington, D.C.
has looked at the Soviet Union's gains and losses in the postwar
period in global terms and has come up with a chronological table
that demonstrates that there is little stability in Soviet advances in
the Third World (see Table XVI).

Table XVI: Gains and Losses for the Soviet Union 1945-1979

	Mongolia	Albania Bulgaria East Germany Poland Romania Yugoslavia	North Korea	Hungary	Czechoslovakia	China		
Gains		1945	1946	1947	1948	1949	1950	1951
Losses					Yugoslavia			

	Mongolia	Albania group	North Korea	Hungary	Syria	China	Indonesia Iraq	Guinea
Gains	1952	1953	1954	1955	1956	1957	1958	1959
Losses							Syria	

	Ghana Mali		Yemen (Sana)	Algeria		Vietnam	Syria	Egypt
Gains	1960	1961	1962	1963	1964	1965	1966	1967
Losses	China	Albania Guinea	Indonesia	Iraq		Algeria	Ghana	

	Congo Iraq	Cuba Somalia Sudan		Guinea India	Bangladesh		Libya	Angola Laos Mozambique
Gains	1968	1969	1970	1971	1972	1973	1974	1975
Losses	Mali	North Korea Yemen (Sana)		Sudan	Egypt			Bangladesh

		Ethiopia	Afghanistan Yemen (Aden)	Cambodia	
Gains	1976	1977	1978	1979	1980
Losses		Guinea India Somalia	Iraq		

Source: The Defense Monitor, Vol. IX (1980) no. 1 (January), p. 24.

While Table XVI indicates a greater number of gains than losses for the Soviet Union, the situation changes if weights are attached to the units and those outside the calculus are considered. In 1945 the Soviet Union had a significant influence in 7 other countries out of a total of 74 countries. In 1980 there was Soviet influence in 19 countries out of a total of 155 according to calculations from the Center for Defense Information (50). The high point of Soviet influence was 1958, when the Soviet Union had not yet "lost" China. At that moment, it controlled, again according to the Center for Defense Information, 31 percent of the world's population and 9 percent of the world's GNP, not counting its own. In 1979, however, the percentage was down to 6 percent of the world population and 5 percent of its GNP, again excluding the Soviet Union's own share in it. Basing itself on the power rating method developed by Ray Cline (a former Deputy Director of Intelligence for the CIA) the Center found that at the end of the 1970s, the pro-Soviet camp (including the Soviet Union) held 20 percent of the Balance of World Power, with the pro-Western countries and China accounting for 70 percent, leaving the rest of the accounted nations, including India, with a remaining total of 10 percent (51).

In the light of such figures, it is difficult to take seriously alarmist views that the Soviet Union is about to cut off the West from the resources of the Third World. Given the often violent process of decolonialization and the charges of Third World nations against the terms of trade imposed on them by the West, it is in fact amazing that not more than 35 out of 155 nations have been at one time or another under significant Soviet influence. The strength of nationalism in these new nations which made them originally turn against Western domination is, however, also a force directed against potential Soviet domination. Having gained a measure of sovereignty after long struggles, it is not likely that most of these nations will throw themselves in the arms of the Soviet Union.

This, of course, is no answer to the question what the Soviet Union wants in the Third World. One Soviet official claimed for his country "an equal right to meddle in Third Areas" (57). Phrased in more ideological terms, the Soviet Defence Minister, Marshall Andrei A. Grechko, put it this way in 1974:

> "at the present state the historic function of the Soviet Armed Forces is not restricted to their function in defending our Motherland and the other socialist countries. In its foreign policy activity the Soviet state purposefully opposes the export of counter-revolution and the policy of oppression, supports the struggle for national liberation, and resolutely resists imperialist aggression in whatever distant region of our planet it may appear." (53)

The language of this statement mirrors the one of the Truman Doctrine of 1947:

> "One of the primary objectives of the foreign policy of the United States is the creation of conditions in which we and other nations will be able to work out a way of life free from coercion. (...) I believe that it must be the policy of the United States to support free peoples who are resisting attempted subjugation by armed minorities or by outside pressures." (54)

The Truman Doctrine of containment of Communism has led to situations of American interventions, whose purpose it was, in the words of Raymond Aron, "to uphold a government favourable to the institutions and ideologies of the United States, even against the people's aspirations" (55). Soviet interventions in Egypt, Iraq and Sudan have been in support of regimes whose internal policy was one of suppressing communists. The world today is one of, roughly, 25 democracies, 20 communist states and 100 authoritarian states, most of the latter in the Third World (56). The stability of the authoritarian regimes is likely to remain shaky due to multiple factors. In this situation the superpowers (and increasingly, also regional powers) will be either invited or tempted to intervene on the side of the tottering regimes or the armed insurgents. Where strategic locations or crucial resources are at stake, interventions to secure these, or to deny these to the other side, will be likely. The renewed commitment to global competition of the superpowers in the

1980s, combined with the ambitions of unstable local actors, make for a gloomy future, as Stanley Hoffmann has pointed out:

> "The collision of the two trends gives one a major reason for pessimism (in addition to the reasons provided by mutual misperceptions and internal developments in the two super-powers): the ability now of clients or proxies to manipulate super-powers or to provoke confrontations. The biggest peril lies in 'grey areas' in which uncertainty exists about the extent of a superpower's commitment to an ally or friend and about the other's likely response." (57)

It is the volatile blend of attractive local actors and geopolitic opportunities rather than a Soviet grand design for world domination which, in our view, lies at the basis of future Soviet military interventions outside its own bloc.

Conclusion: The Soviet Union - expansionist or not?

According to our findings (see table XVII), the Soviet Union has intervened militarily 44 times in the postwar period. (This count excludes mere threats, cases labelled doubtful or not fully in accordance with the definitions of table V, and double countings due to overlap between intra-, inter- and extrabloc interventions.) In the

Table XVII:Soviet Military Interventions in the Postwar Period, according to Periods and Locations

	Intrabloc (+ China)	Interbloc (+ extra-bloc with strong interbloc overtones)	Extrabloc	Total
1945-1955	13	2	0	15
1955-1965	3	5	3	11
1965-1980	5	0	13	18
Total	21	7	16	44

period 1945-1955 most interventions took place within the (emerging) Soviet bloc. Most extrabloc interventions took place after 1965. Interbloc interventions (or extrabloc ones with strong interbloc overtones) were most frequent in the period 1955-1965. This count is probably incomplete and in the absence of comparable data for the other intervening powers in the postwar period, its significance is difficult to assess. Nevertheless, it is safe to say that the Soviet Union, with such an intervention record, has been a highly active military participant of the international system.

In the international system there are a number of states which are hyperactive. In their struggle for survival against inimical surroundings they have built up so much military power that their original inferiority turned into great strength and became a source of insecurity for their neighbours. Cuba and Vietnam are such hyperactive states and so is Israel today. The Soviet Union also became such a state after the October Revolution of 1917. As the first organized opposition to capitalist society on the level of state, it started its existence under the onslaught of local counterrevolution and imperialist intervention, first by Germany and her allies and then by the Entente and her allies. It was not the rising of the toiling masses in the capitalist countries which secured the survival of socialism in one country but the bayonets of the Red Army. The instrument of military power which had formed the basis of the Czarist empire also became the foundation of the Soviet Union.

When the world revolution failed to materialize after the First World War and the Soviet Union was once more subject to foreign intervention - this time by Poland - the opportunity arose in the counteroffensive to "carry the revolution abroad" and to recover the territorial losses suffered in the peace with the German imperialists at Brest-Litovsk. The attempt to defeat Poland failed according to L. Trotsky and M.N. Tukachevsky mainly through the military blunders of the political commissar J.V. Stalin (58).

In the Second World War Stalin obtained a second chance to restore the empire and to carry the revolution abroad. Russia had emerged stronger than ever from this fourth foreign intervention in 25 years and with a few exceptions (northern Iran, the Danish island of Bornholm) Stalin was able to hold his territorial gains. In addition he made claims to military bases on Spitzbergen and on the Dardanelles and demanded a share in the Italian colonies. This he did not get but his appetite created apprehension among his neighbours as well as among the other great powers. With Stalin's death this apprehension diminished. China and Finland were given back naval bases, Austria was released from occupation, the territorial claims on Turkey were dropped. A decrease in international tension, however, proved to be very problematical for the post-Stalinist leaders in the Kremlin and in Eastern Europe.

After the uprisings in Germany, Poland and Hungary, tensions were reestablished over the status of Berlin. Another arena for interbloc conflict waging opened with the process of decolonization in the Third World. For the Soviet Union it offered an opportunity to weaken the position of the Western powers. From the mid-1950s onwards the Soviet Union began to direct an increasing flow of arms into the Third World. Later the "support for national liberation movements" even became codified in the new Soviet constitution of 1977. It gained ideological importance for the Soviet leadership in that it could be presented as a contemporary expression of "proletarian internationalism" even when the class basis of these movements was rarely proletarian. Gradually this military assistance for liberation movements and endangered anti-Western Third World regimes has led the Soviet Union to military interventions of an indirect type.

If we look closely at the genesis of these interventions in the Middle East as well as in Angola and Ethiopia, it is quite clear that the pull factors of local actors rather than an active forward thrust of the Soviet Union stood at the basis of these interventions. Where there were low-risk opportunities in the Third World, the Soviet leaders have generally responded to local intervention requests. Only in the case of Cuba is it likely that the stationing of missiles was an initiative of N. Khrushchev rather than F. Castro. This has so far been the only high-risk operation of the Soviet Union in the Third World and Khrushchev was subsequently removed from office because of his unpredictable gambling. The possibility of nuclear war has been clearly realized by the Soviet Union and forms an element of caution in its military policies. However, this caution has also been one reason why the East-West conflict has been increasingly fought out in the Third World and with the help of third actors. Détente has been interpreted by the Soviet Union as not incompatible with the support of "liberation movements", and also as not incompatible with continued ideological confrontation. It would seem that the continuing tension of the confrontation with the capitalist world has become a necessity for the Soviet power holders in that it legitimizes their rule at home and in Eastern Europe. In that sense, what Richard Lowenthal has written in the early 1970s is still to the point:

> "However convinced the present Soviet leaders are of the need for "peaceful coexistence", i.e. for controlling the forms of their conflict with the West in the interest of their own survival, they are equally convinced of the need for maintaining the conflict itself in the interest of maintaining their power at home. (...)
> The Soviet Union today, then is no longer a revolutionary power committed by its ideology to the struggle for world domination, but neither is it a satisfied power concerned only with its own security to the exclusion of specific ideological motives. It is a world power committed by its ideology to regard a state of hostile tension with the non-Communist World as natural and inevitable, and to interpret its security in the framework of global rivalry with the United States. In that sense, a Soviet policy of global expansion still exists; and its motivation still includes a specific ideological component, and will continue to include it so long as the nature of the party regime at home does not undergo a major change." (59)

The burning question today is whether the next generation of Soviet leaders will be able to develop the kind of pragmatism of Mao Zedong's successors. The new Chinese leaders have openly admitted that Marx, Engels and Lenin are "out of date" when it comes to solving some of their contemporary problems (60).
There is, at present, little reason for hoping for early changes. The Soviet Union has reached the year 1984 unchanged and change is not likely to come from the outside. The outside Western world is, by its existence alone, perceived as a threat by the Soviet leaders and would be considered as a constant challenge even if it were unarmed. A regime like the one of the Soviet Union where a continuously ruling party claims a monopoly of "truth" is bound to feel threatened by societies where open criticism of their own and other societies is accepted and even welcomed and where various parties compete with

each other for offering the population alternative roads to social improvement.

For the present Soviet leaders the Western democracies form an ideological, not a military threat. In this regard history has taken an ironic turn. When the Soviet Union came into existence the situation was reversed: the first Soviet republic formed an ideological challenge to the warring imperialist powers. Today it is the almost seventy year old Soviet Union which has major ideological and imperial problems. The promises of Communism - an end to war and exploitation - have not been realized among and within the socialist countries. The Soviet Union's achievement of having become a military power of the first order is not one which appears to have enhanced its leaders' sense of security. Their insecurity is our insecurity.

NOTES

Notes to Introduction

1) Based on League of Nations figures on military budgets in the 1930s, as refered to in: Ruth Leger Sivard, World Military and Social Expenditures 1983, Washington, D.C., World Priorities, 1983, p. 7. - The figures for Germany might be too low due to evasion of Versailles Treaty obligations and the resulting cover-up.
2) Sipri figures for 1983 at 1980 prices and exchange rates. - Stockholm International Peace Research Institute (Sipri), The arms Race and Arms Control 1984 (The shorter Sipri yearbook), London: Taylor and Francis, 1984, p. 88, Appendix 3A.

Notes to Chapter 1: Intrabloc Conflicts: Eastern Europe and the Special Case of China

1) Zdeněk Mylnář, Nachtfrost. Erfahrungen auf dem Weg vom realen zum menschlichen Sozialismus, Köln: Europäische Verlagsanstalt, 1978, pp. 300-301.
2) Ladislaus Singer, Sowjet-Imperialismus, Stuttgart: Seewald, 1970, pp. 136, 150.
3) Royal Institute of International Affairs, The Soviet-Yugoslav Dispute, London, 1948, p. 38; c. 38; cit. Christopher Civiic, Soviet-East European Relations, in: R. Pipes (Ed.), Soviet Strategy in Europe, New York: Crane, Russak & Co., 1976, p. 114; Milovan Djilas, Conversations With Stalin, New York: Harcourt, Brace & World, 1962, p. 114.
4) Martin McCauley (Ed.), Communist Power in Europe, 1944-1949, London: Macmillan, 1977, p. xii; Siegfried Kogelfranz, '"So weit die Armeen kommen..." Wie Osteuropa nach Jalta kommunistisch wurde', Der Spiegel (Hamburg), Vol. 38 (1984) no. 35 (August 27), p. 108.
5) Malcolm Mackintosh, Stalin's Policies towards Eastern Europe, 1939-1948: The General Picture, in: Thomas T. Hammond (Ed.), The Anatomy of Communist Takeovers, New Haven: Yale University Press, 1975, pp. 234-235; Peter Calvocoressi, World Politics Since 1945, London: Longman, 1982, p. 117.
6) S. Kogelfranz, op. cit. (note 4), No. 36, p. 170.
7) A.Z. Rubinstein, Soviet Foreign Policy Since World War II: Imperial and Global, Cambridge, Mass.: Winthrop Publ., 1981, pp. 56-58; Christopher D. Jones, Soviet Influence in Eastern Europe. Political Autonomy and the Warsaw Pact, New York: Praeger, 1981, pp. 65-67.

8) David Irving, Uprising, London: Hodder and Stoughton, 1981, pp. 34-36.
9) Daniel Yergin, Shattered Peace: The Origin of the Cold War and the National Security State, Harmondsworth: Pelican, 1980, p. 312.
10) Nikolai Tolstoy, Stalin's Secret War, London: Pan Books, 1981, p. 268.
11) Idem, p. 267.
12) P. Calvocoressi, op. cit. (note 5), p. 119; S. Kogelfranz, op. cit. (note 4), No. 37, p. 181.
13) Nissan Oren, A Revolution Administered: The Sovietization of Bulgaria, in: Th.T. Hammond (Ed.), op. cit. (note 5), pp. 337-338.
14) N. Tolstoy, op. cit. (note 10), p. 220.
15) D.C. Watt, Frank Spender, Neville Brown, A History of the World in the Twentieth Century, London: Hodder and Stoughton, 1967, p. 632; N. Tolstoy, op. cit. (note 10), pp. 354-356.
16) David Kirby, The Baltic States 1940-1950, in: M. McCauley (Ed.), op. cit. (note 4), pp. 31-32.
17) Idem, p. 32.
18) M. Mackintosh, op. cit. (note 5), pp. 238-239.
19) Anthony Upton, Finland, in: M. McCauley (Ed.), op. cit. (note 4), p. 148.
20) Adam Ulam, Stalin, the Man and his Era, London: A. Lane, 1974, p. 594; cit. Ch. Civiic, op. cit. (note 3), p. 113; Isaac Deutscher, Stalin. Vol. II, Hilversum: C. de Boer, Jr./Paul Brand, 1963, p. 155.
21) Cit. A.Z. Rubinstein, op. cit. (note 7), p. 42.
22) Vladimir V. Kusin, Czechoslovakia, in: M. McCauley, op. cit. (note 4), p. 77.
23) Philip Selznick, The Organizational Weapon. A Study of Bolshevik Strategy and Tactics, New York: McGraw-Hill, 1952, p. 270n.
24) Idem, pp. 265-267.
25) S. Kogelfranz, op. cit. (note 4), No. 39, p. 194.
26) D. Yergin, op. cit. (note 9), p. 344n.
27) V.V. Kusin, op. cit. (note 4), p. 81.
28) Pavel Tigrid, The Prague Coup of 1948: The Elegant Takeover, in: Th.T. Hammond (Ed.), op. cit. (note 5), p. 414; S. Kogelfranz, op. cit. (note 4), No. 39, p. 204.
29) Idem, pp. 421-424; S. Kogelfranz, op. cit. (note 4), No. 39, p. 206.
30) Cit. ibid., p. 429; S. Kogelfranz, op. cit. (note 4), No. 39, p. 204.
31) Cit. D. Yergin, op. cit. (note 9), pp. 349-350.
32) Cit. P. Tigrid, op. cit. (note 5), p. 429; cit. S. Kogelfranz, op. cit. (note 4), No. 39, p. 206.
33) D. Yergin, op. cit. (note 9), p. 348; Joseph Josten, 'Kampf ohne Waffen', Beiträge für Konfliktforschung, (1972) no. 4, p. 121, as quoted in Heinz Vetschera, Soziale Verteidigung - Ziviler Widerstand - Immerwährende Neutralität, Wien: Universität, 1974, p. 28 (mimeo).
34) D. Yergin, op. cit. (note 9), p. 354.
35) Cit. S. Kogelfranz, op. cit. (note 4), Nos. 39, 35, pp. 199, 111.
36) D. Yergin, op. cit. (note 9), p. 344n.

37) Ethics and Morals in Hungarian Public Life, in: Imre Nagy, On Communism, New York: Praeger, 1957, cit. in: Christopher D. Jones, 'Soviet Hegemony in Eastern Europe: The Dynamics of Political Autonomy and Military Intervention', World Politics, 29 (1976-77), p. 224.
38) Ch.D. Jones, op. cit. (note 37), p. 229.
39) Jiri Valenta, 'Soviet Options in Poland', Survival, Vol 23 (1981), no. 2, p. 54; Information from ex-Polish government official, provided by M. Leitenberg.
40) Ch.D. Jones, op. cit. (note 7), pp. 68-69; Stephen S. Kaplan, Diplomacy of Power. Soviet Armed Forces as a Political Instrument, Washington, D.C.: Brookings Institution, 1981, pp. 77-78.
41) This interpretation is based on Ch.D. Jones, op. cit. (note 37), p. 241n.
42) P. Calvocoressi, op. cit. (note 5), p. 140.
43) Ch.D. Jones, op. cit. (note 37), p. 233; J. Valenta, op. cit. (note 39), pp. 115-117.
44) Ch.D. Jones, op. cit. (note 37), pp. 221-223.
45) Ch.D. Jones, op. cit. (note 37), p. 240; in Ch.D. Jones, op. cit. (note 7), p. ix.
46) Stephen T. Hosmer and Thomas W. Wolfe, Soviet Policy and Practice toward Third World Conflicts, Lexington, Mass.: D.C. Heath, 1983, pp. 5-6.
47) A.Z. Rubinstein, op. cit. (note 7), pp. 61-63.
48) Idem, pp. 124-125.
49) S. Kogelfranz, op. cit. (note 4), No. 35, pp. 113-114.
50) These points have been stressed by Z. Brzezinski, as quoted in S. Kogelfranz, op. cit. (note 4), No. 35, pp. 113-114.
51) Kristian Gerner, The Soviet Union and Central Europe in the Postwar Era. A Study in Precarious Security, Stockholm: The Swedish Institute of International Affairs, 1984, pp. 159-160.
52) Teresa Rakowska-Harmstone, Christopher D. Jones, John Jaworsky, Ivan Sylvain, Warsaw Pact: The Question of Cohesion. Phase II - Vol. I: The Greater Socialist Army: Integration and Reliability, Ottowa: Operational Research and Analysis Establishment, Febr. 1984, p. vii.
53) Treaty text repr. in Document Section of Robin Alison Remington, The Western Pact. Case Studies in Communist Conflict Resolution, Cambridge, Mass.: The MIT Press, 1971, p. 204.

Notes to Case Study I: The Incorporation of the Baltic Republics into the Soviet Union (1941-1949)

1) New Encyclopaedia Britannica (NEB), 15th edition, Chicago etc., 1976, Vol. 2, p. 675.
2) See Albert Kalme, Total Terror: An Exposé of Genocide in the Baltics, New York: Appleton-Century-Crofts, 1951, p. 11, and

Adolfs Šilde, The Profits of Slavery: Baltic Forced Laborers and Deportees under Stalin and Khrushchev, Stockholm: Latvian National Foundation in Scandinavia, 1958, p. 296 n. 27.

3) Edgar Tomson, The Annexation of the Baltic States, in: Thomas T. Hammond (Ed.) and Robert Farrell (Ass. Ed.), The Anatomy of Communist Takeovers, New Haven/London: Yale University Press, 1975, p. 221.

4) A. Kalme, op. cit. (note 2), p. 145.

5) The frequently mentioned number of 34,260 Lithuanian casualties apparently only refers to one week of mass arrests in June 1941.

6) A. Kalme, op. cit. (note 2), p. 83, and NEB, op. cit. (note 1), p. 675.

7) V. Stanley Vardys, 'The Partisan Movement in Postwar Lithuania', in: Slavic Review: American Quarterly of Soviet and East European Studies, Vol. 12 (1963) no. 3 (September), p. 506.

8) A. Kalme, op. cit. (note 2), p. 165.

9) Idem, pp. 164-165; see also pp. 218-219.

10) A. Šilde, op. cit. (note 2), p. 17 and 201.

11) NEB, op. cit. (note 1), p. 676.

12) A. Šilde, op. cit. (note 2), p. 191.

13) Die Deportationen im Baltikum: 25 Jahre sowjetische Verschleppungen in den baltischen Staaten, Stockholm: Estnischer Nationalfond, 1966, p. 10.

14) See NEB, op. cit. (note 1), p. 675; Šilde, op. cit. (note 2), p. 15 comp. with Deportationen im Baltikum, p. 10; and A. Kalme, op. cit. (note 2), p. 8 comp. with p. 83.

15) V.S. Vardys, 'The Partisan Movement in Postwar Lithuania', in: Slavic Review, op. cit. (note 7).

16) Idem, pp. 500-501.

17) A. Kalme, op. cit. (note 2), p. 271.

18) NRC Handelsblad, August 31, 1983, and January 16, 1984.

19) NEB, op. cit. (note 1), p. 676.

Notes to Case Study II: The East German Uprising (1953)

1) Theodor Ebert, Non-Violent Resistance Against Communist Regimes?, in: Adam Roberts (Ed.), The Strategy of Civilian Defence: Non-Violent Resistance to Aggression, London: Faber and Faber Ltd., 1967, p. 177.

2) Idem, p. 179.

3) See François Fejtö, Histoire des Démocraties Populaires: Après Staline, 1953-1968, Paris: Editions du Seuil, 1969, p. 43, and Stephen S. Kaplan, et al., Diplomacy of Power: Soviet Armed Forces as a Political Instrument, Washington: The Brookings Institution, 1981, p. 72.

4) Th. Ebert, op. cit. (note 1), p. 192.

5) J.M. Mackintosh, Strategy and Tactics of Soviet Foreign Policy, London: Oxford University Press, 1963, pp. 77-78, cited in: S.S. Kaplan, op. cit. (note 3), p. 72., comp. also p. 649.

6) F. Fejtö, op. cit. (note 3), pp. 43-44.
7) Martin Jänicke, Der dritte Weg: Die antistalinistische Opposition gegen Ulbricht seit 1953, Köln: Neuer Deutscher Verlag, 1964, p. 48, cited in: Th. Ebert, op. cit. (note 1), p. 187.
8) J.M. Mackintosh, Strategy and Tactics of Soviet Foreign Policy, London: Oxford University Press, 1962, and Raymond L. Garthoff, 'The Military Establishment', in: East Europe, September 1965, p. 11, both cited in: Thomas W. Wolfe, Soviet Power and Europe, 1945-1970, Baltimore/London: The John Hopkins Press, 1970, pp. 43-44.
9) Th.W. Wolfe, op. cit. (note 8), pp. 39-40.
10) S.S. Kaplan, op. cit. (note 3), p. 73.
11) F. Fejtö, op. cit. (note 3), pp. 44-45.

Notes to Case Study III: The Hungarian Uprising (1956)

1) Michel Tatu, Intervention in Eastern Europe, in: Stephen S. Kaplan, Diplomacy of Power: Soviet Armed Forces as a Political Instrument, Washington, D.C.: The Brookings Institution, 1981, p. 215.
2) Idem, p. 216.
3) Idem, pp. 215-216.
4) Veljko Mićunović, Moscow Diary, London: Chatto & Windus, 1980, pp. 131-141.
5) Christina Arber, A Study of Civilian Defence, with Special Reference to the Contrasting Theories of Sharp and Boserup/Mack within the Context of General Civilian Defence Theory, and Illustrated by Events, and Methods Used, in Hungary 1956 and Czechoslovakia 1968, University of Bradford, School of Peace Studies, 1980; p. 36; estimates run from 2,650 to 25,000 casualties.
6) Miklos Molnar, Budapest 1956: A History of the Hungarian Revolution, London: George Allen & Unwin, 1971, p. 240.
7) Robert Thompson (Ed.), War in Peace: An Analysis of Warfare since 1945, London: Orbis Publishing, 1981, p. 303.
8) Ferenc A. Vali, Rift and Revolution in Hungary, Cambridge, Mass.: Harvard University Press, 1961, p. 434, cited in: Dale R. Herspring, 'Political Reliability in the Eastern European Warsaw Pact Armies', in: Armed Forces and Society, Vol. 6 (1980) no. 2 (Winter), p. 279.
9) V. Mićunović, op. cit. (note 4), p. 134.
10) A.J. Jongman, Data omtrent oorlogen, conflicten en politiek geweld [Data concerning Wars, Armed Conflicts and Political Violence], college-documentatiemap, Groningen: Polemologisch Instituut, 1983, p. 169.
11) Robert Lyle Butterworth, with Margaret E. Scranton, Managing Interstate Conflict, 1945-74: Data with Synopses, Pittsburgh: University Center for International Studies, 1976, p. 219.
12) V. Mićunović, op. cit. (note 4), pp. 136-137.

13) C. Arber, op. cit. (note 5), p. 36.

Notes to Case Study IV: Warsaw Pact Intervention in Czechoslovakia
                                (1968)

1) Thomas W. Wolfe, Soviet Power and Europe, 1945-1970,
   Baltimore: The John Hopkins Press, 1970, passim, p. 373 n. 121.
2) Lyman B. Kirkpatrick, The Decision to Intervene: A Comparison
   of Soviet Interventions from 1953 to 1980, Garmisch, Germany:
   U.S. Army Institute, 1980, p. 32, comp. with M.D. Donelan and
   M.J. Grieve, International Disputes: Case Histories 1945-1970,
   London: Europa Publications for The David Davies Memorial
   Institute of International Studies, 1973, p. 277, and Wolfe, op.
   cit. (note 1), pp. 469-470.
3) Michel Tatu, Intervention in Eastern Europe, in: Stephen S.
   Kaplan et al., Diplomacy of Power, Washington, D.C.: The
   Brookings Institution, 1981, p. 230, and Th.W. Wolfe, op. cit.
   (note 1), pp. 469-470.
4) L.B. Kirkpatrick, op. cit. (note 2), p. 33.
5) M. Tatu, op. cit. (note 3), p. 231. Thompson mentions a total of
   70 deads and 1,000 injured (R. Thompson (Cons. Ed.), War in
   Peace: An Analysis of Warfare since 1945, London: Orbis
   Publishing, 1981, p. 303).
6) M. Tatu, op. cit. (note 3), pp. 225-226.
7) Idem, pp. 237, 263.
8) Dale R. Herspring and Ivan Volgyes, 'Political Reliability in the
   Eastern European Warsaw Pact Armies', in: Armed Forces and
   Society, Vol. 6 (1980) no. 2 (Winter), p. 279.
9) Onze Jaren: De wereld na 1945. Geschiedenis van de eigen tijd,
   2nd edition, Amsterdam: Amsterdam Boek, 1975, Vol. 6, p. 3193.
10) Idem, p. 3195.

Notes to Case Study V: The Sino-Soviet Border Dispute (1960s)

1) A.J. Day (Ed.), Border and Territorial Disputes, A Keesing's
   Reference Publication, s.l.: Longman, 1982, p. 266.
2) Thomas W. Robinson, The Sino-Soviet Border Conflict, in: Stephen
   S. Kaplan et al., Diplomacy of Power: Soviet Armed Forces as a
   Political Instrument, Washington: The Brookings Institution, 1981,,
   p. 290.
3) Li Huichuan, in: The People's Daily, June 17, 1981, cited in: A.J.
   Day (Ed.), op. cit. (note 1), p. 267-268.
4) David Downing, An Atlas of Territorial and Border Disputes,
   London: New English Library, 1980, p. 16.
5) A.J. Day (Ed.), op. cit. (note 1), p. 265.
6) Idem, p. 267.

7) See A.J. Day (Ed.), op. cit. (note 1), p. 262, and O.B. Borisov and B.T. Koloskov, Sovetsko-Kitaiskiye otnosheniya, 1945-1970: Kratkii ocherk [Soviet-Chinese Relations, 1945-1970: A Short Outline], Moscow: Mysl', 1971 , p. 302. The latter statement, made by Borisov, is no more specific than that.

8) A.J. Day (Ed.), op. cit. (note 1), p. 264.

9) Ibid.

10) Idem, p. 266.

11) Yao Ming-le (Pseud.), 'De samenzwering tegen Mao', in: Vrij Nederland 44 (1983) no. 19 (May 14), pp. 1, 15-17.

12) The Military Balance, 1978-1979, London/Melbourne: Arms and Armour Press, in ass. with The International Institute for Strategic Studies, 1978., pp. vii, 8-10.

13) Idem, pp. vii, 56-57.

14) Th.W. Robinson, op. cit. (note 2), p. 288.

15) Annual of Power and Conflict: A Survey of Political Violence and International Influence, 1977-78, London: Institute for the Study of Conflict, 1978, p. 301.

16) NRC Handelsblad, November 17, 1983.

17) Th.W. Robinson, op. cit. (note 2), p. 309.

Notes to Chapter 2: Interbloc Conflicts: Military Aspects of the East-West Conflict

1) Alex P. Schmid, 'Die Expansion des Amerikanischen Kapitalismus nach dem Zweiten Weltkrieg - eine sozialimperialistische Interpretation', Schweizerische Zeitschrift für Geschichte, Vol. 27 (1977) no. 4, p. 477.

2) Hans W. Schoenberg, The Partition of Germany and the Neutralization of Austria, in: Thomas T. Hammond (Ed.), The Anatomy of Communist Takeovers, New Haven: Yale University Press, 1975, p. 371; S. Kogelfranz, '"So weit die Armeen kommen..." Wie Osteuropa nach Jalta kommunistisch wurde', Der Spiegel (Hamburg), Vol. 38 (1984) no. 35 (August 23), p. 106.

3) Letter to his daughter, dated 3 March 1948; cit. Margaret Truman, Harry S. Truman, New York: Pocket Books, 1974, pp. 392-393.

4) N. Tolstoy, Stalin's Secret War, London: Pan Books, 1981, p. 362.

5) P.M.E. Volten, 'Het offensief in het militaire denken van de Sovjet-Unie', Jason, Vol. 8 (1983) no. 2, p. 16 and 21.

6) Kaplan's account, as summarized by N. Tolstoy, op. cit. (note 4), pp. 361-362; K. Kaplan spoke about this episode in The Times (May 6, 1977) and Le Monde (May 20, 1977). See also Kaplan's Dans les archives du Comité central. Trente ans de secret du Bloc soviétique, Paris, 1978. Another Czechoslovakian historian, Michael Rejman, has confirmed Kaplan's account. - Michael Heller and A. Nekrich, Geschichte der Sowjetunion. Vol. II: 1940-1980, Königstein: Athenäum, 1982, p. 427 (note 17).

7) Cf. Dale Herspring and Ivan Volgyes, 'Political Reliability in the Eastern European Warsaw Pact Armies', Armed Forces and Society, Vol. 6 (1980) no. 2 (Winter), where they write: "...most observers agree that non-Soviet forces would have been unreliable if deployed against the West in the late fifties or early sixties" (p. 286). - It would appear that this applies for the early fifties as well.

8) Truman Diary, entry for September 13, 1948; cit. D. Yergin, Shattered Peace, Harmondsworth: Pelican, 1980, pp. 391-392.

9) Zhores Medvedev in lecture on the USSR and the Arms Race, Leiden, November 15, 1983; David Alan Rosenberg, '"A Smoking Radiating Ruin at the End of Two Hours". Document on American Plans for Nuclear War with the Soviet Union, 1954-1955', International Security, Vol. 6 (1981/1982) no. 3 (Winter), p. 7; Stephen Ambrose, Eisenhower. Volume II: The President, New York: Simon and Schuster, 1984, as quoted in review by Frans Verhagen, 'De herwaardering van een president', Intermediair (Amsterdam), Vol. 20 (1984) no. 49 (December 7), p. 23; M. Heller and A. Nekrich, op. cit. (note 6); R. Lowenthal in Foreword to Arnulf Baring, Uprising in East Germany: June 17, 1953, Itahca: Cornell University Press, 1972, p. xx.

10) Adam B. Ulam, Expansion and Coexistence. The History of Soviet Foreign Policy 1917-67, New York: Praeger, 1968, pp. 403-404; Matthew A. Evangelista, 'Stalin's Postwar Army Reappraised', International Security, Vol. 7 (1982/1983) no. 3 (Winter), pp. 118-119; Wolf Perdelwitz, Wollen die Russen Krieg?, München: Goldmann, 1982, p. 242.

11) Alternative Defence Commission, Defence Without the Bomb, London: Taylor & Francis, 1983, pp. 72-76.

12) A.P. Schmid, Churchills privater Krieg. Intervention und Konterrevolution im russischen Bürgerkrieg 1918-1920, Zürich: Atlantis, 1975, p. 339.

13) Christy Campbell, War Facts Now, Glasgow: Fontana, 1982, p. 57.

14) D.C. Watt, Churchill und der Kalte Krieg, Zürich: Schweizerische Winston Churchill Stiftung, 1981, p. 14.

15) D. Yergin, op. cit. (note 8), pp. 187-188.

16) D.C. Watt, et. al., A History of the World in the Twentieth Century, London: Hodder and Stoughton, 1967, p. 628.

17) Joseph M. Jones, The Fifteen Weeks, New York, 1955, p. 186; cit. Todd Gitlin, Counter-Insurgency; Myth and Reality in Greece, in: David Horowitz (Ed.), Containment and Revolution. Western Policy towards Social Revolution: 1917 to Vietnam, London: Anthony Blond, 1967, p. 179.

18) T. Gitlin, op. cit. (note 17), p. 167.

19) Stalin to Djilas, February 10, 1948; M. Djilas, Conversations with Stalin, New York, 1962, p. 181; cit. T. Gitlin, op. cit. (note 17), p. 174.

20) Cf. D. George Kousoulas, The Greek Communists Tried Three Times - and Failed, in: Th.T. Hammond (Ed.), op. cit. (note 2), pp. 305-306.

21) W. Friedman, The Allied Military Government of Germany, London: Stevens & Sons, 1947, pp. 229, 236.

22) D. Yergin, op. cit. (note 8), pp. 376-377.
23) Roger Parkinson, Encyclopaedia of Modern War, London: Paladin Books, 1979, p. 57.
24) Marshall D. Shulman, Stalin's Foreign Policy Reappraised, Cambridge: Harvard University Press, 1963, p. 66; cit. D. Yergin, op. cit. (note 8), p. 388.
25) Adam B. Ulam, The Rivals. America & Russia since World War II, New York: The Viking Press, 1971, p. 172.
26) Strobe Talbott (Ed.), Khrushchev Remembers, New York: Bantham, 1970, pp. 400-402.
27) Gavriel D. Ra'anan, The Evolution of the Soviet Use of Surrogates in Military Relations with the Third World, with Particular Emphasis in Cuban Participation in Africa, St. Monica: RAND, Dec. 1979, p. 39; quoting from "Two Different Lines on the Question of War and Peace", Comment on the Open Letter of the Central Committee of the CPSU, November 19, 1963, pp. 221-256, in: The Polemic on the General Line of the International Communist Movement, Peking: Foreign Language Press, 1965, p. 246. - With thanks to Milton Leitenberg for directing my attention to this statement.
28) G.D. Ra'anan, op. cit. (note 27), p. 40.
29) Stephen S. Kaplan, Diplomacy of Power, Washington, D.C.: The Brookings Institution, 1981, pp. 329-331.
30) Idem, pp. 332-333.
31) Edward Friedman, 'Nuclear Blackmail and the End of the Korean War', Modern China, Vol. 1 (1975) no. 1, pp. 75-91, Historical Abstracts DIALOG File summary; Bruce D. Porter, The USSR in Third World Conflicts. Soviet Arms and Diplomacy in Local Wars, 1945-1980, Cambridge: Cambridge University Press, 1984, pp. 15-16; A.B. Ulam, op. cit. (note 10), pp. 403-404.
32) H.W. Schoenberg, op. cit. (note 2), pp. 379-381.
33) Louis Kriesberg, 'Noncoercive Inducements in U.S.-Soviet Conflicts: Ending the Occupation of Austria and Nuclear Weapons Tests', Journal of Political and Military Sociology, Vol. 9 (Spring 1981), p. 9.
34) Manfried Rauchensteiner, Der Sonderfall. Die Besatzungzeit in Oesterreich, 1945 bis 1955, Graz: Verlag Styria, 1979, p. 333; A.Z. Rubinstein, Soviet Foreign Policy Since World War II: Imperial and Global, Cambridge, Mass.: Winthrop Publ., 1981, p. 224.
35) Michel Tatu, Power in the Kremlin. From Khrushchev to Kosygin, New York: Viking, 1967, p. 232.
36) S.S. Kaplan, op. cit. (note 29), pp. 156-157; Francis Fukuyama, 'Nuclear Shadowboxing: Soviet Intervention Threats in the Middle East', Orbis, Fall 1981, p. 586; Erik Dirksen, 'Economische en militaire hulp van de Sovjet-unie aan de Derde Wereld', Internationale Spectator, Vol. 37 (1983) no. 7 (July), p. 445.
37) S.S. Kaplan, op. cit. (note 29), pp. 337, 342; Stephen T. Hosmer and Thomas W. Wolfe, Soviet Policy and Practice toward Third World Conflicts, Lexington, Mass.: D.C. Heath, 1983, pp. 5-6, 133.

38) S.S. Kaplan, op. cit. (note 29), pp. 341, 347; M. Leitenberg, The Impact of the Worldwide Confrontation of the Great Powers: Aspects of Military Power, Stockholm, Swedish Institute of International Affairs, 1982, p. 36.
39) S.T. Hosmer and Th.W. Wolfe, op. cit. (note 37), pp. 129-141.
40) Georgy Arbatov, A Soviet Commentary, in: Arthur Macy Cox, Russian Roulette. The Superpower Game, New York: Times Books, 1982, p. 182; R.J. Barnet, The Giants. Russia and America, New York: Simon and Schuster, 1977, p. 80. - The Kissinger trip to Peking equally served the purpose of restraining North Vietnam so that the United States would be enabled to withdraw with honour from the Vietnam quagmire. - E.A. Molander and R.C. Molander, What About the Russians - and Nuclear War, New York: Pocket Books, 1983, p. 131.
41) Cit. R.J. Barnet, op. cit. (note 40), p. 109.
42) Based on a summary of Brzezinski's scheme made by R.J. Barnet, op. cit. (note 40), pp. 109-113.
43) This overview is partly based on chapter 5 of David Holloway's The Soviet Union and the Arms Race, New Haven: Yale University Press, 1983.

Notes to Case Study VI: The Iranian Crisis (1945-1946)

1) Faramarz S. Fatemi, The U.S.S.R. in Iran: The Background History of Russian and Anglo-American Conflict in Iran, its Effects on Iranian Nationalism, and the Fall of the Shah, South Brunswick & New York/London: A.S. Barnes and Company/Thomas Yoseloff, 1980, pp. 21-22.
2) Idem, pp. 36-37.
3) Daniel Yergin, Shattered Peace: The Origins of the Cold War and the National Security State, Harmondsworth: Penguin Books, 1980 (first published 1977), pp. 179-180.
4) F.S. Fatemi, op. cit. (note 1), p. 37.
5) Lincoln P. Bloomfield and Amelia C. Leiss, Controlling Small Wars: A Strategy for the 1970's, New York: Albert A. Knopf, 1969, p. 63.
6) Idem, p. 63 n. 5.
7) Quassem Massudi, Jarayan Mossaferat Mission Azemie Iran be Moscow [An Account of the Iranian Mission to Moscow], Tehran: Printing Association, 1947, p. 69-70, cited in: F.S. Fatemi, op. cit. (note 1), pp. 104, 131.
8) D. Yergin, op. cit. (note 3), p. 189.
9) Robert Lyle Butterworth with Margaret E. Scranton, Managing Interstate Conflict, 1945-74: Data with Synopses, Pittsburgh: University Center for International Studies, 1976, p. 62.
10) Hubert Druks, Harry S. Truman and the Russians, 1945-1953, 1967, p. 125, cited in: An Analysis of International Crises: Historical Appraisal 1945-1974, Final Report, US Army War College, Strategic Studies Institute, 1974, p. C/2; New York Times, August

25, 1957, and George Lenczowski, The Middle East in World Affairs, 2nd edition, New York: Cornell University Press, 1956, pp. 176-183, both cited in: Stephen S. Kaplan et al., Diplomacy of Power: Soviet Armed Forces as a Political Instrument, Washington, D.C.: The Brookings Institution, 1981, passim, pp. 70-71.
11) L.P. Bloomfield, op. cit. (note 5), p. 71.
12) Idem, p. 72.
13) New York Times, December 14, 1946, cited in: F.S. Fatemi, op. cit. (note 1), pp. 159, 169.
14) New York Times, August 18, 1947, and U.S. Department of State, Foreign Relations of the United States, 1947, Vol. 5: The Near East and Africa, Washington, D.C.: Government Printing Office, 1971, p. 963, both cited in: S.S. Kaplan, op. cit. (note 10), p. 121.
15) D. Yergin, op. cit. (note 3), p. 190.

Notes to Case Study VII: The Greek Civil War (1944-1949) - A Case of Soviet Non-Intervention

1) Evangelos Averoff-Tossizza, By Fire and Axe: The Communist Party and the Civil War in Greece, 1944-1949, New Rochelle, N.Y.: Caratzas Brothers, 1978, pp. 101-102.
2) Joyce Kolko and Gabriel Kolko, The Limits of Power: The World and the United States Foreign Policy, 1945-1954, New York: Harper & Row, 1972, p. 221.
3) M.D. Donelan and M.J. Grieve, International Disputes: Case Histories 1945-1970, London: Europa Publications, 1973, p. 19.
4) Daniel Yergin, Shattered Peace: The Origin of the Cold War and the National Security State, Harmondsworth: Pelican Books, 1980, pp. 288-289.
5) Idem, p. 294.
6) E. Averoff-Tossizza, op. cit. (note 1), p. 266.
7) M.D. Donelan, op. cit. (note 3), p. 20.
8) L.P. Bloomfield and A.C. Leiss, Controlling Small Wars: A Strategy for the 1970s, New York: A.A. Knopf, 1969, p. 174.
9) E. Averoff-Tossizza, op. cit. (note 1), p. 365.

Notes to Case Study VIII: The Korean War (1950-1953)

1) John Keegan, World Armies, New York/London & Basingstoke/Alphen aan den Rijn: Facts on File/The Macmillan Press/Sijthoff & Noordhoff, 1979, p. 404.
2) All times/dates mentioned will be local.
3) P.R. Baehr in co-operation with P.J.G. Kapteyn, De Verenigde Naties: Ideaal en werkelijkheid [The United Nations: Ideal and Reality], Utrecht/Antwerpen: Het Spectrum, 1976, p. 139.

4) F.A. Godfrey, Crisis in Korea, in: Robert Thompson (Consultant Ed.), War in Peace: An Analysis of Warfare since 1945, London: Orbis Publishing, 1981, p. 52.
5) Leland M. Goodrich, Korea: A Study of U.S. Policy in the United Nations, New York: Council on Foreign Relations, 1956, p. 117, cited in: J.G. Stoessinger, Why Nations Go to War, 2nd edition, New York: St. Martin's Press, 1978, p. 85, 102.
6) Istoriya vneshnei politiki SSSR 1945-1975 gg. [A History of the Foreign Policy of the USSR 1945-1975], Vol. 2, p. 165, cited in: I.E. Shavrov (Ed.), Lokalnye Voiny: Istoriya i sovremmenost [Local Wars: History and the Modern Era], Moscow: Voyennoye Izdatelstvo, 1981, pp. 112.
7) At a meeting on October 15, 1950 at Wake Island in the middle of the Pacific, for instance, MacArthur had assured President Truman that a Chinese intervention was unlikely. When the Chinese attacked two weeks later, MacArthur under-estimated their number by some 80 per cent (40-60,000 troops instead of 200-300,000 troops) (M. Carver, War since 1945, London: Weidenfeld and Nicholson, 1980, p. 160; and Samuel B. Griffith II, The Chinese People's Liberation Army, New York: McGraw-Hill, 1967, p. 129, 134, cited in: J.G. Stoessinger, op. cit. (note 5), p. 94, 102).
8) Rober Lyle Butterworth with Margaret E. Scranton, Managing Interstate Conflict, 1945-74: Data with Synopses, Pittsburgh: University Center for International Studies, 1976, pp. 147-148; M. Carver, op. cit. (note 7), p. 169 seems to date the threat earlier.
9) Robert F. Randle, The Origin of Peace: A Study of Peacemaking and the Structure of Peace Settlements, New York/London: The Free Press/ Collier-Macmillan Publishers, 1973, p. 236.
10) NRC Handelsblad, October 10, 1983.
11) J. Keegan, op. cit. (note 1), pp. 404, 411.
12) General MacArthur had implicitly said the same already in 1949 (William Zimmerman, The Korean and Vietnam Wars, in: Stephen S. Kaplan et al., Diplomacy of Power: Soviet Armed Forces as a Political Instrument, Washington, D.C.: The Brookings Institution, 1981, p. 317).
13) J.G. Stoessinger, op. cit. (note 5), p. 98.
14) W. Zimmerman, op. cit. (note 12), pp. 326-327.
15) F.A. Godfrey, Crisis in Korea, in: R. Thompson (Ed.), op. cit. (note 4), p. 42.
16) W. Zimmerman, op. cit. (note 12), p. 333.
17) Estimates vary greatly. According to Röling, 84 per cent of the casualties in the Korean War were civilian (B.V.A. Röling, Vredeswetenschap: Inleiding tot de polemologie [Peace Research: An Introduction to War and Peace Studies], Utrecht/Antwerpen: Het Spectrum, 1981, p. 39 table 2.2). This estimate appears to be on the high side. Reeve mentions 1 million civilian deaths (W.D. Reeve, The Republic of Korea: A Political and Economic Study, London/New York/Toronto: Oxford University Press, 1963, p. 33). In Onze Jaren, p. 851, it is stated that the Korean War had caused more civilian than military victims. From the death rates of military personal and civilians given by Wood (David Wood,

Conflict in the Twentieth Century, in: Adelphi Papers no. 48, London: The Institute for Strategic Studies, 1968), at p. 27, it can be concluded that 40.7 per cent of the Korean War fatalities were civilians; of the South Korean fatalities 80 per cent were civilians, and of the North Korean fatalities 37 per cent. From the Casualties of Armed Conflicts list, it can be infered that 20.4 per cent of all Korean War casualties were civilian; one of the sources mentioned is Wood, op. cit. (Casualties of Armed Conflicts in the Twentieth Century (1900-1970) [mimeographed staff report], Washington, D.C.: U.S. Arms Control and Disarmament Agency, 1971, p. 5).
18) Estimated at 10 million Koreans (NRC Handelsblad, July 23, 1983).

Notes to Case Study IX: The Soviet Role in the Allied Occupation of Austria (1945-1955)

1) In this context, the term 'Allied' will be taken to include France.
2) A pronouncement attributed to Karl Renner (William B. Bader, Austria between East and West 1945-1955, Stanford, California: Stanford University Press, 1966, p. 55). According to American estimates, Soviet troops in Austria numbered some 200,000 in December 1945, American forces numbered 47,000, French forces 40,000 and British forces 65,000 (Report sent to Secretary of State James F. Byrnes by Secretary of War Robert F. Patterson, dated January 11, 1946, added as appendix to Proceedings of the Allied Commission, ALCO/M (46) 14, cited in: W.B. Bader, op. cit., p. 55n.).
3) Manfried Rauchensteiner, Der Sonderfall: Die Besatzungszeit in Österreich, 1945 bis 1955, Graz/Wien/Köln: Verlag Styria, 1979, pp. 307, 317-318, 327, 329; Keesings Historisch Archief: Geïllustreerd dagboek van het hedendaags wereldgebeuren [Keesing's Contemporary Archives], Amsterdam: Uitgevers Systemen Keesing, p. 11902 (May 16-22, 1955).
4) W.B. Bader, op. cit. (note 2), p. 209.
5) The way in which the Soviet Union handled the question of the German properties (seizure to be placed under Soviet direction) has been described as an 'emergency measure', because no agreement could be reached on the foundation of bilateral companies (David J. Dallin, Soviet Foreign Policy after Stalin, Philadelphia, 1961, pp. 192-196, cited in: M. Rauchensteiner, op. cit. (note 3), pp. 331, 401).
6) W.B. Bader, op. cit. (note 2), pp. 190-191.
7) M. Rauchensteiner, op. cit. (note 3), pp. 305-309; W.B. Bader, op. cit. (note 2), pp. 107-108.
8) M. Rauchensteiner, op. cit. (note 3), pp. 310, 316-318.
9) Idem, p. 333.
10) W.B. Bader, op. cit. (note 2), pp. 107-108.
11) M. Rauchensteiner, op. cit. (note 3), p. 334.

12) Ibid.
13) Idem, p. 335, note 49 p. 401.
14) NRC Handelsblad, April 22, 1983.
15) D.J. Dallin, op. cit. (note 5), cited in: M. Rauchensteiner, op. cit. (note 3), pp. 332, 401.
16) W.B. Bader, op. cit. (note 2), pp. 204-205, passim.
17) A Soviet document with such a plan was published by an Austrian daily in 1974. - Oral communication from Dutch defence official.

Notes to Chapter 3: Extrabloc Conflicts: Soviet Military Involvement
in Third World Conflicts

1) Ruth Leger Sivard, World Military and Social Expenditures, Leesburg, VA, World Priorities, 1981, p. 8; as quoted in M.D. Wolpin, State Terrorism and Repression in the Third World: Parameters and Prospects, Potsdam, N.Y.: State University of New York, 1983, Mimeo, p. 41.
2) Does not add up to 100 percent as exports to centrally directed countries in the South (like Cuba) are excluded. Source: U.N. Monthly Bulletin of Statistics, July 1981, as quoted in Jan Joost Teunissen & Hans van Zon (Eds.), De Russische omhelzing. Het Oostblok en de Derde Wereld, Amsterdam: Transnational Institute, 1983, p. 142.
3) Joseph L. Nogee, The Soviet Union in the Third World: Successes and Failures, in: Robert H. Donaldson (Ed.), The Soviet Union in the Third World, Boulder, Colo.: Westview Press, 1981, pp. 448-449.
4) Cit. Arthur Macy Cox, Russian Roulette. The Superpower Game, New York: Times Books, 1982, p. 41 & p. 51.
5) Pravda, 13 Sept. 1919; cit. A.P. Schmid, Churchill's Privater Krieg. Intervention und Kontrarevolution im Russischen Bürgerkrieg, 1918-1920, Zürich: Atlantis, 1975, pp. 294-295.
6) Cit. Jean Laloy, Europe in the Soviet Perspective, in: Christopher Bertram (Ed.), Prospects of Soviet Power in the 1980, London: Macmillan, 1980, p. 47, note 11.
7) Cit. Keith A. Dunn, Soviet Involvement in the Third World: Implications of US Policy Assumption, in: R.H. Donaldson (Ed.), op. cit. (note 3), p. 415.
8) Alvin Z. Rubinstein, Soviet Foreign Policy Since World War II: Imperial and Global, Cambridge, Mass.: Winthrop Publ., 1981, p. 216.
9) A.Z. Rubinstein, op. cit. (note 8), pp. 215-216; Stephen S. Kaplan, Diplomacy of Power. Soviet Armed Forces as a Political Instrument, Washington, D.C.: The Brookings Institution, 1981, pp. 148-152.
10) Gavriel D. Ra'anan, The Evolution of the Soviet Use of Surrogates in Military Relations with the Third World, With Particular Emphasis on Cuban Participation in Africa, St. Monica: Rand, Dec. 1979, pp. 2-3.

11) M. Leitenberg, The Impact of the Worldwide Confrontation of the Great Powers: Aspects of Military Intervention and the Projection of Military Power, Stockholm: Swedish Institute of International Affairs, Conference Paper, 1982, p. 13.

12) V.I. Glunin et al, Noveyshay a Istoria Kitaya, Moscow, 1972, p. 246; cit. Adam B. Ulam, The Soviet Union and the International Game, in: Kurt London (Ed.), The Soviet Union in World Politics, Boulder, Colo., Westview Press, 1980, p. 39.

13) A.Z. Rubinstein, op. cit. (note 8), p. 224.

14) Ronald M. Schneider, Communism in Guatemala 1944-1954, New York: 1959, p. 309; John Gerassi, The Great Fear: The Reconquest of Latin America by Latin Americans, New York, 1963, p. 165.

15) Ernest W. Lefever, Arms Transfers, Military Training, and Domestic Politics, Washington, D.C.: Brookings Institution, n.d., pp. 23-24 (Mimeo).

16) R. Schneider, 'Guatemala: An Aborted Communist Takeover', Studies on the Soviet Union (New Series), Vol. 11 (1971) no. 4, p. 525.

17) Bruce D. Porter, The USSR in Third World Conflicts. Soviet Arms and Diplomacy in Local Wars, 1945-1980, Cambridge: Cambridge University Press, 1984, p. 17; Stephen T. Hosmer and Thomas W. Wolfe, Soviet Policy and Practice toward Third World Conflicts, Lexington, Mass.: D.C. Heath, 1983, p. 11.

18) G.D. Ra'anan, op. cit. (note 10), p. 4.

19) S.S. Kaplan, op. cit. (note 9), p. 152.

20) S.T. Hosmer and Th.W. Wolfe, op. cit. (note 17), pp. 72-74.

21) S.S. Kaplan, op. cit. (note 9), p. 153, citing a 1978 CIA study on Communist Aid Activities in Non-Communist Less Developed Countries; Andrew J. Pierre, The Global Politics of Arms Sales, Princeton, N.J.: Princeton University Press, 1982, p. 45; Ernest W. Lefever, op. cit. (note 15), p. 3; Michael Kidron and Dan Smith, The War Atlas. Armed Conflict - Armed Peace, London: Pluto Press, 1983, map 18.

22) G. Ra'anan, op. cit. (note 10), pp. 5-6.

23) Joseph B. Smith, Portrait of a Cold Warrior, New York: Ballantine Books, 1976, pp. 239-240.

24) S.S. Kaplan, op. cit. (note 9), p. 161.

25) S. Talbott (Ed.), Khrushchev Remembers. The Last Testament, London: André Deutsch, 1974, pp. 325-327; Dutch Ministerial Council, June 8, 1962; cit. Volkskrant, Het Vervolg, July 10, 1982, p. 6.

26) B.D. Porter, op. cit. (note 17), p. 19; Center for Defense Information, 'Soviet Geopolitical Momentum: Myth or Menace. Trends of Soviet Influence Around the World from 1945 to 1980', The Defense Monitor, Vol. 9 (1980) no. 1 (January), p. 21.

27) S. Talbott, op. cit. (note 25), p. 310.

28) A.Z. Rubinstein, op. cit. (note 8), p. 222.

29) S.T. Hosmer and Th.W. Wolfe, op. cit. (note 17), p. 12.

30) '"Eine Fliege vom Himmel holen." Moskaus Kunst der Tarnung und der Rüstungsbluffs', Der Spiegel (Hamburg), Vol. 38 (1984) no. 28 (July 9), p. 80.

31) S.S. Kaplan, op. cit. (note 9), p. 162.
32) Richard E. Bissell, 'Soviet Use of Proxies in the Third World: The Case of Yemen', Soviet Studies, Vol. 30 (1978) no. 1 (January), p. 94.
33) New York Times, 13 Dec. 1967; The Times, 13 Dec. 1967; cit. R.E. Bissell, op. cit. (note 32), p. 100; S.S. Kaplan, op. cit. (note 9), p. 170.
34) B.D. Porter, op. cit. (note 17), p. 23.
35) R.E. Bissell, op. cit. (note 32), p. 104.
36) S.S. Kaplan, op. cit. (note 9), pp. 159-160.
37) Idem, p. 162.
38) Idem, p. 160; B.D. Porter, op. cit. (note 17), p. 20; S.T. Hosmer and Th.W. Wolfe, op. cit. (note 17), p. 19.
39) A.M. Cox, op. cit. (note 4), p. 52; S.T. Hosmer and Th.W. Wolfe, op. cit. (note 17), pp. 24-25.
40) William J. Durch, The Cuban Military in Africa and the Middle East: From Algeria to Angola, Alexandria, Virginia: Center for Naval Analysis, 1977, p. 1; S.T. Hosmer and Th.W. Wolfe, op. cit. (note 17), p. 98.
41) A.J. Pierre, op. cit. (note 21), p. 244; Volkskrant, 3 May, 1984, p. 4 (based on New York Times).
42) H. Kissinger et al., Report of the National Bipartisan Commission on Central America, Washington, D.C.: G.P.O., January 1984; reprinted in part in NRC Handelsblad, 12 January, 1984, p. 4; Volkskrant, 3 May, 1984, p. 4 (based on New York Times).
43) Ibid, p. 4.
44) Cit. Bertil Dunér, 'Proxy Intervention in Civil Wars', Journal of Peace Research, Vol. 18 (1981) no. 4, p. 358, 355.
45) S.T. Hosmer and Th.W. Wolfe, op. cit. (note 17), p. 13.
46) G.D. Ra'anan, op. cit. (note 10), p. 8; B.D. Porter, op. cit. (note 17), p. 19.
47) G.D. Ra'anan, op. cit. (note 18), pp. 6-7.
48) Idem, p. 17.
49) A.Z. Rubinstein, op. cit. (note 8), pp. 217-218.
50) B.D. Porter, op. cit. (note 17), pp. 18-19.
51) S.S. Kaplan, op. cit. (note 9), p. 161.
52) David Holloway, The Soviet Union and the Arms Race, New Haven: Yale University Press, 1983, p. 35.
53) Idem, pp. 40-41.
54) Leon Goure and Morris Rothenberg, Latin America, in: K. London (Ed.), The Soviet Union in World Politics, Boulder, Colo.: Westview Press, 1980, p. 235.
55) Jan van der Putten, Er waart een spook door Latijns-Amerika. De 'Real-politiek' van de Sovjet Unie, in: J.J. Teunissen en H. van Zon (Eds.), op. cit. (note 2), pp. 108-109; S.T. Hosmer and Th.W. Wolfe, op. cit. (note 17), p. 45.
56) L. Goure and M. Rothenberg, op. cit. (note 54), p. 249.
57) NRC Handelsblad (Rotterdam), June 4, 1982, p. 5; Volkskrant (Amsterdam), 6 March 1984, p. 4 (basing itself on the book The Sinking of the Belgrano, by Desmond Rice and Arthur Gavshon, 1984).
58) Volkskrant, 3 May, 1984, p. 4 (based on New York Times).

59) The Defense Monitor, Vol. 12 (1983) no. 1, p. 15.
60) Joseph L. Nogee and Robert H. Donaldson, Soviet Foreign Policy Since World War Two, New York: Pergamon Press, 1981, p. 268; A.M. Cox, op. cit. (note 4), p. 52.
61) Caspar W. Weinberger, Soviet Military Power, Washington, D.C.: GPO, 1984, pp. 128-131; S.T. Hosmer and Th.W. Wolfe, op. cit. (note 17), pp. 58-59, 102-103.
62) Roger Hamburg, Soviet Perspectives on Military Intervention, in: Ellen P. Stern (Ed.), The Limits of Military Intervention, Beverly Hills: Sage, 1977, pp. 61-62.
63) J.L. Nogee, in: R.H. Donaldson (Ed.), op. cit. (note 3), p. 446.
64) Ruth Leger Sivard, World Military and Social Expenditures 1983, Washington, D.C.: World Priorities, 1983, p. 8; Lovell Finley, 'Raising the Stakes. The Major Powers Still Play for Keeps in Indochina', Southern Asia Chronicle, No. 64, 1978, p. 24.
65) A.Z. Rubinstein, op. cit. (note 8), p. 225.
66) Max Spoor, Huwelijk uit wederzijds belang. De strategie van Moskou in Zuid-Oost Azië, in: J.J. Teunissen and H. van Zon, op. cit. (note 2), p. 100; cit. B.D. Porter, op. cit. (note 17), p. 33.
67) Werner Levi, The Coming End of War, Beverley Hills: Sage, 1981, p. 68; S.T. Hosmer and Th.W. Wolfe, op. cit. (note 17), pp. 95, 230, 132.
68) Jiri Valenta, 'From Prague to Kabul. The Soviet Style of Invasion', International Security, Vol. 5 (1980) no. 2 (Fall), p. 120; S.T. Hosmer and Th.W. Wolfe, op. cit. (note 17), p. 186; In the period 1957 to 1974, sub-Saharan African nations received economic credits worth about $ 780 million from the USSR; Afghanistan received about $ 850 million. - A.Z. Rubinstein, op. cit. (note 8), p. 230.
69) William J. Barnds, South Asia, in: Kurt London (Ed.), The Soviet Union in World Politics, Boulder, Colorado: Westview Press, 1980, pp. 214-215.
70) Peter Gosztony, Die Rote Armee. Machtfaktor der Weltpolitik, München: Goldmann, 1983, p. 368.
71) Fred Halliday, Threat from the East? Soviet Policy from Afghanistan and Iran to the Horn of Africa, Harmondsworth: Pelican Books, 1982, pp. 90-91; J.L. Nogee, in: R.H. Donaldson (Ed.), op. cit. (note 3), p. 445.
72) Volkskrant (Amsterdam), June 24, 1983, p. 4. - Based on Reuter report from Tehran. Quotes are retranslations from Dutch.
73) David Holloway, The Soviet Union and the Arms Race, New Haven: Yale University Press, 1983, p. 96; F. Halliday, op. cit. (note 70), p. 111.
74) The Defense Monitor, Vol. 12 (1983) no. 1, p. 4.
75) Cit. D. Holloway, op. cit. (note 73), p. 97.
76) K. London (Ed.), op. cit. (note 54), p. 338; S.S. Kaplan, op. cit. (note 9), p. 184.
77) S.S. Kaplan, op. cit. (note 9), p. 184; H. Kissinger, White House Years, Boston: Little Brown, 1979, p. 913, as quoted in B.D. Porter, op. cit. (note 17), p. 25; Seymour M. Hersh, The Price of Power. Kissinger in the Nixon White House, New York: Summit Books, 1983, p. 444.

78) A.J. Pierre, op. cit. (note 21), p. 75.
79) A.Z. Rubinstein, op. cit. (note 8), p. 223.
80) Keesings Historisch Archief, May 21, 1971, p. 334.
81) G.D. Ra'anan, op. cit. (note 10), p. 1.
82) A.Z. Rubinstein, op. cit. (note 8), p. 228; F. Halliday, op. cit. (note 70), p. 47.
83) Reproduced from J.J. Teunissen and H. van Zon, op. cit. (note 2), p. 139.
84) Data from SIPRI Yearbooks, 1968-1981.
85) Data derived from Robert Harkavy, Strategic Access, Bases and Arms Transfers: The Major Powers' Evolving Geopolitical Competition in the Middle East, in: Milton Leitenberg and Gabriel Sheffer (Eds.), Great Powers Intervention in the Middle East, New York: Pergamon, 1979, pp. 165-187; Galia Golan, Soviet Power and Policies in the Third World: The Middle East, in: Christopher Bertram (Ed.), Prospects of Soviet Power in the 1980s, London: Macmillan, 1980, pp. 59-60; M. Leitenberg, op. cit. (note 11), pp. 22-23).
86) Francis Fukuyama, 'Nuclear Shadowboxing: Soviet Intervention Threats in the Middle East', Orbis, Fall 1981, p. 586.
87) John. C. Campbell, Communist Strategies in the Mediterranean, in: Erik P. Hoffmann and Frederic J. Fleron, Jr. (Eds.), The Conduct of Soviet Foreign Policy, New York: Aldine Publishing Company, 1980, pp. 547-548; A.Z. Rubinstein, op. cit. (note 8), p. 243; Nadav Safran, From War to War. The Arab-Israeli confrontations 1948-1967, New York: Bobbs-Merrill, 1969, pp. 274-275, 277.
88) S.S. Kaplan, op. cit. (note 9), p. 167.
89) S.T. Hosmer and Th.W. Wolfe, op. cit. (note 17), pp. 36, 142; J.C. Campbell, op. cit. (note 87), p. 548.
90) A.Z. Rubinstein, op. cit. (note 8), p. 243; B.D. Porter, op. cit. (note 17), p. 23.
91) S.T. Hosmer and Th.W. Wolfe, op. cit. (note 17), pp. 46, 144; F. Fukuyama, op. cit. (note 86), pp. 584-585; B.D. Porter, op. cit. (note 17), pp. 1-2.
92) S.S. Kaplan, op. cit. (note 9), p. 170; A.Z. Rubinstein, op. cit. (note 8), p. 244.
93) J.L. Nogee and R.H. Donaldson, op. cit. (note 60), p. 181.
94) G.D. Ra'anan, op. cit. (note 10), p. 12.
95) S.S. Kaplan, op. cit. (note 9), p. 194, p. 170; S.T. Hosmer and Th.W. Wolfe, op. cit. (note 17), pp. 49, 62, 130.
96) Idem, p. 181; S.T. Hosmer and Th.W. Wolfe, op. cit. (note 17), p. 47; S.M. Hersh, op. cit. (note 77), p. 242.
97) Idem, p. 185; S.T. Hosmer and Th.W. Wolfe, op. cit. (note 17), pp. 50-51.
98) John C. Campbell, op. cit. (note 87), p. 549; B.D. Porter, op. cit. (note 17), p. 124; S.T. Hosmer and Th.W. Wolfe, op. cit. (note 17), p. 143.
99) S.S. Kaplan, op. cit. (note 9), p. 188.
100) Idem, p. 194; S.T. Hosmer and Th.W. Wolfe, op. cit. (note 17), p. 130; The Pike Papers, repr. The Village Voice (New York), Vol. 21 (1976) no. 7 (February 16), p. 85.

101) J.L. Nogee, op. cit. (note 3), p. 443.
102) Bradford Dismukes and James M. McConnell, Soviet Naval Diplomacy, New York: Pergamon Press, 1979, p. 117.
103) A.Z. Rubinstein, op. cit. (note 8), p. 257.
104) A.M. Cox, op. cit. (note 4), p. 48; G.D. Ra'anan, op. cit. (note 10), p. 55; S.T. Hosmer and Th.W. Wolfe, op. cit. (note 17), pp. 96, 171; B.D. Porter, op. cit. (note 17), p. 33.
105) R. Barnet, The Giants. Russia and America, New York: Simon and Schuster, 1977, p. 19.
106) G.D. Ra'anan, op. cit. (note 10), pp. 36-37; W.J. Durch, Revolution from Afar. - The Cuban Armed Forces in Africa and the Middle East, Alexandria: Center for Naval Analysis, 1977, pp. 4, 9; S.T. Hosmer and Th.W. Wolfe, op. cit. (note 17), p. 25.
107) F. Halliday, op. cit. (note 70), p. 47.
108) William Beecher, 'Behind Soviet decision to give Syria missiles', Boston Globe, October 17, 1983, p. 13; Mustafa Tlas in interview with Der Spiegel (Hamburg), Vol. 38 (1984) no. 37 (September 10), p. 140.
109) M. Leitenberg, 1982, op. cit. (note 11), p. 28; A.J. Pierre, op. cit. (note 21), p. 198.
110) A.J. Pierre, op. cit. (note 21), p. 189.
111) J.L. Nogee, in R.H. Donaldson, op. cit. (note 3), p. 448.
112) Cit. Daniel Volman, A Continent Besieged: Foreign Military Activities in Africa since 1975, Washington, D.C.: IPS, ca. 1982, p. 5.
113) Cit. A.M. Cox, op. cit. (note 4), p. 59.
114) Cit. in review article of Kenneth Grundy, 'Moscow, Havana, and Africa', Problems of Communism, Vol. 30 (1981) no. 4 (August), p. 66.
115) A.Z. Rubinstein, op. cit. (note 8), p. 231; A.J. Pierre, op. cit. (note 21), pp. 75-76.
116) Mahmood Mamdani, Imperialism and Fascism in Uganda, London: Heinemann, 1984; cit. Martin Ros, 'Een Afrikaanse prinses op oorlogspad' (2), NRC Handelsblad, 3 March 1984, p. 6; also M. Leitenberg, op. cit. (note 11), p. 38.
117) Robin Luckham, 'Underdevelopment and Demilitarization in Africa', Alternatives, No. 6, July 1980, p. 226.
118) B.D. Porter, op. cit. (note 17), pp. 24, 90-111.
119) R.H. Donaldson (Ed.), op. cit. (note 3), p. 442; Hans van Zon, Het gemak waarmee vrienden vijanden werden. Russische invloed in Africa beperkt, in: I.I. Teunissen and H. v. Zon, op. cit. (note 2), p. 72; S.T. Hosmer and Th.W. Wolfe, op. cit. (note 17), pp. 48-49; R. Luckham, op. cit. (note 117), pp. 242-243.
120) Figures from R.L. Sivard, op. cit. (note 64), pp. 8-9.
121) Robin Luckham, 'French Militarism in Africa', Review of African Political Economy, No. 24, May-August 1982, p. 57, Table I.
122) Colin Legum, I. William Zartman et al., Africa in the 1980s. A Continent in Crisis, New York: McGraw Hill, 1979, pp. 45-46.
123) R. Luckham, op. cit. (note 121), p. 55.
124) A.Z. Rubinstein, op. cit. (note 8), p. 232.
125) W.J. Durch, op. cit. (note 40), pp. 18-22.
126) Idem, p. 7.

127) S.S. Kaplan, op. cit. (note 9), pp. 195-196.
128) The Pike Papers, op. cit. (note 100), p. 85.
129) John Stockwell, In Search of Enemies, New York: Norton, 1978, as quoted in F. Halliday, op. cit. (note 70), p. 137, note 12.
130) Nelson P. Valdes, Revolutionary Solidarity in Angola, in: Cole Blasier and Carmelo Mesa-Lago (Eds.), Cuba in the World, Pittsburgh: University of Pittsburgh Press, 1979, pp. 97-98.
131) Bertil Dunér, The Intervenor: Lone Wolf or...? Co-operation between Interveners in Civil Wars, Stockholm: Institute for International Affairs, 1983, Mimeo, pp. 9-11 (later published in Cooperation and Conflict, No. 4, 1983).
132) Colin Legum, in C. Legum and I.W. Zartman et al., op. cit. (note 122), p. 46.
133) N.P. Valdes, op. cit. (note 130), p. 101; Brian Crozier, The Surrogate Forces of the Soviet Union, London: ISC, 1978, p. 2.
134) N.P. Valdes, op. cit. (note 130), p. 103.
135) Idem, pp. 103-108; R.B. Barnet, op. cit. (note 105), p. 44.
136) René Lemarchand, 'The C.I.A. in Africa: How Central? How Intelligent?', The Journal of Modern African Studies, Vol. 14 (1976) no. 3, p. 408.
137) Newsweek, May 22, 1978, quoting John Stockwell, cit. in: John L.S. Girling, America and the Third World. Revolution and Intervention, London: Routledge & Kegan Paul, 1980, p. 270; R. Lemarchand, op. cit. (note 136), p. 414.
138) N.P. Valdes, op. cit. (note 130), p. 103.
139) S.S. Kaplan, op. cit. (note 9), p. 196.
140) A.M. Cox, op. cit. (note 4), pp. 34, 36.
141) Cit. N.P. Valdes, op. cit. (note 130), p. 109.
142) A.M. Cox, op. cit. (note 4), p. 37.
143) Cit. N.P. Valdes, op. cit. (note 130), p. 110.
144) Cit. B.D. Porter, op. cit. (note 17), p. 169.
145) N.P. Valdes, op. cit. (note 130), p. 111; S.S. Kaplan, op. cit. (note 9), p. 196.
146) Cit. A.M. Cox, op. cit. (note 4), p. 39.
147) D. Volman, op. cit. (note 112), p. 7; N.P. Valdes, op. cit. (note 130), p. 105; A.M. Cox, op. cit. (note 4), p. 38.
148) Cit. N.P. Valdes, op. cit. (note 130), p. 105.
149) David T. Twining, 'Soviet Activities in the Third World: A New Pattern', Military Review, No. 6, June 1980, p. 5; S.T. Hosmer and Th.W. Wolfe, op. cit. (note 17), p. 83.
150) K. Grundy, op. cit. (note 114), p. 66.
151) See K. Grundy's review of literature on the Soviet Union in Africa, op. cit. (note 114), p. 64.
152) Colin Legum, in C. Legum and I.W. Zartman et al., op. cit. (note 122), pp. 49-51.
153) Kenneth G. Weiss, The Soviet Involvement in the Ogaden War, Alexandria: Center for Naval Analysis, 1980, pp. 2-4.
154) B.D. Porter, op. cit. (note 17), p. 192; W.J. Durch, op. cit. (note 40), pp. 53-54.
155) K.G. Weiss, op. cit. (note 153), pp. 4-5.
156) F. Halliday, op. cit. (note 70), p. 98.

157) Richard Remnek, Soviet Policy in the Horn of Africa: The Decision to Intervene, Alexandria, Virg.: Center for Naval Analysis, 1980, pp. 24-27.
158) Idem, p. 31.
159) K.G. Weiss, op. cit. (note 153), p. 7.
160) Mohammad Ayoob, The Horn of Africa, in: M. Ayoob (Ed.), Conflict and Intervention in the Third World, London: Croom Helm, 1980, p. 155; R. Remnek, op. cit. (note 157), p. 48.
161) F. Halliday, op. cit. (note 70), p. 106.
162) K.G. Weiss, op. cit. (note 153), p. 10.
163) K.G. Weiss, op. cit. (note 153), p. 8; F. Halliday, op. cit. (note 70), p. 106-107.
164) Newsweek, September 26, 1977, pp. 42-43, as quoted in R. Remnek, op. cit. (note 157), pp. 48-49.
165) K.G. Weiss, op. cit. (note 153), pp. 10-12.
166) A.M. Cox, op. cit. (note 4), p. 41; M. Ayoob, op. cit. (note 160), p. 157.
167) R. Remnek, op. cit. (note 157), p. 27; S.T. Hosmer and Th.W. Wolfe, op. cit. (note 17), p. 91.
168) F. Halliday, op. cit. (note 70), p. 100; M. Ayoob, op. cit. (note 160), p. 158.
169) A.M. Cox, op. cit. (note 4), p. 41; S.T. Hosmer and Th.W. Wolfe, op. cit. (note 17), p. 92.
170) A.Z. Rubinstein, op. cit. (note 8), p. 231; A.M. Cox, op. cit. (note 4), p. 41; R. Remnek, op. cit. (note 157), p. 33.
171) K.G. Weiss, op. cit. (note 153), p. 17; S.T. Hosmer and Th.W. Wolfe, op. cit. (note 17), p. 228.
172) D.T. Twining, op. cit. (note 149), p. 6; B.D. Porter, op. cit. (note 17), p. 201; S.T. Hosmer and Th.W. Wolfe, op. cit. (note 17), pp. 92, 131.
173) A.J. Pierre, op. cit. (note 21), p. 258.
174) 'Report of the National Bipartisan Commission on Central America', Washington, D.C.: GPO, 1983; as partly repr. in NRC Handelsblad, January 12, 1984, p. 4.
175) D.T. Twining, op. cit. (note 149), p. 6.
176) S.S. Kaplan, op. cit. (note 9), p. 200.
177) R. Remnek, op. cit. (note 157), pp. 38, 43.
178) G. Golan, op. cit. (note 85), pp. 59-60.
179) F. Halliday, Bij het nekvel naar het socialisme. Het Sovjetmodel in de Derde Wereld, in: J.J. Teunissen and H. van Zon (Eds.), op. cit. (note 2), p. 125; F. Halliday, Moskou en de Derde Wereld. Een golf van revoluties, in: Idem, p. 24.
180) Cit. A.J. Pierre, op. cit. (note 21), p. 141.
181) S.S. Kaplan, op. cit. (note 9), p. 663.
182) Idem, p. 77.
183) Cit. S.S. Kaplan, op. cit. (note 9), p. 192.
184) A.Z. Rubinstein, op. cit. (note 8), p. 235.
185) M. Leitenberg, op. cit. (note 11), pp. 34, 29).
186) Evening Star (Washington, D.C.) November 19, 1969; cit. Richard Pipes, 'Russia's Mission, America's Destiny. The Premises of U.S. and Soviet Foreign Policy', Encounter, Vol. 35 (1970) no. 4 (October), p. 8n.

187) C.R. Mitchell, 'Civil Strife and the Involvement of External Parties', International Studies Quarterly, Vol. 14 (1970) no. 2 (June), p. 192.
188) B. Crozier, op. cit. (note 133), titel.
189) B. Dunér. op. cit. (note 131), p. 3.
190) K. Grundy, op. cit. (note 114), p. 67.
191) S.T. Hosmer and Th.W. Wolfe, op. cit. (note 17), p. 79.
192) Cit. George A. Glass, 'East Germany in Black Africa: a new special role?', The World Today, Aug. 1980, p. 311.
193) R.E. Bissell, op. cit. (note 32), p. 103.
194) This table is based on: M. Leitenberg, The Military Implications of Arms Sales to the Third World: What Do We Know, and What Don't We Know, Ithaca: Cornell University, 1979, draft paper, 1979, p. 21; M. Leitenberg, op. cit. (note 11), p. 4.
195) J.L. Nogee, op. cit. (note 3), p. 448.
196) M. Leitenberg, 1979, op. cit. (note 194), p. 15.
197) Michael T. Klare, Resurgent Militarism, Washington, D.C.: IPS, 1979, pp. 9-10; Stockholm International Peace Research Institute, World Armaments and Disarmaments, Sipri Yearbook 1984, London: Taylor and Francis, 1984, pp. 176-178.
198) Thomas G. Hart, The Spread of Extra-European Conflict to Europe. Concepts and Analysis, Stockholm: Swedish Institute for International Affairs, 1979, p. 7.
199) Barry M. Blechman, Outside Military Forces in Third World Conflicts, in: Christopher Bertram et al. (Eds.), Third World Conflict and International Security. Part I, London: IISS, 1981, p. 37.
200) James M. McConnell and Anne M. Kelly, as quoted in S.S. Kaplan, op. cit. (note 9), p. 181; B. Dismukes and J. McConnell, op. cit. (note 102), p. 277.
201) B.D. Porter, op. cit. (note 17), p. 5.
202) V.M. Kulish, Military Force in International Relations, in: Kulish et al., Voennaya sila i mezhdunarodnye otnosheniy a, Moscow, 1972, pp. 19, 24, as quoted in B. Dismukes and J. McConnell, op. cit. (note 102), pp. xv-xvi - Emphasis added, AS.

Notes to Case Study X: The Soviet Intervention into Afghanistan
(1979-)

1) Fred Halliday, Threat from the East? Soviet Policy from Afghanistan and Iran to the Horn of Africa, revised edition, Harmondsworth: Penguin Books, 1982, pp. 89-90.
2) Current History, February 1980, p. 91, cited in: Berto Jongman, War, Armed Conflict and Political Violence: A Pilot Study, Groningen: Polemologisch Instituut, 1983, p. 133.
3) A conflicting but undocumented interpretation is offered by the Annual of Power and Conflict, 1979-80: A Survey of Political Violence and International Influence, London: Institute for the Study of Conflict, 1980. According to the APC Taraki "was killed

on Soviet instructions by Amin, whose policies displayed closer alignment to Soviet requirements". (Op. cit., p. 408.) - The Soviets later accused Amin as being a CIA agent.

4) De Volkskrant, January 6, 1981.
5) Michael Orr, Invasion of Afghanistan, in: Robert Thompson (Consultant Ed.), War in Peace: An Analysis of Warfare since 1945, London: Orbis Publishing, 1981, p. 288.
6) Idem, p. 289.
7) NRC Handelsblad, April 2, 1983. According to B. Jongman, op. cit. (note 2), p. 132, the decimation of the Afghan army was mainly a result of the factional struggle between the Khalq and the Parcham factions in the PDPA.
8) NRC Handelsblad, October 19, 1983, and January 3, 1984.
9) Joris Versteeg, 'Ooggetuige in Afghanistan' [Eye-witness in Afghanistan], in: Vrij Nederland, June 4, 1983, bijvoegsel no. 22, p. 12.
10) NRC Handelsblad, June 8, 1983. However, the number of 15,000 casualties is also often mentioned, of which 5,000 would be fatalities (e.g. De Volkskrant, March 26, 1983; comp. with NRC Handelsblad, April 2, 1983). Western diplomats estimated Soviet fatalities in late 1983 at 15,000 to 20,000; according to an Afghan press agency, narrowly linked up with the guerrilla resistance, over 50,000 Soviets had been killed from the December 1979 invasion (NRC Handelsblad, December 24, 1983).
11) S. Enders Wimbush and Alex Alexiev, 'Soviet Central Asian Soldiers in Afghanistan', in: Conflict, Vol. 4 (1983) nos. 2/3/4, pp. 325-338.
12) R.D.M. Furlong and Theodor Winkler, 'The Soviet Invasion of Afghanistan', in: International Defense Review, Vol. 13 (1980) no. 2, p. 169.
13) Imtiaz H. Bokhari, 'The War in Afghanistan: A Study of Insurgency and Counter-Insurgency', in: Strategic Studies, Vol. 5 (1982), no. 3, pp. 35-40; Bokhari refers to a 'scorched earth' strategy.
14) Estimates vary greatly: between $ 7 to $ 18 million per day to fight the war (Bokhari, op. cit. (note 13), p. 43); $ 15 million per day to suppress the Afghan resistance (Nake M. Kamrany, 'Afghanistan under Soviet Occupation', in: Current History, no. 475 (May 1982), p. 230; several million dollars a day to sustain the Afghan state (F. Halliday, op. cit. (note 1), p. 115).
15) Keesings Historisch Archief: Geïllustreerd dagboek van het hedendaags wereldgebeuren, Amsterdam/Antwerpen: Keesings uitgeversmaatschappij, November 12, 1982, p. 752.
16) F. Halliday, op. cit. (note 1), p. 92.
17) CIA estimates which were published in 1977 and confirmed in 1979, still expected the Soviet Union to become an oil importer by 1982 with rapidly increasing requirements (R.D.M. Furlong and Th. Winkler, op. cit. (note 12), p. 170).
18) Interview with the correspondent of the Arab newspaper Al Sharq Al Awsat (Sunday Times, January 6), 1980, cited in: F. Halliday, op. cit. (note 1), p. 93 and 144; comp. also D. Rees,

'Afghanistan's Role in Soviet Strategy', in: Conflict Studies, no. 118 (May 1980), p. 3).

19) D. Rees, ibid.

20) Idem, p. 9.

21) Roy Medvedev, 'The Afghan Crisis' (interview), in: New Left Review, no. 121 (May/June 1980), pp. 94-95, quotation p. 94.

22) Cox and Arbatov, in: Arthur Macy Cox with a Soviet Commentary by Georgy Arbatov, Russian Roulette: The Superpower Game, New York: Times Books, 1982, see p. 57 and 177.

23) F. Halliday, op. cit. (note 1), p. 116.

Notes to Epilogue: Past and Future of Soviet Military Interventions

1) K.V. Tauras, Guerilla Warfare on the Amber Coast, New York: Voyages Press, 1962, p. 8n. - The events listed in Table VIII are not derived from Tauras.

2) Cit. Thede Palm, The Finnish-Soviet Armistice Negotiations of 1944, Stockholm: Almqvist & Wiksell, 1971, p. 88.

3) Cit. Ladislaus Singer, Sowjet-Imperialismus, Stuttgart: Seewald, 1970, pp. 133-134.

4) Cit. Kristian Gerner, The Soviet Union and Central Europe in the Post-War Era. A Study in Precarious Security, Stockholm: The Swedish Institute of International Affairs, 1984, p. 165.

5) Cit. L. Singer, op. cit. (note 3), pp. 64-67.

6) Herman de Lange, De bewapeningswedloop tussen de Verenigde Staten en de Sovjetunie, 1945-1983, Leeuwarden: Eisma, 1983, pp. 253-255.

7) Veljko Mićunović, Moscow Diary, London: Chatto and Windus, 1980, pp. 133-134.

8) Ibid., p. 134.

9) Peter Gosztony, Die Rote Armee. Machtfaktor der Weltpolitik, München: Goldmann, 1983, pp. 328-329.

10) K. Gerner, op. cit. (note 4), p. 170.

11) Idem, p. 183.

12) Milovan Djilas, Conversations With Stalin, New York, 1962; cit. Todd. Gitlin, 'Counter-Insurgency: Myth and Reality in Greece', in: David Horowitz (Ed.), Containment and Revolution. Western Policy towards Social Revolution: 1917 to Vietnam, London: Anthony Blond, 1967, p. 174.

13) Robin Alison Remington, The Warsaw Pact. Case studies in Communist Conflict Resolution, Cambridge, Mass.: The MIT Press, 1971, p. 64; Klaus von Beyme, Die Sowjetunion in der Weltpolitik, München: Piper, 1983, p. 85.

14) L. Singer, op. cit. (note 3), pp. 154-155.

15) Christopher D. Jones, Soviet Influence in Eastern Europe. Political Autonomy and the Warsaw Pact, New York: Praeger, 1981, pp. 104-105.

16) Richard D. Anderson, Jr., 'Soviet Decision-Making and Poland', in: Problems of Communism (1982) (March-April), pp. 32, 35-36.

17) Andrzej Kutylowski, 'Review Essay: Interpretations of Peace and War in Poland. A Review of Recent Literature', Journal of Peace Research, Vol. 21 (1984) no. 3, p. 297.

18) A. Ross Johnson, Robert W. Dean and Alexander Alexiev, East European Military Establishments: The Warsaw Pact Northern Tier, New York: Crane Russak, 1982, p. 148.

19) Sipri, The Arms Race and Arms Control 1984. The shorter Sipri Yearbook, London: Taylor and Francis, 1984, p. 88, Table 3A, for 1983.

20) Teresa Rakowska-Harmstone, Christopher D. Jones, John Jaworsky, Ivan Sylvain, Warsaw Pact: The Question of Cohesion. Phase II - Vol. I: The Greater Socialist Army: Integration and Reliability, Ottawa: Operational Research and Analysis Establishment, Febr. 1984, pp. v-vi.

21) Zdeněk Mlynář, Krisen und Krisenbewältigung im Sowjetblock, Köln: Bund-Verlag, 1983, p. 170.

22) Idem, p. 166-167.

23) Stephen T. Hosmer and Thomas W. Wolfe, Soviet Policy and Practice toward Third World Conflicts, Lexington, Mass.: D.C. Heath, 1983, p. 188.

24) Submarine Defence Commission, Countering the Submarine Threat, Submarine violations and Swedish security policy, Stockholm: Swedish Official Reports Series, 1983, p. 106.

25) Cf. G. Kade, Die Bedrohungslüge. Zur Legende von der 'Gefahr aus dem Osten', Köln: Pahl-Rugenstein, 1982.

26) A.R. Johnson et al., op. cit. (note 18), pp. 145-148.

27) Figures from a Soviet pamphlet The Threat to Europe (1981), as quoted in A. Cockburn, The Threat. Inside the Soviet Military Machine, New York: Random House, 1983, p. 8.

28) ISS, Military Balance 1982/83, as quoted in Andrew Wilson, Das Abrüstungshandbuch. Analysen, Zusammenhänge, Hintergründe, Hamburg: Hoffmann und Campe, 1984, p. 128.

29) Statement of D.F. Fleming, in: U.S. Congress, House, Subcommittee on Europe of the Committee on Foreign Affairs, 92nd Congress, 1st Session, Hearings, The Cold War Origins and Developments, Washington, D.C.: GPO, 1971, p. 12; see also Rem. A. Beloussow, 'Wie leben nun die Russen?', in: Der Spiegel, Nr. 29, 12 June 1976, p. 101.

30) John Keegan, World Armies, London: Macmillan, 1979, p. 736.

31) John J. Mearsheimer, 'Why the Soviets Can't Win Quickly in Central Europe', in: International Security, Vol. 7 (1982) no. 1 (Summer), pp. 32-33.

32) Idem, p. 7n.

33) Leopold Labedz, 'The Soviet Union and Western Europe', in: Survey, (1973) no. 3, p. 14, as quoted in George Ginsburg and Alvin Z. Rubinstein (Eds.), Soviet Foreign Policy Toward Western Europe, New York: Praeger, 1978, p. 289.

34) Figure from J.Th. Degenkamp, 'P.v.d.A. moet beter nadenken over defensie', in: Volkskrant, November 10, 1984, p. 17.

35) Source: Gallup surveys as reported in Newsweek, 15 March, 1982, p. 9. - Quoted from Bruce Russett and Donald R. DeLuca, 'Theatre Nuclear Forces: Public Opinion in Western Europe', in:

Political Science Quarterly, Vol. 98 (1983) no. 2 (Summer), p. 189; for USA: 1981 Gallup Survey as reported in John Barron, KGB heute. Moskaus Spionagezentrale von innen, Bern: Scherz, 1983, p. 402n.

36) G. Ginsburg and A.Z. Rubinstein, op. cit. (note 33), pp. 9-117; as summarized in Robert Woito, To End War. A New Approach to International Conflict, New York: The Pilgrim Press, 1982, p. 240.

37) B. Russett and D.R. DeLuca, op. cit. (note 35), p. 188.

38) Hannes Adomeit, The Soviet Union and Western Europe. Perceptions, Policies, Problems, Kingston, Ontario: Center for International Relations, 1979, p. 162.

39) K. von Beyme, op. cit. (note 13), p. 60.

40) Jan M. Meijer (Ed.), The Trotsky Papers 1917-1922. Vol. I: 1917-1919, The Hague: Mouton, 1964, p. 627.

41) Mose L. Harvey in Foreword to Morris Rothenberg's The USSR and Africa, as quoted in Kenneth Grundy, 'Moscow, Havana, and Africa', Problems of Communism, Vol. 30 (1981) no. 4 (August), p. 65.

42) Stanley Hoffmann, Dead Ends. American Foreign Policy in the New Cold War, Cambridge, Mass.: Ballinger, 1983, p. 99.

43) Cit. Guillermo Toriello, La Batalla de Guatemala, Mexico, D.F., 1955; as quoted in Eduardo Galeano, Guatemala: Occupied Country, New York, 1969, p. 52.

44) Barry M. Blechman, Outside Military Forces in Third World Conflicts, in: Christopher Bertram et al., Third World Conflict and International Security. Part I, London: IISS, 1981, p. 31 (Adelphi Papers, no. 166); Robin Luckham, 'French Militarism in Africa', Review of African Political Economy, (1982) no. 24 (May-August), pp. 55-57.

45) Daniel Volman, A Continent Besieged: Foreign Military Activities in Africa since 1975, Washington, D.C.: IPS, ca. 1982, pp. 8, 4.

46) K. von Beyme, op. cit. (note 13), p. 47.

47) S. Kogelfranz, "So weit die Armeen kommen..." Wie Osteuropa nach Jalta kommunistisch worde', Der Spiegel, Vol. 38 (1984) no. 37 (September 10), p. 180.

48) Cit. The Defence Monitor, Vol. 9 (1980) no. 1 (January), p. 6.

49) Data arrived at on the basis of statistical information provided in Michael Kidron and Dan Smith, The War Atlas. Armed Conflict - Armed Peace, London: Pan Books, 1983, Country Tables: The International Military Order. These figures should be treated with great caution since the Cold War orientation of mid-1982 is an arbitrary yardstick given the many "switchers". The definition of alignments (core, pro, non-aligned) is also a matter of some dispute. Nicaragua, for instance, is treated as "non-aligned", while Afghanistan appears as "core-east" in the Kidron/Smith classification.

50) 'Soviet Geopolitical Momentum: Myth or Menace. Trends of Soviet Influence Around the World From 1945 to 1980', The Defense Monitor, Vol. 9 (1980) no. 1 (January), pp. 3-4.

51) The Power index is based on a combination of demographic, geographical, economic and military factors and covered 78 countries (13 pro-Soviet ones, 15 other non-aligned and 49

pro-Western ones plus China. The United States and its military allies scored 1,449 points on the power index, the other pro-Western countries 351 and China 139 points. The non-aligned scored 250 points while the Soviet Union and its clients were given 556 points. Idem, pp. 5-6; for methodology, see: Ray S. Cline, World Power Trends and U.S. Foreign Policy for the 1980s, Boulder, Colorado: Westview Press, 1980.

52) David Holloway, The Soviet Union and the Arms Race, New Haven: Yale University Press, 1983, p. 91.

53) Cit. D. Holloway, op. cit. (note 52), p. 91.

54) Cit. Foster Rhea Dulles, The United States, since 1865, Ann Arbor: The University of Michigan Press, 1974, p. 490.

55) Cit. John L.S. Girling, America and the Third World. Revolution and Intervention, London: Routledge & Kegan Paul, 1980, pp. 148-149.

56) Michael Nacht, Internal Change and Regime Stability, in: Christopher Bertram et al., Third-World Conflict and International Security. Part I, London: International Institute for Strategic Studies, 1981 (Adelphi Paper no. 166), p. 53.

57) Stanley Hoffmann, Security in an Age of Turbulance: Means of Response, in: Stanley Hoffmann et al., Third-World Conflict and International Security. Part II, London: International Institute for Strategic Studies, 1981 (Adelphi Papers no. 167), p. 6.

58) Harry Wilde, Trotzki, Reinbek: Rowohlt, 1970, p. 125.

59) R. Lowenthal, 'The Soviet Policy of Global Expansion: Political/Ideological Perspectives', in: U.S. Army Institute for Advanced Russian and East European Studies. 5th Annual Soviet Affairs Symposium, 20-22 April 1971. The Present Stage of Soviet Global Expansion: Sources and Prospects. Garmish, 1971, p. 6.

60) China Daily (Peking), December 7, 1984, as quoted in Volkskrant, December 8, 1984, p. 1.

BIBLIOGRAPHY

Adomeit, Hannes	The Soviet Union and Western Europe. Perceptions, Policies, Problems. - Kingston, Ontario: Centre for International Relations, 1979.
Allard, Sven	Russia and the Austrian State Treaty: A Case Study of Soviet Policy in Europe. - London: The Pennsylvania State University Press, 1970.
Annual	Annual of Power and Conflict: A Survey of Political Violence and International Influence, 1976-77, 1977-78, 1978-79, 1979-80, 1980-81. - London: Institute for the Study of Conflict.
Arbatov, Georgy	A Soviet Commentary in: Arthur Macy Cox, Russian Roulette. The Superpower Game. - New York: Times Books, 1982.
Arber, Christina	A Study of Civilian Defence, with Special Reference to the Contrasting Theories of Sharp and Boserup/Mack within the Context of General Civilian Defence Theory, and Illustrated by Events, and Methods Used, in Hungary 1956 and Czechoslovakia 1968. - University of Bradford, School of Peace Studies, 1980.

Averoff-Tossizza, Evangelos
By Fire and Axe: The Communist Party and the Civil War in Greece, 1944-1949. - New Rochelle, N.Y.: Caratzas Brothers, 1978.

Ayoob, Mohammed	The Horn of Africa in: M. Ayoob (Ed.), Conflict and Intervention in the Third World. - London: Croom Helm, 1980.
Bader, William B.	Austria between East and West, 1945-1955. - Stanford, California: Stanford University Press, 1966.

Baehr, P.R., in co-operation with P.J.G. Kapteyn
De Verenigde Naties: Ideaal en werkelijkheid [The United Nations: Ideal and Reality]. - Utrecht/ Antwerpen: Het Spectrum, 1976.

Baltic   The Baltic States and the Soviet Union, reprinted
                          from a Report of the Council of Europe, with a
                          Preface   and   Supplementary   Comments.   -
                          Stockholm: Skanska Centraltryckeriet, 1962. -
                          (Problems of the Baltics no. 1)

Baltic   Baltic States: A Study of Their Origin and
                          National   Development;   Their   Seizure   and
                          Incorporation into the U.S.S.R., Third Interim
                          Report of the Select Committee on Communist
                          Aggression, House of Representatives Eighty-
                          Third Congress, Second Session 1954; 3rd repr.
                          edition
                          in: International Military Law & History, Reprint
                          Series Vol. IV. - Buffalo/New York: William S.
                          Hein & Co., 1972.

Barber, Noel   De Hongaarse opstand: Zeven dagen vrijheid [The
                          Hungarian Uprising: Seven Days of Freedom],
                          transl. - Amsterdam/Brussel: Elsevier Nederland,
                          1976.

Barnds, William J.   South Asia
                          in: Kurt London (Ed.), The Soviet Union in World
                          Politics. - Boulder, Colorado: Westview Press,
                          1980.

Barron, John   KGB heute. Moskaus Spionagezentrale von innen.
                          - Bern: Scherz, 1983.

Behrens, Henning   Die Afghanistan-Intervention der UdSSR: Unab-
                          hängigkeit und Blockfreiheit oder Mongolisierung
                          Afghanistan: Eine Herausforderung für das inter-
                          nationale Krisenmanagement. - München: Tuduv-
                          Buch, 1982.

Berchin, J.B.   Istoriya SSSR 1917-1978 [A History of the USSR
                          1917-1978], 3rd edition. - Moscow: Vysshaya
                          Shkola, 1979.

Beyme, Klaus von   Die Sowjetunion in der Weltpolitik. - München:
                          Piper, 1983.

Bissell, Richard E.   'Soviet Use of Proxies in the Third World: The
                          Case of Yemen'
                          Soviet Studies, vol. 30 (1978) no. 1 (January).

Blechman, Barry M., Stephen S. Kaplan et al.
                          Force without War: U.S. Armed Forces as a
                          Political Instrument. - Washington, D.C.: The
                          Brookings Institution, 1978.

Blechman, Barry M. Outside Military Forces in Third World Conflicts
in: Christopher Bertram et al. (Eds.), Third World
Conflict and International Security. Part I. -
London, IISS, 1981. - (Adelphi Papers, no. 166)

Bloomfield, L.P., and A.C. Leiss
Controlling Small Wars: A Strategy for the
1970s. - New York: A.A. Knopf, 1969.

Bokhari, Imtiaz H. 'The War in Afghanistan: A Study of Insurgency
and Counter-Insurgency'
Strategic Studies, vol. 5 (1982) no. 3.

Bolshaya Bolshaya Sovetskaya Entisklopediya [Great Soviet
Encyclopaedia], 3rd edition. - Moscow: Izdatel-
stvo Sovetskaya Entsiklopediya, vol. 14, 1973,
s.v. 'Latviiskaya Sovetskaya Sotsialisticheskaya
Respublika' [Latvian Soviet Socialist Republic]
and 'Litovskaya Sovetskaya Sotsialisticheskaya
Respublika' [Lithuanian Soviet Socialist Repub-
lic]; vol. 30, 1978, s.v. 'Estonskaya Sovetskaya
Sotsialisticheskaya Respublika' [Estonian Soviet
Socialist Republic].

Booth, Ken The Military Instrument in Soviet Foreign Policy,
1917-1972. - London: Royal United Services
Institute, 1973.

Borisov, O.B., and B.T. Koloskov
Sovetsko-Kitaiskiye otnoshenija, 1945-1970: Kra-
tkii ocherk [Soviet-Chinese Relations, 1945-1970:
A Short Outline]. - Moscow: Mysl', 1971.

Butterworth, Robert Lyle, with Margaret E. Scranton
Managing Interstate Conflict, 1945-74: Data with
Synopses. - Pittsburgh: University Center for
International Studies, 1976.

Calvocoressi, Peter World Politics Since 1945. - London: Longman,
1982.

Campbell, Christy War Facts Now. - Glasgow, Fontana, 1982.

Campbell, John C. Communist Strategies in the Mediterranean
in: Erik P. Hoffmann and Frederic J. Fleron, Jr.
(Eds.), The Conduct of Soviet Foreign Policy. -
New York: Aldine Publishing Company, 1980.

Carver, Michael War since 1945. - London: Weidenfeld and
Nicholson, 1980.

Casualties   Casualties of Armed Conflicts in the Twentieth
                       Century (1900-1970). - Washington, D.C.: U.S.
                       Arms Control and Disarmament Agency, 1971. -
                       (mimeographed staff report)

Civiic, Christopher   Soviet-East European Relations
                       in: R. Pipes (Ed.), Soviet Strategy in Europe. -
                       New York: Crane, Russak & Co, 1976.

Cline, Ray S.   World Power Trends and U.S. Foreign Policy for
                       the 1980s. - Boulder, Colo.: Westview Press,
                       1980.

Cox, Arthur Macy, with a Soviet Commentary by Georgy Arbatov
                       Russian Roulette: The Superpower Game. - New
                       York: Times Books, 1982.

Crozier, Brian   The Surrogate Forces of the Soviet Union. -
                       London: ISC, 1978.

Day, A.J. (Ed.)   Border and Territorial Disputes, A Keesing's
                       Reference Publication. - s.l.: Longman, 1982.

Defense   The Defense Monitor, vol. 9 (1980) no. 1 & vol.
                       12 (1983) no. 1.

Deportationen   Die Deportationen im Baltikum, 25 Jahre
                       sowjetische Verschleppungen in den baltischen
                       Staaten. - Stockholm: Estnischer Nationalfond,
                       1966.

Dirksen, Erik   'Economische en militaire hulp van de Sovjetunie
                       aan de Derde Wereld'
                       Internationale Spectator, vol. 37 (1983) no. 3
                       (July).

Dismukes, Bradford, and James M. McConnell
                       Soviet Naval Diplomacy. - New York: Pergamon
                       Press, 1979.

Djilas, Milovan   Conversations with Stalin. - New York: Harcourt,
                       Brace & World, 1962.

Donaldson, Robert H. (Ed.)
                       The Soviet Union in the Third World. - Boulder,
                       Colo.: Westview Press, 1981.

Donelan, M.D., and M.J. Grieve
                       International Disputes: Case Histories 1945-1970.
                       - London: Europa Publications for the David
                       Davies Memorial Institute of International
                       Studies, 1973.

Downing, David   An Atlas of Territorial and Border Disputes. -
                        London: New English Library, 1980.

Dunér, Bertil   'Proxy Intervention in Civil Wars'
                        Journal of Peace Research, vol. 18 (1981) no. 4.

Dunér, Bertil   The Intervenor: Lone Wolf or...? Co-operation
                        between Interveners in Civil Wars. - Stockholm,
                        Institute for International Affairs, 1983. - (later
                        published in Cooperation and Conflict, 1983, no.
                        4).

Dunér, Bertil   'The Many-Pronged Spear: External Military
                        Intervention in Civil Wars in the 1970s'
                        Journal of Peace Research, vol. 20 (1983) no. 1.

Dunn, Keith A.   Soviet Involvement in the Third World:
                        Implications of US Policy Assumption
                        in: Robert H. Donaldson (Ed.), The Soviet Union
                        in the Third World. - Boulder: Westview Press,
                        1981.

Dunn, Stephen P.   Cultural Processes in the Baltic Area under
                        Soviet Rule. - Berkely: Institute of International
                        Studies, University of California, 1966. -
                        (Research Series no. 11)

Durch, William J.   The Cuban Military in Africa and the Middle
                        East: From Algeria to Angola. - Alexandria,
                        Virginia: Center for Naval Analysis, 1977.

Durch, William J.   Revolution from Afar: the Cuban Armed Forces
                        in Africa and the Middle East. - Alexandria:
                        Center for Naval Analysis, 1977.

Ebert, Theodor   Non-Violent Resistance Against Communist
                        Regimes?
                        in: Adam Roberts (Ed.), The Strategy of Civilian
                        Defence: Non-Violent Resistance to Aggression. -
                        London: Faber and Faber Ltd., 1967.

Evangelista, Matthew A.
                        'Stalin's Postwar Army Reappraised'
                        International Security, vol. 7 (1982/83) no. 3
                        (Winter).

Fejtö, François   Histoire des Démocraties Populaires: Après
                        Staline, 1953-1968. - Paris: Editions du Seuil,
                        1969.

Finley, Lovell   'Raising the Stakes. The Major Powers Still Play
                        for Keeps in Indochina'
                        Southern Asia Chronicle, (1978) no. 64.

Freedman, Lawrence
                        The Evolution of Nuclear Strategy. - London:
                        Macmillan, 1981.

Friedman, Edward   'Nuclear Blackmail and the End of the Korean
                        War'
                        Modern China, vol. 1 (1975) no. 1.

Friedman, W.   The Allied Military Government of Germany. -
                        London: Stevens & Sons, 1947.

Furlong, R.D.M., and Theodor Winkler
                        'The Soviet Invasion of Afghanistan'
                        International Defense Review, vol. 4 (1980), no.
                        2.

Fukuyama, Francis   'Nuclear   Shadowboxing: Soviet   Intervention
                        Threats in the Middle East'
                        Orbis, Fall 1981.

Galeano, Eduardo   Guatemala: Occupied Country. - New York, 1969.

Geeraerts, Gustaaf   Sociale   verdediging: Situering   van   een   idee
                        [Social Defence: the Setting of an Idea]
                        in: G. Geeraerts & P. Stouthuysen (Eds.),
                        Veiligheid en alternatieve defensie: De idee van
                        sociale verdediging [Security and Alternative
                        Defence: The Concept of Social Defence]. -
                        Brussels: I.O.T., 1983.

Gerassi, John   The Great Fear: The Reconquest of Latin
                        America by Latin Americans. - New York, 1963.

Gerner, Kristian   The Soviet Union and Central Europe in the
                        Postwar Era. A Study in Precarious Security. -
                        Stockholm: The Swedish Institute of International
                        Affairs, 1984.

Girling, John L.S.   America and the Third World. Revolution and
                        Intervention. - London: Routledge & Kegan Paul,
                        1980.

Gitlin, Todd   Counter-Insurgency; Myth and Reality in Greece
                        in: David Horowitz (Ed.), Containment and
                        Revolution. Western Policy towards Social
                        Revolutions: 1917 to Vietnam. - London: Anthony
                        Blond, 1967.

Glass, George A.   'East Germany in Black Africa: A New Special
                        Role?'
                        The World Today, August 1980.

Godfrey, F.A.   Crisis in Korea
                        in: Robert Thompson (Consultant Ed.), War in
                        Peace: An Analysis of Warfare since 1945. -
                        London: Orbis Publishing, 1981.

Golan, Galia   Soviet Power and Policies in the Third World:
                        The Middle East
                        in: Christopher Bertram (Ed.), Prospects of
                        Soviet Power in the 1980s. - London: Macmillan,
                        1980.

Gosztony, Peter   Die Rote Armee. Machtfaktor der Weltpolitik. -
                        München: Goldmann, 1983.

Goure, Leon, and Morris Rothenberg
                        Latin America
                        in: K. London (Ed.), The Soviet Union in World
                        Politics. - Boulder, Colo.: Westview Press, 1980.

Grundy, Kenneth   'Moscow, Havana, and Africa'
                        Problems of Communism, vol. 30 (1981) no. 4
                        (August).

Halliday, Fred .   Threat from the East? Soviet Policy from
                        Afghanistan and Iran to the Horn of Africa. -
                        Harmondsworth: Pelican Books, 1982.

Halliday, Fred   Bij het nekvel naar het socialisme. Het
                        Sovjetmodel in de Derde Wereld
                        in: J.J. Teunissen and H. van Zon (Eds.), De
                        Russische omhelzing: het Oostblok en de Derde
                        Wereld. - Amsterdam: Transnational Institute,
                        1983.

Halliday, Fred   Moskou en de Derde Wereld. Een golf van
                        revoluties
                        in: J.J. Teunissen and H. van Zon (Eds.), De
                        Russische omhelzing: het Oostblok en de Derde
                        Wereld. - Amsterdam: Transnational Institute,
                        1983.

Halliday, Fred   The Making of the Second Cold War. - London:
                        Verso, 1983.

Hamburg, Roger   Soviet Perspectives on Military Intervention
                        in: Ellen P. Stern (Ed.), The Limits of Military
                        Intervention. - Beverly Hills: Sage, 1977.

Hammond, Thomas H.
                    The Anatomy of Communist Takeovers. - New
                    Haven: Yale University Press, 1975.

Harkavy, Robert   Strategic Access, Bases and Arms Transfers: The
                    Major Powers' Evolving Geopolitical Competition
                    in the Middle East
                    in: Milton Leitenberg and Gabriel Sheffer (Eds.),
                    Great Powers Intervention in the Middle East. -
                    New York: Pergamon, 1979.

Hart, Thomas G.   The Spread of Extra-European Conflict to
                    Europe. Concepts and Analysis. - Stockholm:
                    Swedish Institute for International Affairs, 1979.

Heller, Michael, and Alexander Nekrich
                    Geschichte der Sowjetunion. - 2 vols. -
                    Königstein: Athenäum, 1982.

Hersh, Seymour M. The Price of Power. Kissinger in the Nixon White
                    House. - New York: Summit Books, 1983.

Herspring, Dale R., and Ivan Volgyes
                    'Political Reliability in the Eastern European
                    Warsaw Pact Armies'
                    Armed Forces and Society, vol. 6 (1980) no. 2
                    (Winter).

Hoffmann, Stanley Dead Ends. American Foreign Policy in the New
                    Cold War. - Cambridge, Mass.: Ballinger Publ.,
                    1983.

Holloway, David   The Soviet Union and the Arms Race. - New
                    Haven: Yale University Press, 1983.

Hosmer, Stephen T., and Thomas W. Wolfe
                    Soviet Policy and Practice toward Third World
                    Conflicts. - Lexington, Mass.: D.C. Heath, 1983.

Irving, David   Uprising. - London: Hodder and Stoughton, 1981.

Jones, Christopher D.
                    Soviet Influence in Eastern Europe. Political
                    Autonomy and the Warsaw Pact. - New York:
                    Praeger, 1981.

Jongman, A.J.   Data omtrent oorlogen, conflicten en politiek
                    geweld [Data relating to Wars, Armed Conflicts
                    and Political Violence]. - Groningen: Polemolo-
                    gisch Instituut, 1983. - (College-documentatie
                    map)

Jongman, A.J.   War, Armed Conflict and Political Violence: A
                       Pilot Study. - Groningen: Polemologisch Instituut,
                       1983.

Jukes, Geoffrey   Soviet Strategy
                       in: Desmond Ball (Ed.), Strategy & Defence: Aus-
                       tralian Essays. - Sydney: Allen & Unwin, 1982.

Kade, G.   Die Bedrohungslüge. Zur Legende von der
                       "Gefahr aus dem Osten". - Köln: Pahl-Rugen-
                       stein, 1982.

Kalme, Albert   Total Terror: An Exposé of Genocide in the Bal-
                       tics. - New York: Appleton-Century-Crofts, 1951.

Kamrany, Nake M.   'Afghanistan under Soviet Occupation'
                       Current History, (1982) no. 475 (May).

Kanet, Roger E. (Ed.)
                       Soviet Foreign Policy in the 1980s. - New York:
                       Praeger, 1982.

Kaplan, Stephen S., et al.
                       Diplomacy of Power: Soviet Armed Forces as a
                       Political Instrument. - Washington: The Brookings
                       Institution, 1981.

Kareda, Endel   Estonia in the Soviet Grip: Life and Conditions
                       under Soviet Occupation, 1947-1949. - London:
                       Boreas Publishing Co., 1949. - (East and West:
                       Facts from behind the Iron Curtain no. 5)

Keegan, John   World Armies. - New York: Facts on File, 1979.

Keesings   Keesings Historisch Archief: Geïllustreerd dag-
                       boek van het hedendaags wereldgebeuren, 1950-
                       1952, 1955, 1961 [Keesing's Contemporary Ar-
                       chives, 1950-1952, 1955, 1961]. - Amsterdam:
                       Uitgevers Systemen Keesing.

Kirby, David   The Baltic States 1940-1950
                       in: Martin McCauley (Ed.), Communist Power in
                       Europe, 1944-1949. - London: Macmillan, 1977.

Kirkpatrick, Lyman B.
                       The Decision to Intervene: A Comparison of
                       Soviet Interventions from 1953 to 1980. -
                       Garmisch, Germany: U.S. Army Institute, 1980.

Kissinger, H., et al.
                       Report of the National Bipartisan Commission on
                       Central America. - Washington, D.C.: G.P.O.,

                              January 1984; reprinted in part in NRC
                              Handelsblad, January 12, 1984.

Klare, Michael T.   Resurgent Militarism. - Washington, D.C.: IPS,
                              1979.

Kogelfranz, Siegfried
                              '"So weit die Armeen kommen..." Wie Osteuropa
                              nach Jalta kommunistisch wurde'
                              Der Spiegel (Hamburg), vol. 38 (1984) nos. 35-39
                              (Aug. 27 - Sept. 24).

Kolko, J., and G. Kolko
                              The Limits of Power: The World and the United
                              States Foreign Policy, 1945-1954. - New York:
                              Harper and Row, 1972.

Koreaanse   De Koreaanse oorlog en de Verenigde Naties [The
                              Korean War and the United Nations]. -
                              's-Gravenhage: Staatsuitgeverij, 1951-1955. -
                              (Ministerie van Buitenlandse Zaken, nos. 26, 31,
                              35 en 38)

Kousoulas, D. George
                              The Greek Communist Tried Three Times - and
                              Failed
                              in: Thomas T. Hammond (Ed.), The Anatomy of
                              Communist Takeovers. - New Haven: Yale
                              University Press, 1975.

Kriege   Kriege des 20. Jahrhunderts, transl. from the
                              English. - Zollikon-Schweiz: Albatros Verlag, s.a.

Kriesberg, Louis   'Noncoercive Inducements in U.S.-Soviet Con-
                              flicts: Ending the Occupation of Austria and
                              Nuclear Weapons Tests'
                              Journal of Political and Military Sociology, vol. 9
                              (Spring 1981).

Kulish, V.M.   Military Force in International Relations
                              in: V.M. Kulish et al., Voennaya sila i
                              mezhdunarodnye otnosheniy a. - Moscow, 1972.

Laloy, Jean   Europe in the Soviet Perspective
                              in: Christopher Bertram (Ed.), Prospects of
                              Soviet Power in the 1980s. - London: Macmillan,
                              1980.

Lange, Herman de   De bewapeningswedloop tussen de Verenigde
                              Staten en de Sovjetunie 1945-1983. Een
                              onderzoek naar de relatie tussen politiek en
                              militaire macht. - Leeuwarden: Eisma, 1983.

Laqueur, Walter   Europe Since Hitler. - Harmondsworth: Penguin,
                      1972.

Lefever, Ernest W.   Arms Transfers, Military Training, and Domestic
                      Politics. - Washington, D.C.: Brookings Institu-
                      tion, n.d.

Legum, Colin, I. William Zartman et al.
                      Africa in the 1980s. A Continent in Crisis. - New
                      York: McGraw Hill, 1979.

Leitenberg, Milton   The Military Implications of Arms Sales to the
                      Third World: What Do We Know, and What Don't
                      We Know. - Ithaca, Cornell University, 1979. -
                      (draft paper)

Leitenberg, Milton   The Impact of the Worldwide Confrontation of
                      the Great Powers; Aspects of Military
                      Intervention and the Projection of Military
                      Power. - Stockholm: Swedish Institute of
                      International Affairs, 1982. - (Conference Paper)

Lemarchand, René   'The C.I.A. in Africa: How Central? How
                      Intelligent?'
                      The Journal of Modern African Studies, vol. 14
                      (1976) no. 3.

Levi, Werner   The Coming End of War. - Beverley Hills: Sage,
                      1981.

Lomax, Bill   Hungary 1956. - New York: St. Martin's Press,
                      1976.

Luckham, Robin   'Underdevelopment and Demilitarization in Afri-
                      ca'
                      Alternatives, (1980) no. 6 (July).

Luckham, Robin   'French Militarism in Africa'
                      Review of African Political Economy, (1982) no.
                      24 (May-August).

Luttwak, Edward N.   The Grand Strategy of the Soviet Union. -
                      London: Weidenfeld and Nicolson, 1983.

McCauley, Martin (Ed.)
                      Communist Power in Europe, 1944-1949. -
                      London: Macmillan, 1977.

McCune, George M.   'The Occupation of Korea'
                      Foreign Policy Reports, vol. 33 (1947) no. 15
                      (October 15).

Mackintosh, Malcolm
                    Stalin's Policies towards Eastern Europe,
                    1939-1948: The General Picture
                    in: Thomas T. Hammond (Ed.), The Anatomy of
                    Communist Takeovers. - New Haven: Yale
                    University Press, 1975.

Medvedev, Roy   'The Afghan Crisis' (interview)
                    New Left Review, no. 121 (May/June 1980).

Meissner, Boris   Die Sowjetunion, die Baltischen Staaten und das
                    Völkerrecht. - Köln: Verlag für Politik und
                    Wirtschaft, 1956.

Meijer, Jan M. (Ed.) The Trotsky Papers 1917-1922. Vol. I: 1917-1919.
                    - The Hague: Mouton & Co., 1964.

Mićunović, Veljko   Moscow Diary, transl. - London: Chatto &
                    Windus, 1980.

Military   The Military Balance, 1978-1979. - London: Arms
                    and Armour Press, in ass. with The International
                    Institute for Strategic Studies, 1978.

Mitchell, C.R.   'Civil Strife and the Involvement of External
                    Parties'
                    International Studies Quarterly, vol. 14 (1970) no.
                    2 (June).

Mlynář, Zdeněk   Nachtfrost. Erfahrungen auf dem Weg vom realen
                    zum menschlichen Sozialismus. - Köln: Euro-
                    päische Verlagsanstalt, 1978.

Mlynář, Zdeněk   Krisen und Krisenbewältigung im Sowjetblock. -
                    Köln: Bund-Verlag, 1983.

Molander, E.A., and R.C. Molander
                    What About the Russians and Nuclear War. - New
                    York: Pocket Books, 1983.

Molnar, Miklos   Budapest 1956: A History of the Hungarian
                    Revolution, transl. - London: George Allen &
                    Unwin Ltd., 1971.

New   The New Encyclopaedia Britannica, 15 edition. -
                    Chicago etc., 1976, vol. 2, s.v. 'Baltic States,
                    History of the'.

Nogee, Joseph L.   The Soviet Union in the Third World: Successes
                    and Failures

in: Robert H. Donaldson (Ed.), The Soviet Union in the Third World. - Boulder, Colo.: Westview Press, 1981.

Nogee, Joseph L., and Robert H. Donaldson
Soviet Foreign Policy Since World War Two. - New York: Pergamon Press, 1981.

Onze   Onze jaren: De wereld na 1945. Geschiedenis van de eigen tijd [Our Time: The World after 1945. A History of the Contemporary Period], 2nd edition. - Amsterdam: Amsterdam Boek, 1975.

Oren, Nissan   A Revolution Administered: The Sovietization of Bulgaria
in: Th.T. Hammond (Ed.), The Anatomy of Communist Takeovers. - New Haven: Yale University Press, 1975.

Orr, Michael   Invasion of Afghanistan
in: Robert Thompson (Consultant Ed.), War in Peace: An Analysis of Warfare since 1945. - London: Orbis Publishing, 1981.

Palm, Thede   The Finnish-Soviet Armistice Negotiations of 1944. - Stockholm: Almqvist & Wiksell, 1971.

Parkinson, Roger   Encyclopaedia of Modern War. - London: Paladin Books, 1979.

Perdelwitz, Wolf   Wollen die Russen Krieg? Ein Portrait der Roten Armee - die militärische Stärke der Sowjetunion. - München: Goldmann, 1982.

Petersen, Ib Damgaard
Laws of Development of Cybernetic Systems: The Case of the Sino-Soviet Border Conflict 1963-1973. - (Paper presented to the ECPR Workshop on Non-Standard Data Analysis) in: Forskningsrapport. - Institute of Political Studies, University of Copenhagen, 1979.

Pike   The Pike Papers
repr. in The Village Voice, vol. 21, (1976) no. 7 (February 16).

Porter, Bruce D.   The USSR in Third World Conflict. Soviet Arms and Diplomacy in Local Wars, 1945-1980. - Cambridge: Cambridge University Press, 1984.

Putten, Jan van der   Er waart een spook door Latijns-Amerika. De 'Real-politiek' van de Sovjet Unie

In: Jan Joost Teunissen en Hans van Zon (Eds.), De Russische omhelzing: het Oostblok en de Derde Wereld. - Amsterdam: Transnational Institute, 1983.

Ra'anan, Gavriel D. The Evolution of the Soviet Use of Surrogates in Military Relations with the Third World, With Particular Emphasis on Cuban Participation in Africa. - St. Monica: Rand, 1979.

Rakowska-Harmstone, T., Chr. D. Jones, J. Jaworsky, and I. Sylvain Warsaw Pact: The Question of Cohesion. Phase II - Vol. I: The Greater Socialist Army: Integration and Reliability. - Ottawa: Operational Research and Analysis Establishment, Febr. 1984.

Randle, Robert F. The Origins of Peace: A Study of Peacemaking and the Structure of Peace Settlements. - New York: The Free Press, 1973.

Rauch, Georg von Geschichte der baltischen Staaten. - Stuttgart: Kohlhammer Verlag, 1970.

Rauchensteiner, Manfried Der Sonderfall: Die Besatzungszeit in Österreich, 1945 bis 1955. - Graz: Verlag Styria, 1979.

Rees, David 'Afghanistan's Role in Soviet Strategy' Conflict Studies, no. 118 (May 1980).

Reeve, W.D. The Republic of Korea: A Political and Economic Study. - London: Oxford University Press, 1963.

Remington, Robin Alison The Warsaw Pact. Case Studies in Communist Conflict Resolution. - Cambridge, Mass.: The MIT Press, 1971.

Remnek, Richard Soviet Policy in the Horn of Africa: The Decision to Intervene. - Alexandria, Virg.: Center for Naval Analysis, 1980.

Robinson, Thomas W. The Sino-Soviet Border Conflict in: Stephen S. Kaplan et al., Diplomacy of Power: Soviet Armed Forces as a Political Instrument. - Washington, D.C.: The Brookings Institution, 1981.

Röling, B.V.A. Vredeswetenschap: Inleiding tot de polemologie [Peace Research: An Introduction to War and

Peace Studies]. - Utrecht/Antwerpen: Het Spectrum, 1981.

Rosenberg, David Alan
'"A Smoking Radiating Ruin at the End of Two Hours." Documents on American Plans for Nuclear War with the Soviet Union, 1954-1955' International Security, vol. 6 (1981/82) no. 3 (Winter).

Rubinstein, Alvin Z. Soviet Foreign Policy Since World War II: Imperial and Global. - Cambridge, Mass.: Winthrop Publ., 1981.

Safran, Nadav   From War to War. The Arab-Israeli Confrontation 1948-1967. - New York: Bobbs-Merrill, 1969.

Schmid, Alex P.   Churchill's Privater Krieg. Intervention und Kontrarevolution im Russischen Bürgerkrieg, 1918-1920. - Zürich: Atlantis, 1975.

Schmid, Alex P.   'Die Expansion des Amerikanischen Kapitalismus nach dem Zweiten Weltkrieg - eine sozialimperialistische Interpretation' Schweizerische Zeitschrift für Geschichte, vol. 27 (1977) no. 4.

Schneider, Ronald M.
Communism in Guatemala 1944-1954. - New York, 1959.

Schneider, R.   'Guatemala: An Aborted Communist Takeover' Studies on the Soviet Union (New Series), vol. 11 (1971) no. 4.

Schoenberg, Hans W.
The Partition of Germany and the Neutralization of Austria in: Th.T. Hammond (Ed.), The Anatomy of Communist Takeovers. - New Haven: Yale University Press, 1975.

Selznick, Philip   The Organizational Weapon. A Study of Bolshevik Strategy and Tactics. - New York: McGraw-Hill, 1952.

Shavrov, I.E. (Ed.) Lokalnye Voiny: Istoriya i sovremmenost [Local Wars: History and the Modern Era]. - Moscow: Voyennoye Izdatelstvo, 1981.

Shulman, Marshall D.

Stalin's Foreign Policy Reappraised. - Cambridge: Harvard University Press, 1963.

Šilde, Adolfs   The Profits of Slavery: Baltic Forced Laborers and Deportees under Stalin and Khrushchev. - Stockholm: Latvian National Foundation in Scandinavia, 1958.

Singer, Ladislaus   Sowjet-Imperialismus. - Stuttgart: Seewald, 1970.

Singleton, Seth   'The Soviet Invasion of Afghanistan' The Atlantic Community Quarterly, 19 (1981) no. 2.

Sivard, Ruth Leger   World Military and Social Expenditures. - Leesburg, VA: World Priorities, 1981.

Small, Melvin, and J. David Singer
                       Resort to Arms: International and Civil Wars, 1816-1980. - Beverly Hills: Sage, 1982.

Smith, Joseph B.   Portrait of a Cold Warrior. - New York: Ballantine Books, 1976.

Spoor, Max   Huwelijk uit wederzijds belang. De strategie van Moskou in Zuid-Oost Azië in: J.J. Teunissen and Hans van Zon (Eds.), De Russische omhelzing: het Oostblok en de Derde Wereld. - Amsterdam: Transnational Institute, 1983.

Stockwell, John   In Search of Enemies. - New York: Norton, 1978.

Stoessinger, John G.

Why Nations Go to War, 2nd edition. - New York: St. Martin's Press, 1978.

Submarine Defence Commission
                       Countering the Submarine Threat. Submarine violations and Swedish security policy. - Stockholm: Swedish Official Report Series, 1983.

Survel, Jaak   Estonia To-Day: Life in a Soviet-Occupied Country. - London: Boreas Publishing Co., 1947. - (East and West: Facts from behinds the Iron Curtain no. 1)

Talbott, S. (Ed.)   Khrushchev Remembers. The Last Testament. - London: Deutsch, 1974.

Tatu, Michel   Power in the Kremlin. From Khrushchev to
                      Kosygin. - New York: Viking, 1967.

Tatu, Michel   Intervention in Eastern Europe
                      in: Stephen S. Kaplan et al., Diplomacy of Power.
                      - Washington, D.C.: The Brookings Institution,
                      1981.

Teeuw, Wout   Het conflict Afghanistan (27 december 1979 - ??)
                      [The Afghan Conflict (December 27, 1979 - ??)].
                      - Rijksuniversiteit Groningen, 1983. - (unpublish-
                      ed paper).

Teunissen, Jan Joost, & Hans van Zon (Eds.)
                      De Russische omhelzing. Het Oostblok en de
                      Derde Wereld. - Amsterdam: Transnational
                      Institute, 1983.

Thompson, Robert (Cons. Ed.)
                      War in Peace: An Analysis of Warfare Since
                      1945. - London: Orbis Publishing, 1981.

Tigrid, Pavel   The Prague Coup of 1948: The Elegant Takeover
                      in: Thomas T. Hammond (Ed.), The Anatomy of
                      Communist Takeovers. - New Haven: Yale
                      University Press, 1975.

Tillema, Herbert K.   Appeal to Force: American Intervention in the
                      Era of Containment. - New York: Thomas Y.
                      Cromwell Company, 1973.

Tillema, H.K.   Law, Power and Military Intervention since
                      World War II: Use of Force by forty-two States,
                      1946-1982. - Mexico City, April 5-9, 1983. -
                      (Paper prepared for the International Studies
                      Association)

Tolstoy, Nikolai   Stalin's Secret War. - London: Pan Books, 1982.

Tomson, Edgar   The Annexation of the Baltic States
                      in: Thomas T. Hammond (Ed.), The Anatomy of
                      Communist Takeovers. - New Haven: Yale
                      University Press, 1975.

Toriello, Guillermo   La Batalla de Guatemala. - Mexico, 1955.

Twining, David T.   'Soviet Activities in the Third World: A New
                      Pattern'
                      Military Review, (1980) no. 6 (June).

Ulam, Adam B.   Expansion and Coexistence. The History of Soviet
                         Foreign Policy. 1917-67. - New York: Praeger,
                         1968.

Ulam, Adam B.   The Rivals. America & Russia since World War
                         II. - New York: The Viking Press, 1971.

Ulam, Adam B.   The Soviet Union and the International Game
                         in: Kurt London (Ed.), The Soviet Union in World
                         Politics. - Boulder, Colo.: Westview Press, 1980.

Valdes, Nelson P.   Revolutionary Solidarity in Angola
                         in: Cole Blasier and Carmelo Mesa-Lago (Eds.),
                         Cuba in the World. - Pittsburgh: University of
                         Pittsburgh Press, 1979.

Valenta, Jiri   'Soviet Options in Poland'
                         Survival, vol. 23 (1981) no. 2.

Vardys, V. Stanley   'The Partisan Movement in Postwar Lithuania'
                         Slavic Review: American Quarterly of Soviet and
                         East European Studies, vol. 12 (1963) no. 3
                         (September).

Versteeg, Joris   'Ooggetuige in Afghanistan' [Eye-witness in
                         Afghanistan]
                         Vrij Nederland, (1983) (June 4). - (Bijvoegsel no.
                         22).

Volman, Daniel   A Continent Besieged: Foreign Military Activi-
                         ties in Africa since 1975. - Washington, D.C.:
                         IPS, ca. 1982.

Volten, P.M.E.   Brezhnev's "Peace Program". Success or Failure?.
                         - Emmen: Inrichting Uitgeven Boekwerken, 1981.

Volten, P.M.E.   'Het offensief in het militaire denken van de
                         Sovjet-Unie'
                         Jason, vol. 8 (1983), no. 2.

Watt, D.C.   Churchill und der Kalte Krieg. - Zürich,
                         Schweizerische Winston Churchill Stiftung, 1981.

Watt, D.C., Frank Spender, and Neville Brown
                         A History of the World in the Twentieth
                         Century. - London: Hodder and Stoughton, 1967.

Weinberger, Caspar W.
                         Soviet Military Power. - 3rd ed. - Washington,
                         D.C.: GPO, 1984.

Weiss, Kenneth G.   The Soviet Involvement in the Ogaden War. -
                     Alexandria: Center for Naval Analysis, 1980.

Wieringa, T.J., and B.R.C. ten Voorde
                     "Afghanistan is ons Vietnam!": Verslag van de
                     gebeurtenissen omtrent de Russische inval in
                     Afghanistan ["Afghanistan is our Vietnam!":
                     Report of the events regarding the Russian
                     invasion of Afghanistan]. - Groningen: Rijksuni-
                     versiteit Groningen, 1982. - (unpublished paper).

Wimbush, S. Enders, and Alex Alexiev
                     'Soviet Central Asian Soldiers in Afghanistan'
                     Conflict, vol. 4 (1983) nos. 2/3/4.

Windsor, Philip, and Adam Roberts
                     Czechoslovakia 1968: Reform, Repression and
                     Resistance. - London: Chatto and Windus, 1969.

Wolfe, Thomas W.   Soviet   Power   and   Europe,   1945-1970.   -
                     Baltimore: The Johns Hopkins Press, 1970.

Wolpin, M.D.   State Terrorism and Repression in the Third
                     World: Parameters and Prospects. - Potsdam,
                     N.Y.: State University of New York, 1983.

Wood, David   Conflict in the Twentieth Century. - London:
                     The Institute for Strategic Studies, 1968. -
                     (Adelphi Paper no. 48).

Yao Ming-le (Pseud.)
                     'De samenzwering tegen Mao' [The Conspiracy
                     against Mao]
                     Vrij Nederland, vol. 44 (1983) no. 19 (May 14).

Yergin, Daniel   Shattered Peace: The Origin of the Cold War
                     National Security State. - Harmondsworth:
                     Pelican Books, 1980.

Zacher, Mark W.   International Conflicts and Collective Security,
                     1946-77: The United Nations, Organization of
                     American States, Organization of African Unity,
                     and Arab League. - New York etc.: Praeger
                     Publishers, 1979.

Zagoria, Donald S., and Janet D. Zagoria
                     Crises on the Korean Peninsula
                     in: Stephen S. Kaplan et al., Diplomacy of Power:
                     Soviet Armed Forces as a Political Instrument. -
                     Washington: The Brookings Institution, 1981.

Zimmerman, William   The Korean and Vietnam Wars
                     in: Stephen S. Kaplan et al, Diplomacy of Power:
                     Soviet Armed Forces as a Political Instrument. -
                     Washington: The Brookings Institution, 1981.

Zon, Hans van   Het gemak waarmee vrienden vijanden werden.
                     Russische invloed in Africa beperkt
                     in: J.J. Teunissen and H. van Zon (Eds.), De
                     Russische omhelzing: het Oostblok en de Deerde
                     Wereld. - Amsterdam: Transnational Institute,
                     1983.

INDEX

Acheson, D.: 67
Afghanistan: 37, 88-90, 126, 127-132, 152
Ahmad (Imam of North Yemen): 79
Albania: 1, 11, 13, 139; Greek Civil War: 44, 61, 62
Algeria: Czech-Soviet arms supplies: 83
Allende, S.: 85, 110
Alvarado, J.V.: 85
Amin, H.: 88-90, 127-128, 130-131
Amin, I.: 100, 118
Amri, Hassan al-: 80
Amstutz, B.: 89
Anderson, R.D.: 141
Angola: 102-110, 120
Arafat, Y.: 119
Arbenz, J.: 77
Argentina, Falklands War: 85
Assad, Hafez al-: 98, 99
Austria: 6, 47-48, 52, 69-72
Azerbaijan: 43, 54-58

Badr, Muhammad al-: 79
Baghdad Pact: 78, 92
Balkan, Communist takeovers: 2-6
Baltic States: 4-5, 18-22
Bandaranaike, S.: 91
Beaufre, A.: 17
Benes, E.: 7-10
Beria, L.: 24-25
Berlin: 48-52; blockade 1948: 44-45; conference 1954: 71; crisis 1958-1961: 48, 144
Bessarabia: 19
Biafra: 101
Bishop, M.: 86
Bokassa, J.B.: 118, 151
Brandt, W.: 52
Brezhnev, L.I.: 12, 14, 52, 74, 75, 90, 91, 96, 97, 108, 109, 118, 126, 136, 141; doctrine: 1, 33

Brown, S.: 108
Brzezinski, Z.: 50, 51, 87, 100, 116
Bukovina: 19
Bulganin, N.: 79
Bulgaria: 2, 3, 4, 56, 139; Greek Civil War: 43-44, 61-62
Byelorussia: 5

Caetano, M.: 103
Cahill, K.: 113
Carlucci, F.: 100
Carter, J.: 74, 86, 114, 116
Castro, F.: 82, 85, 99, 108, 109, 112, 160
Ceausescu, N.: 13, 140
Cerník, O.: 30
Chad: 121
Chiang Kai-shek: 14, 67
Chile: 85
China: 160; Afghanistan: 90, 131; Angola: 102, 103; Biafra: 101; Civil War: 76; Guinea: 78; Korea: 45-47, 65-67, 76; North Yemen: 80-81; relation with Soviet Union: 14-15, 140; Sino-Indian border conflict: 79; Sino-Soviet border conflict: 35-38, 86; Tanzania: 100-101; Vietnam: 49-50, 87-88
Churchill, W.S.: 2, 4, 59
CIA: 28, 51; Angola: 103-107; Bay of Pigs: 82; Guatemala: 76-77; Bangladesh War: 90-91; Indonesia 1958: 78; Ogaden War: 114
Colby, W.: 103
Cold War: 10, 39-53, 70, 75, 155; Iranian Crisis: 54-58, 152; Korean War: 66-67
Comecon: 30
Cominform: 3, 75
Communist takeovers: Balkan, Eastern Europe: 2-6; Czecho-

slovakia: 7-10, 15-16
Cooperative intervention: 119-122
Congo-Leopoldville: 82
Cuba: 85, 159; African liberation movements; 83-84; Angola: 102-110; Guinea: 78; military potential: 82-83; Ogaden War: 112-117; Soviet arms supplies: 82, 88, 159; Soviet military presence: 82, 86, 88; Syria: 99
Cyprus: 49
Czarism: 133-136, 159
Czechoslovakia: 1, 2, 6, 83; Prague Coup 1948: 7-10; Prague Spring: 12-13, 30-34

Dacka, D.: 151
Daud, M.: 89, 127
Dekanozov, V.G.: 19
De Gaulle, Ch.: 78
Deportations: Balts: 5, 20-21; Bulgarians: 4; East Germans: 40; Hungarians: 4; Romanians: 4
Denmark: 43
Djilas, M.: 2
Dubček, A.: 13, 30-34
Dulles, J.F.: 28, 88

East Germany: 1, 6, 30, 31, 40, 57; Berlin blockade: 44-45; uprising 1953: 12, 23-25
Eastern Europe: Communist takeovers: 2-6; Soviet military presence: 14, 25, 33
Egypt: Afghanistan: - 90, 131; break with the Soviet Union: 95, 97; Czech-Soviet arms supplies 1955: 77; Canal War 1970: 94-95; June War 1967: 93-94; North Yemen: 79-81; October War 1973: 96-97; Suez Crisis 1956: 92
Eisenhower, D.D.: 9, 47, 66, 77, 88
El Salvador: 77, 86
Eritrea: 115, 121
Ethiopia: 120-121, 125; Ogaden War: 110-116

Feisal (King of Saudi Arabia): 80

Figl, L.: 69
Finland: 2, 6, 19, 52, 134
Finlandization: 42, 147-149
France: Angola: 104; Austria: 69-72; Biafra: 101, Chad: 121; Guinea: 78; military presence in Africa: 102, 151; Vietnam: 49
Frey-Bielecki, Gen.: 11

Geneva conference 1954: 49
George II (King of Greece): 59, 60
Germany: see East and West Germany
Gerö, E.: 26, 27
Ghana: 78, 83
Gomulka, W.: 1, 10-13, 26, 140
Gorshkov, S.G.: 110, 111
Gottwald, K.: 7, 9
Govorov, L.A.: 141
Gowon, Y.: 101
Great Britain: 63, 85, 91, 92, 134; Austria: 69-72; early Cold War: 3, 42, 43; Greece: 59-62; Iran: 54-58; Nigeria: 101; North Yemen: 79
Grechko, A.A.: 157
Greece: 2, 43-44, 59-62, 137, 144
Grenada: 86
Gromyko, A.: 108, 136
Guatemala: 76-77, 151
Guevara, E. "Ché": 85, 103
Guinea: 78, 83, 101

Haile Selassie: 102, 112
Helsinki Agreement 1975: 52
Henq-Samrin: 87
Herrnstadt, R.: 23-25
Hitler, A.: 2
Ho Chi Minh: 49, 76
Holden, R.: 104
Honduras: 77
Hoxha, E.: 13, 93, 140
Hua Guofeng: 38
Hungary: 1, 2, 3, 4, 72; uprising 1956: 12-13, 26-29
Husak, G.: 34
Hussein (King of Jordan): 96

India: 77-79, 90-92

Indonesia: 77-79
Interventions: definition: 123
Iran: Afghanistan: 131; Baghdad
    Pact: 92; Iranian Crisis 1945-
    1946: 43, 54-58
Iraq: 78, 92, 97-98
Israel: Canal War 1970: 94-95;
    Czech-Soviet arms supplies:
    76; June War 1967: 93-94;
    October War 1973: 52, 96-97
Ivan III (Czar of Russia): 134

Japan: 14, 52, 133, 134
Jaruzelski, W.: 13, 141
Johnson, L.B.J.: 32
Jordan: 90, 96

Kádár, J.: 12, 27-29
Kampuchea: 86-88, 119
Kania, S.: 141
Kaplan, K.: 41, 144
Karmal, B.: 89, 90, 128
Kennedy, J.F.: 48, 84, 86
Khrushchev, N.S.: 11, 15, 26, 28,
    41, 45, 48, 52, 72, 75, 77, 79,
    80, 83, 84, 86, 93, 122, 136,
    160
Khuzistan: 57
Kim Il Sung: 45, 63, 140
Kissinger, H.A.: 50, 90-91, 97,
    100, 103, 107, 108, 116
Komar, W. Gen.: 11
Korea: 45-47, 49, 63-68, 76, 140
Kostov: 10
Kosygin, A.: 36, 49
Kovâcs, B.: 3
Kreisky, B.: 72
Kurds: 56, 97-98

Laos: 49, 82, 84, 85, 87
Latin America: 85
Lebanon: 49, 99
Lenin, V.I.: 136
Libya: 74, 90, 99
Lin Biao: 37
Lippmann, W.: 40
Lockhart, B.: 9
Lumumba, P.: 82, 84

MacArthur, D.: 64, 65, 67
McNamara, R.: 51
Malenkov, G.: 23-25, 26

Maleter, P.: 28
Mali: 78
Malik, Ya. A.: 45, 67
Manchuria: 14, 57
Maniu, I.: 4
Mao Zedong: 14-15, 37, 45, 76
Marshall, G.C.: 10
Marshall Aid: 8, 41, 44, 70
Masaryk, J.: 9
Mengistu Haile Mariam: 112,
    114, 116
Michael I (King of Romania): 4
Mićunović, V.: 136
Mikolayczyk, S.: 3
Mikoyan, A.I.: 27
Mobutu, J.D.: 82, 103-105
Molotov, V.: 71, 74, 134
Molotov-Ribbentrop Pact: 18
Mongolia: 15, 37
Moose, R.: 114
Morocco: 49, 96

Nagy, I.: 10, 12, 13, 26, 27
Nasser, G.A.: 77, 79, 80, 81, 84,
    94, 95
NATO: 33, 39, 42, 47, 72, 142,
    146
Netherlands (The): 78-79
Neto, A.: 104, 107, 110
Nicaragua: 86
Nigeria: 101
Nimeiry, Jaafar el-: 95
Nixon, R.M.: 50, 86, 96
Nkrumah, J.: 83
North Yemen: 79-81, 121-122
Novotny, A.: 30
Nuclear arms: Cold War: 40-42,
    50-52; Korean War: 47, 66;
    October War: 97; strategic
    balance: 39, 52-53; Suez
    Crisis: 79

Ogaden War: 110-116, 125
Ojukwu, E.: 101

Pakistan: Afghanistan: 90, 129,
    131; Baghdad Pact: 78, 92;
    Indo-Pakistan War 1965: 79;
    Bangladesh War: 90-91
Palach, J.: 33
Palestine Liberation Organiza-
    tion: 93, 94, 96

Papandreou, G.: 59
Paputin, V.S.: 128
Patton, G.S.: 9
Peru: 85
Petkov, N.: 4
Petrov, V.I.: 115, 141
Phoumi Nosavan: 82
Pinochet Uguarte, A.: 85
PLO: 93, 94, 96
Podgorny, N.: 112
Poland: 1, 2, 3, 5, 6, 11-14, 18,
   26, 52, 133, 159; events since
   1981: 126, 141-142
Pol Pot: 87, 119
Popkov, M.D.: 141
Portugal: 144; Angola: 102-106;
   decolonization: 83-84
Potsdam conference 1945: 70,
   74, 134
Purges: Afghanistan: 127; Baltic
   States: 19-21; Czechoslovakia:
   34; East Germany: 24; Hun-
   gary: 29

Qaddafi, M.: 99, 121
Qavam, A.: 43, 56, 57, 58

Rabbot, B.: 108, 144
Radford, A.: 88
Rajk, L.: 10
Rákosi, M.: 3, 10, 26
Rejman, M.: 144
Remnek, R.: 112, 116
Renner, K.: 69
Reza Shah: 54, 58
Rhee, S.: 63
Ridgway, M.B.: 65
Rokossovsky, K.K.: 3, 11
Romania: 2, 4, 11, 13, 31, 32,
   72, 139, 140, 152
Rosa Coutinho: 107

Sadat, A.: 95-97
Safronchuk, V.S.: 89
Said, Qabus bin: 98
Saleh, Ali-Abdallah: 81
Sallal, Abdullah-al: 80-81
Saudi Arabia: Afghanistan: 90,
   131; Ogaden War: 113; Yemen:
   80-81
Savimbi, J.: 104
Schwiesau, H.: 89

Scobie, Gen.: 59
Semyonov, V.: 23
Shaba: 121
Shelepin, A.: 108
Siad Barre, M.: 112-114
Sik, O.: 30
Slanský, R.: 8
Somalia: 74; Ogaden War: 110-
   116, 125; territorial claims:
   111
Somoza, A.: 86
Sonnenfeldt, H.: 50
South Africa: Angola: 104-110
South Yemen: 81, 98
Souvanna Phouma: 82
Soviet Union: arms supplies:
   76-84, 85-86, 90-93, 94-101,
   109, 111, 115, 153; military
   interventions: see tables IX,
   X, XII, XVII; military person-
   nel abroad: table XIV; Ango-
   la: 109-110; Cuba: 82-83, 88;
   Egypt: 94-95; Ethiopia: 115;
   Ghana: 83; Iraq: 97; Libya:
   99; Somalia: 112; Syria: 99;
   military presence in Eastern
   Europe: 14, 25, 33, table I;
   relation with China: 14-15;
   relation with Vietnam: 76,
   86-88; see also Cold War
Spheres of influence: Europe: 2,
   3, 59-60; Third World: 117-
   126
Sri Lanka: 91
Stalin, J.V.: 2-6, 8, 10, 14-16,
   25-26, 40-42, 44-47, 50-51,
   59, 62, 66, 70, 71, 74, 75, 76,
   77, 133-137, 144, 159
Stalin, S.: 40
Sudan: 95
Suez Canal: Canal War 1970:
   94-95; Suez Crisis 1956; 79,
   84, 92
Sukarno: 77-79
Suslov, M.: 27
Svoboda, L.: 7, 30
Sweden: 144
Switzerland: 71
Syria: Golan Heights 1973-74:
   98-99; intervention in Jordan
   1970: 96; June War 1967; 93;
   Lebanese Civil War 1975: 99;

October War 1973: 96-97

Taiwan: 15, 46, 67
Taraki, N.M.: 89-90, 127-128
Thailand: 45, 84
Tito, J.B.: 2, 3, 11, 13, 60, 62, 139, 140
Tlas, M.: 99
Touré, A.S.: 78, 101
Trotzky, L.: 159
Truman, H.S.: 9, 40, 41, 45, 56, 61, 65, 66, 67; doctrine: 43, 157
Tukhachevsky, M.N.: 136, 159
Turkey: 49, 56, 74, 75, 91, 92, 139, 152

Uganda: 100
Ukraine: 5
Ulbricht, W.: 12, 23, 24, 25
United Nations: 28-29, 32-33, 43, 45, 56-57, 63-67, 71, 82, 131
United States: Afghanistan: 90, 126, 127, 131; Angola: 103-110; Austria: 69-71; Baghdad Pact: 78; Bangladesh War: 90-91; Chad: 121; Chile: 85; China: 38; Cuba: 88; Czechoslovakia: 32; Egypt: 77; Ethiopia: 112; Greece: 61-62; Guatemala: 76-77; Indonesia: 78-79; Iran: 54-58; June War 1967: 94-95; Korea: 45-47, 63-68; Laos: 84; October War 1973: 96-97; Syrian-Jordanese crisis: 96; Thailand: 84; Vietnam: 49-50, 84-85, 88; see also Cold War; see also NATO
Vaculík, L.: 31
Vafiades, M.: 44, 60
Valdes, N.P.: 106
Van Fleet, Lt.-Gen.: 61
Vietnam: Chinese incursion 1979: 87-88; Kampuchea: 86-88; relation with Soviet Union: 76, 86-88; Syria: 99; Vietnam War: 49-50, 84-85, 88
Vyshinsky, A.Y.: 19

War by proxy: see cooperative intervention

Warsaw Pact: 13, 16-17, 27, 28-29, 39, 47, 72, 144, 146; Czechoslovakia 1968: 30-34
West Germany: 44-45, 47
Witte, S.: 136
World War II: 18-20, 54-55, 59-60

Yalta: 3, 134
Yugoslavia: 1-3, 32, 44, 59, 60, 62, 70, 91, 137, 140

Zaire: Angola: 102-110
Zaisser, W.: 23-25
Zanjan: 57
Zaytsev, A.N.: 141
Zdhanov, A.A.: 19
Zhou Enlai: 36
Zia Ul Haq: 131
Zorin, V.: 9

РЕЗЮМЕ

Это исследование базируется, главным образом, на вторичных западных источниках, некоторых переведенных советских источниках и нескольких официальных советских сообщениях. Рассматривается около 50 предполагаемых и фактических советских военных акций, 10 из которых анализируются в более глубоком исследовании характерных случаев, написанном Э. Берендс. Зарубежные военные акции подразделены на 11 категорий:

1. Размещение воинских частей в мирное время в качестве сдерживающего средства против третьей стороны;

2. Обеспечение личной и дворцовой охраны для местного правительства;

3. Военная миссия при штабах для планирования локальных операций без прямого военного участия;

4. Боевое участие специальных зарубежных сил (операторы танков, радарных установок, пилоты и т.д.);

5. "Доброволцы", участвующие в боевых действиях;

6. "Регулярные части", участвующие в боевых действиях;

7. Обеспечение морской и воздушной защиты в зоне боевых действий или вблизи нее;

8. Мобилизация, передвижения войск в пограничных областях, развертывание специального вооружения на передовых позициях;

9. Поставки специального вооружения во время боевых действий;

10. Военная блокада для предотвращения доставки вооружения противнику поддерживаемой стороны;

11. Обеспечение перевозок и снабжения (воздушный и морской транспорт) для стороны, участвующей в боевых действиях.

Учитывая тайный характер некоторых из этих операций и неравноценность источников информации, советские военные акции описываются в табличных обзорах (таблицы IX, X, XII) как подтвержденные - "+"; правдоподобные, но не подтвержденные - "+?"; возможные - "?"; сомнительные - "??"; угроза интервенции - "!" и не полностью соответствующие вышеприведенным определениям -"()". Общее количество военных советских акций за период с 1945 г., без учета случаев, обозначенных "??" и "()", равно 44. За период с 1945 по 1955 гг. имело место 15 акций: 13 - внутри социалистического блока, включая Китай; 2 акции между блоками (или вне блоков, но на фоне выраженного противостояния блоков Восток - Запад) и ни одной акции вне блоков (в Третьем Мире). За период 1955-1965 гг. имело место 11 акций (3 внутри блока, 5 между блоками, 3 вне блоков). За период 1965-1980гг. зарегистрированно 18 акций (5 внутри блока, 0 между блоками, 13 вне блоков).

Защита "завоеваний социализма" была главным мотивом советских военных акций внутри блока в Восточной Европе. Однако советизация Восточной Европы была мало связана с

пролетарскими революциями, скорее - с "экспортом революции
на штыках", концепцией, которую впервые пропагандировал
генерал Тухачевский в 1920 г. Отсюда проистекают восстания
против советского господства в Восточной Европе и
советские военные акции по их подавлению.

Идея прозондировать Западную Европу штыками Красной Армии -
операция вторжения между блоками - рассматривалась Сталиным в
январе 1951 г. Одновременно были приняты решения о
громадном росте оборонных бюджетов Советского Союза и стран
- сателлитов. Сталин, однако, колебался между планами войны
и мира, так что эта идея не была осуществлена. План посылки
"добровольцев" в революционную Португалию в 1974/75 гг.,
предложенный А. Шелепиным, также не был материализован. За
исключением многочисленных проникновений советских
подлодок в шведские территориальные воды в начале 80-х
годов, не имеется никаких признаков военных акций между
блоками. Становление СССР как военной державы первой
величины не привело к тому типу политического
запугивания и подчинения, которого опасаются приверженцы
тезиса "финляндизация". Ввиду имеющегося приблизительного
баланса сил в Европе можно ожидать, что на этом фронте военное
столкновение не произойдет. Малой оценивается также
опасность горизонтальной эскалации конфликтов в Третьем Мире
на центральный фронт холодной войны.

Хотя Третий Мир не представляет собой главную зону советских
военных интересов, он играет определенную роль в советском
стратегическом мышлении. Там, где речь идет о стратегических
пунктах или критических ресурсах, акции для их захвата или
для исключения доступа к ним США могут рассматриваться как
вероятные при условии, что будут найдены местные союзники,
которые легитимируют советскую военную акцию. Обзор 16 случаев
советских военных акций в Третьем Мире показывает переход
от тайной продажи вооружения через третьи стороны
(Чехословакия) в случаях Израиля (1948) и Гватемалы (1954) к
открытой продаже в случае Египта (1955), к угрозе
"добровольческой" интервенции (Суэц, 1956), к демонстративным
маневрам в зонах, примыкающих к странам Среднего Востока
(Сирия, 1957, Ливан-Ирак, 1958). В 60-е годы отмечается
переход от транспортировки воинских частей воюющих сторон
в Конго (1960) и Северном Йемене (1962) к снабжению оружием
в длительных конфликтах (война в Биафре, 1967-1970).
Зарегистрировано участие советских пилотов в боевых действиях
в Северном Йемене, Египте, Судане и Шри Ланка. В 70-е годы на
арене появляются советские военно-морские силы,обеспечивающие
защиту Гвинеи и Индии в их конфликтах с американскими
союзниками. Все более частыми становятся операции
по транспортировке войск третьих сторон морским и воздушным
путем (Марокко, Южный Йемен, Куба, Вьетнам) к театрам
военных действий. В случае Эфиопии СССР берет на себя даже
командование местными и кубинскими войсками. Угроза прямой

интервенции советских боевых частей была использована в
арабо-израильских войнах 1967 и 1973 гг. Подобная угроза стала
реальностью, когда в 1979 г. советские воздушнодесантные и
регулярные наземные части численностью в одну дивизию
пересекли границу Афганистана. По мнению авторов, афганская
интервенция не является прологом последующих завоеваний
в Западной Азии, а дальнейшим развитием доктрины Брежнева.

В заключительной главе ставится вопрос, является ли Советский
Союз экспансионистским государством. Считается, что СССР
унаследовал экспансионистскую политику царизма, которая
базировалась на постоянном ксенофобном ощущении неуверенности
по отношению к внешнему миру. Эта советская неуверенность
поддерживается увеличивающимся экономическим и технологическим
отставанием от Запада. В конечном счете, однако, режим,
подобный советскому, где постоянно правящая партия
претендует на монополию "правды", всегда ощущает угрозу со
стороны обществ, в которых открытая критика своего и других
обществ разрешена и даже поощряется, в которых различные
партии борются друг с другом, предлагая населению
альтернативные пути социального прогресса. Для обеспечения
сплоченности и контроля внутри страны и в Восточной Европе
советские лидеры, несомненно, нуждаются в спектре внешних угроз
и поддержании конфликтных отношений с внешним миром, не
прибегая к прямым военным операциям , в качества средства
узаконивания однопартийного режима. Советский Союз, который
в прошлом четырежды (дважды в 1918, 1920 и 1941 гг.)
подвергался нападениям со стороны Запада, не является
более объектом военной угрозы с этой стороны. Вызов имеет
идеологический характер, и этот вызов ощущался бы
советскими лидерами как угроза, даже если бы западные
демократии разоружились.

Считается, что будущие советские акции наиболее вероятны в
Восточной Европе, особенно если сохранятся экономические
проблемы. Военные акции в Третьем Мире возможны только, если
существуют возможности с малым риском, т.е. где не ожидается
существенной реакции Запада. Военные акции между блоками в
Европе рассматриваются как в высшей степени маловероятные
ввиду большого риска, сопряженного с подобными акциями -
риска ядерной эскалации, в первую очередь, и, если война
продолжается без ядерных средств, риска потери Советским
Союзом контроля над Восточной Европой в затянувшемся
безъядерном конфликте.

SUMMARY

This study is mainly based on secondary sources of Western origin, a selection of translated Soviet sources and a few official Soviet accounts. It surveys about fifty alleged and real Soviet interventions of which ten are treated in more depth in case studies written by E. Berends. Foreign military interventions are defined in terms of eleven categories.

1. Peacetime stationing of troops as deterrent against third parties;
2. Providing body guards and palace guards to local government;
3. Military mission at headquarters for planning local operations without direct combat participation;
4. Combat participation of foreign special forces (tank operators, pilots, radar, etc.);
5. "Volunteers" serving in combat;
6. "Regular troops" engaged in combat;
7. Providing naval or air protection in or near combat zone;
8. Mobilization, troop movements in border areas, deployment of special weapons into forward positions;
9. Special weapons supplies during combat phase;
10. Armed blockades to prevent weapons reaching opponent of supported party;
11. Providing logistics (air and naval transport) for combattants.

Given the covert nature of some of these activities and the uneven source situation, Soviet interventions have been described in the tabulatory surveys (Tables IX, X, XII) as + = verified; +? = probably but not verified; ? = possible; ?? = doubtful; ! = threat of intervention, and () = not fully in accordance with the definitions above. Leaving out cases labelled () and ??, a total of 44 cases of Soviet military interventions were found for the period since 1945. In the period 1945-1955 there were 15 of these; 13 within the socialist bloc, including China; 2 interbloc ones (or extrabloc ones with strong interbloc East-West-overtones) and no extrabloc ones (Third World). In the period 1955-1965 there were 11 cases (3 intrabloc, 5 interbloc, 3 extrabloc). In the period 1965-1980 18 cases were recorded (5 intrabloc, 0 interbloc and 13 extrabloc).

Defending the "gains of socialism" was the primary motive for Soviet intrabloc interventions in Eastern Europe. However, the sovietization of Eastern Europe had little to do with proletarian revolutions and much with the "export of the revolution on the points of bayonets", a concept first advocated by General Tukhachevsky in 1920. Hence the recurring uprisings against Soviet rule in Eastern Europe and Soviet interventions to suppress these.

The idea to probe Western Europe with the bayonets of the Red Army - an interbloc invasion - was considered by Stalin in January 1951. At the same time, huge defence budget increases were decided upon for the Soviet Union and her satellites. However, Stalin vacillated between war and peace plans and nothing came of it. A plan to send "volunteers" to revolutionary Portugal in 1974/75, advocated by A. Shelepin, also did not materialize. Except for

numerous Soviet submarine intrusions into Swedish territorial waters
in the early 1980s, there are no signs of interbloc interventions. The
rise of the USSR to a military power of the first order has not led to
the kind of political intimidation and subordination feared by the
adherents of the "Finlandization"-thesis. Given the rough force
balance in Europe it can be expected that no armed clash wil occur
on this front. The danger of horizontal escalation of Third World
conflicts to the central cold war front is considered small.
While the Third World is not the principal area of Soviet military
interest, it plays a role in Soviet strategic thinking. Where strategic
locations or crucial resources are at stake, interventions to secure
these or to deny these to the USA will be likely, provided local allies
can be found which legitimize Soviet intervention. The survey of 16
instances of Soviet interventions in the Third World shows a
progression from covert arms sales through third parties
(Czechoslovakia) in the case of Israel (1948) and Guatemala (1954), to
overt arms sales in the case of Egypt (1955), to threat of
intervention by "volunteers" (Suez, 1956), to demonstrative exercises
in areas adjacent to Middle East countries (Syria, 1957; Lebanon-Iraq,
1958). In the 1960s one notices a progression from troop transports
for belligerents in the Congo (1960) and North Yemen (1962), to the
provision of arms in ongoing conflicts (Biafran war, 1967-1970). One
also notices combat participation of Soviet pilots in North Yemen,
Egypt and Sudan and Sri Lanka. In the 1970s the Soviet navy enters
the picture, providing protection to Guinea and India in their
conflicts with American allies. The transport of troops of third
parties by sea and air (Moroccans, South Yemeni, Cubans,
Vietnamese) to theatres of armed conflict becomes more frequent. In
the case of Ethiopia, the USSR even takes charge of the battlefield
command of local and Cuban troops. Soviet direct combat troop
intervention was threatened in the Arab-Israeli wars of 1967 and
1973. It became a reality when in 1979 Soviet airborne and regular
ground troops in divisional strength crossed the borders into
Afghanistan. In the view of the authors, the Afghanistan intervention
is not a prelude to further conquests in West Asia but a further
extension of the Brezhnev Doctrine.
In the final chapter the question is posed whether or not the Soviet
Union is expansionist. It is held that the USSR is heir to the
expansionist policies of the Czars which were based on a continuous
xenophobic sense of insecurity regarding the outside world. This
Soviet insecurity is enhanced by the threat of a widening economic
and technological gap vis-à-vis the West.
In the last analysis, however, a regime such as that in the Soviet
Union where a continuously ruling party claims a monopoly of "truth"
is bound to feel threatened by societies where open criticism of their
own and other societies is accepted and even welcomed, and where
various parties compete with each other for offering the population
alternative roads to social improvement. In order to maintain cohesion
and control at home and in Eastern Europe, the Soviet leaders
apparently need the spectre of an outward threat and will maintain a
conflictuous relationship with the outer world without taking resource
to actual warfare as a means of legitimizing the one-party regime.

The Soviet Union, which in the past has been attacked four times from the West (twice in 1918, and in 1920 and 1941) is no longer threatened by a Western military intervention. The challenge is an ideological one, and would be perceived as threatening by the Soviet leaders even if the Western democracies were unarmed.

It is held that future Soviet interventions are most likely in Eastern Europe, especially if economic problems continue. Interventions in the Third World are only likely if there are low risk opportunities where no major Western response is expected. Interbloc interventions in Europe are considered highly unlikely given the risks involved - the risk of nuclear escalation on the one hand and, if the war stays conventional, of the disintegration of Soviet control over Eastern Europe in a drawn-out conventional conflict.